D0998595

GORBACHEV GLASNOST & THE GOSPEL

GORBACHEV GLASNOST & THE GOSPEL

Michael Bourdeaux

Hodder & Stoughton
LONDON SYDNEY AUCKLAND TORONTO

British Library Cataloguing in Publication Data
Bourdeaux, Michael *1934–*
    Gorbachev, glasnost and the Gospel.
    1. Soviet Union. Christians. Religious freedom
    I. Title
    323.4420947

ISBN 0-340-51739-5
ISBN 0-340-54193-8 Pbk

Published by Hodder and Stoughton,
a division of Hodder and Stoughton Ltd,
Mill Road, Dunton Green, Sevenoaks, Kent TN13 2YA
Editorial Office: 47 Bedford Square, London WC1B 3DP

Printed in England by Clays Ltd, St Ives plc

Keston College Book Number 31

To Lara Clare

Acknowledgments

It has been a great privilege to write the substance of this book back in Oxford after thirty years away, so my first thanks go to the Leverhulme Trust, whose financial assistance made this possible. My old college, St Edmund Hall, welcomed me graciously as a Visiting Fellow and St Antony's College elected me as a Senior Associate Member, enabling me to benefit from the stimulus of their lecture programme.

The Trust provided me also with a research assistant, Suzanne Oliver, without whose tireless work I would not have finished in double the time. She has been my mind-reader and critic, but has provided considerable original material of her own, particularly for Chapter 5. The amount of information was overwhelming: perhaps enough is left over for a book to follow up each chapter. The staff at Keston College in Kent have gathered this material day by day and it reposes there in the archive.

I am grateful to several people for helpful suggestions, particularly Professor Sir Dimitri Obolensky and Professor Archie Brown of Oxford University, and Michael Rowe, Jane Ellis, John Anderson and others at Keston College.

Professor and Mrs John Fennell and Lady Joya Roberts provided havens of peace in Oxford and generous refreshment along the way.

Most of all I once again pay tribute to the inspiration of those Christians in the Soviet Union, contact with whom over the years has never failed to inspire and enrich.

Michael Bourdeaux   March 1990
Iffley, Oxford

Contents

Photographs

Fr Alexander Men (*Keston College*)
Fr Tavrion (*Keston College*)
Boris Talantov (*Aid to Russian Christians*)
The laying of a foundation stone (*Jim Forest*)
Millennium press conference (*NCCC-USA*)
The Danilov Monastery (*NCCC-USA*)
Fr Mark (Valeri) Smirnov (*Aid to Russian Christians*)
Archbishop Kirill of Smolensk (*Jim Forest*)
Archbishop Chrysostom of Irkutsk (*Jim Forest*)
Alexander Ogorodnikov (*Cahiers du Samizdat*)
Metropolitan Filaret of Kiev (*Jim Forest*)
Viktor Popkov (*James Stark*)
Fr Gleb Yakunin (*Keston College*)
Deacon Vladimir Rusak (*Aid to Russian Christians*)
Church Council (*Jim Forest*)
The unofficial exhibitions of photographs (*Keston College*)
Fifty Christian volunteer workers (*Aid to Russian Christians*)
Baptism in River Dnieper, Kiev (*Aid to the Persecuted*)
Alexander Semchenko (*Keston College*)
Ivan Fedotov (*Keston College*)
Celebrations of Odessa unregistered Baptist church (*Aid to Russian Christians*)
Valeri Barinov (*Keston College*)
Nijole Sadunaite (*Keston College*)
Bishop Julijonas Steponavicius (*Keston College*)
Bishop Pavlo Vasylyk (*Ukrainian Catholic Church*)
Ivan Hel (*John Hands*)
Procession of bishops at Lviv demonstration (*Keston College*)
Iosyp Terelya (*Ukrainian Catholic Church*)
Wife and grand-daughter of Ivan Hel (*Bill Hampson/Jubilee Campaign*)
Young Baptist volunteer (*Keston College*)

1 The Crisis of History

For seventy years a state, for the first time in history, attempted to eradicate all concept of God from society. Regimes in the past have misused religion in every conceivable way, enforcing the worship of idols, relentlessly persecuting those who raised altars to other deities and marching off to war against the infidel under the flag of their own god. Never before, however, had men stood up and said, 'There are no gods in our state; mankind has all the potential within himself; science, equality and economic progress hold the key to the future.'

In 1988, Soviet leaders not only realised they had failed, but they put the process into reverse. This book recounts how it happened and what the consequences have been.

The reinstatement of God in the Kremlin – at one point literally, when the Patriarch celebrated the liturgy in the Cathedral of the Dormition – preceded the collapse of communism in Central and Eastern Europe in a way that is slightly more than symbolic. Christianity, in a different way in every one of those countries, is now a force in the affairs of the nation and therefore of the world.

The inability to comprehend this aspect of culture under communism – the enforcement of atheist dogma – inhibits the West from fully understanding the processes which are now occurring. Western church leaders, commentating on the Soviet Union throughout the seventy years of its history, more often than not lacked the insight to interpret events with a prophetic word. One prominent Western theologian, confronted with one of the first lists of Baptist prisoners in the Soviet Union in the early 1960s, held it up before a meeting of the Central Committee of the World Council of Churches and asked, 'What are 200 prisoners in a country of 200 million people?' By this he intended to say that there was freedom enough for believers in Russia. There was no need to break the law and those who did so were troublemakers. He had missed the prophetic element in the conduct of those men and women. He had assumed that the Christian norm should be a general acceptance of the society around them.

Such attitudes to some extent permeated Western thinking. Some new social experiment was taking place in the East. There were a thousand obstacles on the road and individual non-conformists were still being sacrificed to the Gulag, but overall there was progress and a general acceptance that, in the words of George Bernard Shaw on his return from the Soviet Union, 'I have seen the future, I have been there.' Despite some excellent reporting by journalists from Moscow over many years and the abundance of publications on such topics as the abuse of psychiatry for political ends and the prevalence of religious persecution, there was little real understanding of the indignity visited on human beings by the communist system, leading eventually to their rejection of it.

The old way of looking at the world as a confrontation between two massive power blocs, with the third world suffering as a result, has disappeared. There are few human beings on earth whose lives are not potentially affected in one way or the other – especially those who continue to live under other oppressive regimes. The perspective for religion in the new era is transformed. Early in 1990 a sage of our generation, Lord Jakobovits, reflected on these events thus:

> What is taking place is of seismic dimensions and there is more to it than just liberalizing. The collapse of communism itself will be a major factor in bringing back the religious influence in world affairs. It means the collapse of the view that the essential features of human progress were of a materialistic nature. It provides the present religious leadership with a more exciting contemporary challenge than they have had in the past.[1]

Another consequence of our misunderstanding of communist society is that only those in the West bold enough to face the accusation of being cold war warriors dared expose the true nature of communism – and for a Christian this led to exclusion from the mainstream of acceptance, at least in some church circles. It is still somehow an unpopular view to rate Stalin as a worse tyrant than Hitler. Zbigniew Brzezinski, formerly President Carter's National Security Adviser, reckons that communism in one form or another cost the lives of fifty million people, counting those whose deaths were consequent upon mistaken political or economic decisions, as well as the victims of direct persecution. Stalin therefore has no rival as the greatest tyrant in human history. In his book, *The Grand Failure*, written in 1988 and published in the USA early in 1989, well before the cracks in the Berlin Wall opened into the fissures which destroyed the system, Brzezinski spectacularly predicted the imminent fall of communism. In 1988 he delivered a précis of his views at the Hugh Seton Watson Memorial Lecture in London before an astonished and partly sceptical audience.

Too many people in the West, and perhaps especially Christians, who should have known better, simply failed to appreciate the totality with which communism in practice rejected every proven human and religious value, stripping men and women of trust in each other, excising any sense of individual responsibility for the destiny of society, robbing people of their future, just as the rewriting of history had robbed them of their past. It is impossible for anyone who does not know the Soviet system well to appreciate the extent of the deprivation which believers have experienced. Therefore it is difficult, without a great effort of the imagination, to start on the right wavelength to enable one to appreciate the scale of the changes which Mr Gorbachev's policies have brought into religious life.

Churches – Open and Closed

Even in these days of *glasnost*, it is impossible to assess the full extent of Stalin's persecution of religious believers, their persons, their beliefs, their institutions. So many died in the general purges and famines that no figures can be extracted to indicate those who were victims primarily because of their faith. In Stalin's Russia simply to be a priest warranted a prison sentence which, in its turn, was often the equivalent of a death sentence.

Even in the midst of such horror, there was an act of violence against property which Soviet believers would never forgive: the systematic closure and destruction of the churches. Often they were the only stone construction in a locality where dwellings were wooden, so the ready-made policy was to commandeer them as agricultural stores or use them to house the village club or cinema, after removing all the crosses and any other visible symbols of the faith. But it is not so easy to make a church look like a barn, especially a Russian one, with its onion domes and elevated walls. As Solzhenitsyn so vividly put it:

> When you travel the by-roads of Central Russia you begin to understand the secret of the pacifying Russian countryside. It is in the churches. They trip up the slopes, ascend the high hills, come down to the broad rivers, like princesses in white and red, they lift their bell-towers – graceful, shapely, variegated – high over mundane timber and thatch, they nod to each other from afar, from villages that are cut off and invisible to

each other they soar to the same heaven. And wherever you wander in the fields or meadows, however far from habitation, you are never alone: from over the hayricks, the wall of trees, and even the curve of the earth's surface, the head of some bell-tower will beckon you from Borki Lovetskiye, Lyubichi or Gavrilovskoye.

But when you reach the village you find that not the living, but the dead greeted you from afar. The crosses were knocked off the roof or twisted out of place long ago. The dome has been stripped and there are gaping holes between its rusty ribs. Weeds grow on the roofs and in the cracks in the walls. Usually the graveyard has been neglected, its crosses flattened and the graves churned up. Over the years rain has penetrated to the murals over the altar and obscene inscriptions are scrawled over them.

In the porch there are barrels of lubricating oil and a tractor is turning in towards them, or a lorry has backed into the church doorway to pick up some sacks. One church reverberates to the shudder of lathes, another is locked and silent. In others various groups and clubs are meeting: 'Aim at high milk yields!' 'A poem on peace.' 'A heroic deed.'

People were always selfish and often unkind, but the evening chimes would ring out, floating over villages, fields and woods, reminding people to abandon the trivial concerns of this world and give time and thought to eternity . . . our forefathers put all that was finest in themselves, all their understanding of life into these stones, into these bell-towers.

Ram it in, Vitka, give it a bash, don't be afraid! Film show at six, dancing at eight![2]

Solzhenitsyn had not openly declared himself as a Christian at the time when he wrote these words (about 1961), but the outrage which he felt at this desecration of Russia's heritage was shared by the two generations since Lenin. By the time he wrote, Khrushchev's policies were again further devastating churches in the countryside. These buildings made a statement about Russia's past and were a symbol of hope for the future – hardly surprising, then, that the local authorities wished to eradicate them. For ordinary believers the struggle for freedom of religion has usually focused on the longing to win back their place of worship. They were not impressed by the handful of churches converted into museums and shown off with pride to demonstrate the glory of old Russian architecture.

By the outbreak of the Second World War only a few hundred churches throughout the Soviet Union were open for worship. However, so desperate was Stalin for support in the war effort that he encouraged the Russian Orthodox Church to collaborate with him and rewarded it for doing so. This led to the return of several thousand churches in the 1940s which were lovingly and carefully restored by believers, a process which took many years because of the universal shortage of building materials. To these were added many more in the lands conquered by the Red Army as the Nazis retreated; they had not formerly been on Soviet soil and had therefore not undergone persecution.

By 1959 the church had returned to some kind of regular life, at least by Soviet standards, and the public face of Christianity was more normal than it had been at any time since the Revolution. This, then, made Khrushchev's renewed campaign all the more devastating. It coincided with my arrival in Moscow as a member of the first-ever British Council exchange in a country where no students from Western countries had ever spent a length of time.

I was able, therefore, gradually to gauge the atmosphere among believers. This took time, because there were no believers at all, at least overt ones, in the university where I was studying. However, by then even the newspapers were beginning to announce that churches were closing again and trials of believers as enemies of the state were reported with attendant accusations of drunkenness, homosexuality, robbery and embezzlement. Monasticism almost ceased to exist and the Soviet Union's theological seminaries were reduced from eight in number to three.

Khrushchev's persecution of religion stood out more sharply, because in other ways society was moving in a more liberal direction, following the denunciation of Stalin at the Twentieth Party Congress in 1956. There has never been an explanation of why believers were singled out and treated with a savagery which would have undermined Mr Khrushchev's benign image round the world, had this policy become better known. Most likely the ideologues in the Kremlin were dismayed at what Khrushchev had done and put him under severe pressure. To justify himself as a true communist, he attacked the enemy in the midst – and a defenceless one at that – claiming that the Soviet Union was well on the way to attaining communism and there would be no place for religion in the ideal state of the future.

No one in these early days of Khrushchev had ever heard of Solzhenitsyn and it seemed at first that no voice could be heard expressing the outrage that millions felt at this assault. A phrase often used at the time was 'the church of silence', but the improvement in the life of the ordinary believer in the post-war years, followed by the death of Stalin in 1953, gradually gave people the courage to overcome the fear born of the new terror. The church did not suffer the renewed persecution in silence. At first the voices were isolated, apparently crying in the wilderness. It was my privilege to be the person *in situ*, but with the outside contacts, to pick up their distant signals and eventually, as the work of Keston College developed, to transmit them to the world. The task was always to focus the antennae in the right direction and to pick out the true voice from the torrent of propaganda which official church representatives presented after 1961 in such forums as the World Council of Churches and the Prague Christian Peace Conference.

While no one would assert that Christian prottest was the sole motivator of an emergent human rights movement, it unquestionably played a role which academic research, even to this day, has never fully acknowledged. Soon the intelligentsia would protest over the trial of the authors Andrei Sinyavsky and Yuli Daniel, who had evaded the literary straitjacket by sending their satirical works abroad for publication under a pseudonym. Even Jewish protest, which for many people came to symbolise the human rights movement in the Soviet Union, did not emerge until almost a decade after isolated Christians had first begun to call for justice.

The Russian and Ukrainian Baptists, about whom we shall say more in Chapter 6, were the very first to co-ordinate their protests and by April 1965 Gennadi Kryuchkov and Georgi Vins had made the first detailed analysis of the injustices of Soviet legislation.[3] The drive and co-ordination of this movement, which rapidly broke away from the Moscow-dominated and officially registered structure when its demands received a blank rebuttal, remains unique even today in the clarity of its legal formulations in campaigning for justice. The scrutiny to which they subjected the existing processes for the regulation of church–state relations was a model for any human rights movement, though its influence remained relatively limited, because the Baptists did not have many connections with mainstream activism. However, there was one group right outside their normal range of contacts with which the Baptists did establish useful relations, the circle around Gleb Yakunin, which later became the Christian Committee for the Defence of Believers' Rights.

If any one man or woman in the Soviet Union embodies the Christian's cry for a new deal, the ability to organise other people to achieve it and the readiness of that individual to suffer in the process, it is Fr Gleb. He comes from a religious family, but lost his faith after the war, at the age of fifteen, under the influence of communist propaganda. His yearning for an open air life led him to become a student of forestry at Irkutsk, Siberia, where he came under the influence of one of Russia's great Orthodox evangelists, Fr Alexander Men. In the age of *perestroika* Fr Alexander has frequently addressed a whole roomful of atheists and 'seekers', holding them spellbound for up to three hours (a videotape is available, showing him doing this). Back in the days of Stalin or Khrushchev, it was infinitely more dangerous to wean a young man away from some technical institute and into the ordained ministry, but this is what happened with Fr Gleb, showing that the religious revival, at least in a modest form, goes back to the immediate post-war years.

Fr Gleb's temporary break with the church ensured that he returned to it with renewed zeal. He came to Moscow determined to seek ordination. His mother told him to finish his forestry studies first, which he did, by which time he had married Iraida, who was to prove his faithful consort during a life of great testing. Only with great difficulty did he manage to pursue his theological studies, because he was exactly the sort of young man that the state was concerned to keep out of the seminary, but even in those days there were some brave bishops who were set on helping those who had a true vocation. Fr Gleb's mentor was Archbishop Leonid of Mozhaisk, later Metropolitan of Riga.

Ordination followed in 1962, but his work as a dedicated parish priest in Moscow lasted only for a brief spell, for this was now the heyday of the Khrushchev persecution. Knowing both the provinces and the capital city as he did, and rapidly acquiring a reputation as a fearless preacher at a time when most proclamation of the Gospel stopped well short of any practical application to an atheist society, Fr Gleb found that people visiting Moscow from distant corners of the Soviet Union sometimes made their way to his church. The tales they brought with them were horrifying: closure of churches by the local authorities in disregard of all the legal norms, brutal treatment of those who tried to resist, frequent imprisonment of believers after rigged trials.

Fr Gleb began to collect such information systematically and the word soon spread that he was the person to contact. Before long he and a fellow-priest, Fr Nikolai Eshliman, had compiled a considerable dossier. He quietly sounded out one or two older priests, asking the question why no one was willing to take an open stand against this new policy of the state. Eleven or so people said they were prepared to do something, but the promised solidarity failed to materialise, as a result of pressure from the KGB. Just one bishop made his own representations. From others there was always the same answer: 'It's wiser to keep quiet. The storm will pass. Speaking out will only make things worse.'

However, Fr Gleb's temperament would not allow him to watch others suffer in silence, particularly when people were approaching him for help. The initiative he and Fr Nikolai took was bold and unprecedented. In November and December 1965 they wrote two lengthy and detailed letters summarising the facts they had collected, setting them in a legal framework reminiscent of the Baptists' initiative of earlier in the year. They addressed one to the Soviet Government requesting justice and the other to the Patriarch begging him to speak out in defence of the persecuted church.

A quarter of a century later it is almost impossible to indicate just how brave this unprecedented action was. Except for the Baptists, no one in any field had ever defied the Soviet Government in such an open or organised way. Instead of bringing them to trial and imprisoning them alongside those they were trying to defend, the authorities leaned upon the Patriarch to act in their stead. The two priests were suspended from their parishes and subjected to an injunction of silence. Yet this in no way dimmed the impact of what they had done. Their words looked at again in the Gorbachev era read like a blueprint for church *perestroika*:

> No less than ten thousand churches and dozens of monasteries have been closed [during the Khrushchev campaign], among which we should specially mention the Monastery of the Caves at Kiev, the most ancient sacred place of our Orthodox people . . . Moreover, we consider it our right as citizens to call your attention to the undeniable fact that the mass closure of churches, a campaign instigated from above, has created an atmosphere of anti-religious fanaticism which has led to the barbaric destruction of a large number of superb and unique works of art.[4]

During his ten years of silence, a self-effacing act of ecclesiastical obedience, Fr Gleb watched the Brezhnev era become established. Whatever modest hopes accompanied its early years soon evaporated. Its economic policies moved nowhere and Mr Gorbachev later called the resulting mess the period of 'stagnation' (*zastoi*). In the field of human rights and culture, the writers' trials set the tone. Although it may have seemed, from the outside at least, that vigorous persecution of the church had subsided, persecution on the 'administrative' level became the main tool employed by the state in restricting church activity during this time. Churches found it difficult to register their communities, buildings were closed on the slightest pretext and there were petty restrictions at all levels – for example the refusal to provide electricity supplies to church buildings. Close monitoring of church activity was maintained at all levels. Active Christians continued to face difficulties in embarking upon or completing higher education or finding jobs in their chosen field. All of these factors combined showed how believers would continue to be treated as second class citizens: where there was not outright persecution, believers faced universal discrimination.

This era did, however, see increased 'dissident' and human rights activity, no doubt spurred on by the Helsinki agreements of 1975 as such issues began to feature more prominently on the international agenda. There was a crack-down in the republics against nationalism and in prison nationalists found themselves alongside Baptist activists, writers and Jews, as well as an assortment of political prisoners who refused to keep silent. In 1979 and 1980 the arrest and trial took place of religious activists such as Alexander Ogorodnikov, with others who had become involved in his unofficial Christian discussion group, the 'Christian Seminar'.

Among them were Christian activists from all the main denominations. Fr Gleb Yakunin had become their champion, acting with his supporters old and new to establish in 1976 the Christian Committee for Believers' Rights. This time the emphasis was more on ecumenical action. The documents he collected came from various denominations, again representing the most remote geographical areas of the Soviet Union. He did this after he had written an open letter to the Fifth General Assembly of the World Council of Churches in Nairobi begging for help for the persecuted church from the whole international Christian community. The debate which his letter provoked led him to believe – wrongly, as it turned out – that the WCC was behind him. His energy was prodigious. He collected no fewer than 423 documents, totalling nearly 3,000 pages, most of which he managed to send abroad, a record of contemporary church history in the USSR and of state persecution which could never be rivalled. He added to his growing world reputation by including Jews in his defence of religious rights.

By 1979 the lack of support from his own hierarchy and the unyielding attitude of the state led Fr Gleb to throw out a challenge which seemed to many at the time to be preposterous, but which now appears to have been totally justified: believers who wished to evade the straitjacket of state control should deliberately create unregistered – and therefore illegal – parishes and there should be secret ordination of clergy to set up a church structure parallel to the Moscow Patriarchate, but free of its domination.

The authorities could no longer tolerate such a firebrand and they came for him on 1 November 1979. Ten months later they sentenced him to ten years, five in labour camp, five in exile. His trial even more clearly indicated that Brezhnev had started a pointed drive against all democratic activity and many other human rights activists were soon to follow him to gaol.

Fr Gleb Yakunin served over eight years of his sentence before being released a little early in 1987 as a result of the new *perestroika*. During those years of silence, punctuated only by one or two letters smuggled out of the camps, including one begging me to intercede with the Soviet Government and with world opinion to allow him to have a Bible, he did not lose his symbolic status. He and a few others like him had done much to restore the moral authority of Russian Orthodoxy for those of the younger generation seeking a guiding principle in life. Without the likes of Fr Gleb the ground would not have been prepared for the period of church *perestroika* which followed his release.

Incredible as it may seem, there were three times as many churches open on the day Stalin died as when Gorbachev came to power in 1985. This is due solely to Khrushchev's destruction of the churches, not to the mass abandonment of the faith which propagandists claimed.

From 1987 the Soviet press began to publish articles in which believers in many different parts of the country demanded the reopening of their churches. This was still the focus of the aspirations of millions: to have an open church in which to pray and sing the liturgy celebrated clearly and reverently by their own priest. The press not only began in an unprecedented way to reflect the feelings of believers; it actually became a forum for them and unquestionably caused many who would never have dared to act in this way openly to campaign for change.

One of the most amazing examples of this was in *Moscow News*, which became a mouthpiece for *glasnost*. Alexander Nezhny, a campaigning journalist who would later identify himself as a Christian, wrote an indictment of the current policy of refusing to allow new churches to open, even where the building still existed, following its earlier confiscation. He wrote (the words are original, from the English-language version of the publication):

> Before 1962, Kirov had two Russian Orthodox Church communities, two churches – St. Feodor and St. Serafim. In 1962, in line with the then official policy that we should enter communism (which was believed to be close at hand) without religious people, or at least with a minimal quantity of such, St. Feodor Church was closed and its parish disbanded. Because the city authorities had rebuilding plans for the riverside, the church on the Vyatka bank was torn down. The plans called for erecting in its place

a monument celebrating the city's 600th anniversary. But the intriguing plan has so far given us only an ugly concrete slab buried under which is a capsule with a message to future generations.

An irreverent thought came to me when I faced the slab. For some unaccountable reason I thought that our wiser descendants would feel uneasy because of our desire to project a better image of ourselves than that which exists. I thought it would have been much more fair and moral to leave a two-word message buried in the high bank – 'Forgive us!' – because we have failed to preserve here, on the bank of the Vyatka, either St. Feodor Church or the striking [sic] beautiful seventeenth-century cathedral.[5]

These words, as a harbinger of church *perestroika*, would have been impressive enough in any context as early as August 1987 when they appeared. However, an additional and very special circumstance gave them an extraordinary resonance. When Fr Gleb Yakunin began his campaign in 1965 and ensured that his open letters were published in the West, one of the few people to give him open allegiance was a layman, Boris Talantov, a mathematics teacher from that very city of Kirov, formerly called Vyatka before the communists renamed it after a Party hero. In 1966 Talantov had written:

In the period 1960–63 the Kirov regional officials of the Council for Russian Orthodox Church Affairs [now called the Council for Religious Affairs] . . . arbitrarily removed 21 of the 80 priests active in 1959 and registered no-one in their place . . . At the same time the regional executive committee would pass a resolution to close the church and it would assign the building to the local *kolkhoz* or town *soviet* . . . When liquidating places of worship there would be a show of brute force. This would be carried out under the protection of the militia and auxiliary police, often at night. Believers would be forbidden to enter the church. The valuables would be removed without any inventory being made. In the Kirov region, when places of worship were liquidated, the interiors would always be barbarically destroyed, icons and holy vessels burned and all the valuables stolen . . .

Thus in the autumn of 1962 the congregation of St. Feodor's Church in Kirov was, with the agreement of the clergy, merged with St. Serafim's Church. The building itself was then destroyed and thrown into the river Vyatka. At the beginning of 1964 Bishop Ioann of Kirov shut the prayer house in the settlement of Rudnichnoye, which had been built by believers themselves in 1947. Officially this was described as merging one church with another situated forty kilometres away![6]

Six months after Boris Talantov had written his lengthy indictment, no less detailed and documented than Fr Gleb Yakunin's of two years earlier and of which we have quoted only the briefest extract, the local newspaper, *Kirovskaya pravda*, launched into a savage attack. Metropolitan Nikodim, then the chief spokesman for the Russian Orthodox Church, chimed in and claimed during a visit to London that Talantov's letter was anonymous, was therefore untrustworthy and should be disregarded. Under the immense strain of interrogations, accusations and criticism from the church leadership itself, Talantov's wife collapsed and died in September 1967. He himself was arrested two years later, though by this time a sick old man, and sentenced to two years' imprisonment under Article 190–1 (anti-Soviet slander). He did not live to regain his freedom. Betrayed by his own bishops, he died alone in a prison hospital on 4 January 1971. This did not prevent a large crowd from attending his funeral in Kirov. His death showed that nothing had changed under Brezhnev. In 1987 he and his work were reinstated in all but name in the Soviet press itself. Over the next few months there would be a spate of articles reporting demands of believers for the reopening of their churches all over the Soviet Union.

Clearly, religion never came anywhere near to dying out and Stalin was mistaken in thinking that closure of a church or imprisonment of a priest would lead to the demise of the faith in any given area. Nevertheless, systematic persecution eradicated virtually every Christian institution in the land, and the devastation will take generations to repair. Broadly speaking, religious revival can take two forms: first, the restoration of the formal life of the churches, flourishing worship, lively theological education, the publication of Christian literature – these we will discuss presently; and second, the restoration of religious values in society – a trend much harder to monitor.

Restoration of Religious Values

In a very real sense, religious values never died out, even in the years of the most brutal repression. It is hardly coincidental that Alexander Blok, poet of the Revolution, became a Christian at the end of his life. All four of his greatest successors embraced the faith in one way or another and kept it alive between the wars, even though they could not publish their works at the time. Mandelstam, Akhmatova, Tsvetaeva and Pasternak upheld values which communism could suppress, but not eradicate.

The war saw overt Christian revival, with Stalin needing the support of the churches when the Nazis were overrunning the Soviet Union.

The reopening of thousands of churches sent a signal that at some time society would again be able to acknowledge religious values.

The lifting of the terror after Khrushchev's secret speech of 1956 permitted people to begin discussing their feelings and aspirations more openly, if tentatively. Then followed the renewed persecution, the closure of churches, the response of believers, the imprisonment of those who defended the faith. In the absence of any significant official Christian publishing, the resulting circulation of manuscripts, typescripts and sometimes even beautifully home-bound books (*samizdat*) played an incalculable role in this rediscovery of belief. With a few exceptions, the new martyrs did not die for their faith, but they witnessed to it steadfastly in the prisons and camps. After their release their renewed presence revitalised their own communities and impressed literally tens of thousands of young people, who were beginning to be sickened by the inculcation of mindless atheism as a central part of their education in school.

In 1977 I visited a secret Sunday school in Kiev. The teacher had just been released from prison. Young, attractive, fearless, she risked further imprisonment by recounting her experiences to a group of fourteen- to sixteen-year-olds who hung on her every word:

> When I was in prison the language during every waking hour was foul and appalling. Sometimes we went to the punishment cells for proclaiming the Gospel to these poor lost souls, these criminals who had often fallen into sin simply because nobody had ever held the ideal of Christ before them. But we sometimes needed a rest from punishment. Then we would simply smile at their curses. When we came into a room where they were, they would know at once that we belonged to Christ because they could hear a tone of love in our voices. Children, you have to face mockery in school every day from your teachers and fellow-students. But you don't need to be punished every single day. Just show people your faith by the radiance on your faces, even when you're not saying a word.

The lesson continued for nearly an hour, unbroken by singing or by question and answer. Never before or since have I observed boys and girls of that age group so utterly absorbed in listening to a single voice. The suffering the teacher had herself so recently undergone endowed her with a moral authority which knit those young people together in a shared experience.

Gradually in recent years published literature, the cinema, and more recently the general press, have expressed an interest in religious themes, leading in the time of *glasnost* to what one can only call a rehabilitation of Christian values in the media. It is a fascinating story.

The very first example of this was as early as 1962, curiously enough at the time when the persecution under Khrushchev was at its worst. He personally sanctioned the publication of Solzhenitsyn's *One Day in the Life of Ivan Denisovich*, mainly to justify the accusations which he had made against Stalin. Here was an autobiographical account of prison-camp life which riveted just about every literate person in the Soviet Union. It did not escape this vast readership that there were two unforgettable portrayals of Christians in it: Alyosha, the Baptist, who told Ivan Denisovich the way a believer must pray; and a nameless priest who treats every meal as a sacrament, appearing as an icon of Christ as, with immense dignity, he unfolds his scrap of clean cloth on the filthy table before laying his hunk of bread on it and keeping his head upright while he takes his soup spoon to his mouth, just as every Orthodox believer does when he receives communion.

In the Brezhnev years this kind of writing could not develop, but the hiatus was gradually broken by the emergence of a group of writers who have been called the *derevenshchiki* (men of the countryside), who began to write naturalistically and with reverence about the persistence of old customs, among which, of course, religion had its place. Believers, although old, simple and often illiterate, gradually emerge as good people. There was plenty of criticism in the hard-line ideological journals of the Party, but this did not lead to suppression of these works. Gradually religion seemed to be seeping out of the confines of the scattered churches and back into the fabric of society.

Daniil Granin is a novelist who has always displayed a high moral purpose and would later, in Gorbachev's day, make an influential plea for a return to moral standards in society (see p.189). Here is a paragraph from his novel *The Picture*, describing a minor official and member of the Party (Losev) who takes his girlfriend to a town where they are not known. They visit the cathedral as tourists:

> It was the first time Losev had been inside a big, working church while a service was going on . . . The proceedings at the altar – the appearances and disappearances of the white-clad servers, the deacon swinging his censer, the procession of young priests in their brocade robes – it all seemed vaguely familiar, and he began remembering words he had never used and did not even know he knew . . . There must be something in all this, he thought: in the smoky gilded faces on the icons, in the resonance within the dome, in his own reflections about the shortness of life here on earth and about what is to follow that life.[7]

Losev is deeply impressed with the service, but is determined not to succumb to the lure of the faith. His schoolteacher girlfriend, Tanya, has less resistance and comes out of church on the brink of belief. She tells him that she has been praying, even though she did not know how to go about it. Later they talk to one of the servers from the church, who maintains that the way to faith is through doubt and recommends reading the Book of Job as a vehicle for bringing a doubter to the faith.

This is already a long step from the sentimental portrayal of believers as ageing and simple people. It is hard to believe that this novel saw the light of day in 1980, while Brezhnev was still in power and there were hundreds of men and women still in prison for their Christian activities.

More recently the historian Vadim Chubinsky reviewed a novel, *The Scaffold*, by the popular Central Asian writer, Chingiz Aitmatov, and commented on his choice of a Christian believer as his main character:

A significant (and strangely enough, not diminishing) section of the Soviet population – Christians and Muslims – believe in God, and a smaller section, also not insignificant in numbers, belong to the various cults. These people live and work alongside us, think and suffer and search for the meaning of life, argue amongst themselves; and even those of them who are professional 'churchmen' increasingly co-operate with us – for instance, in the peace movement. So is it right for them to be banished from our literature? Common sense replies – no; the very nature of the mission of literature says – no. Now Aitmatov has boldly broken into this virgin soil in literature; this first attempt may be imperfect in some ways, but surely it is worthy of recognition?[8]

Some *samizdat* authors of the Khrushchev–Brezhnev period much more openly embrace Christianity. Andrei Sinyavsky, now in exile in Paris, is an Orthodox believer. Nadezhda Mandelstam's biography of her late husband movingly recounts the role the faith played in their brief life together. The passionate Christian poetry of Irina Ratushinskaya, who belongs to the generation born in the 1950s, did not come out of a vacuum, but continues a tradition from the days of Tolstoy and Dostoevsky which was never completely ruptured.

In the world of art and music dozens of artists have expressed their faith in one way or another. The cellist Mstislav Rostropovich has shown that his dedication to music is grounded firmly in his allegiance to the faith of the Russian Orthodox Church. Among composers of the present day, Edison Denisov and Sofia Gubaidulina have expressed religious influences in their work, while Christian idealism so dominated the thinking of the Estonian, Arvo Pärt, that he had to emigrate to evade discrimination and unofficial banning of his compositions.

Religious themes are no less evident in the Soviet cinema. Naturally, these were usually implied rather than explicit, in order to stand some chance (not always successful) of circumventing the censor, more active here than in the field of literature, because a popular film would make a much more widespread impact.

Andrei Tarkovsky (1932–86) was brought up by his divorced mother in a Christian atmosphere, even though Stalin's terror reigned outside the house. The author of a recent perceptive study of his work writes:

> While it is doubtful that Tarkovsky gained much of an understanding of the liturgical life of the Orthodox Church or of its theology – books on theology, including the writings of the Church Fathers, would have been unavailable, though Tarkovsky was able to read the Bible – he seems to have been raised in an attitude of sympathy towards a church which was being harshly persecuted, indeed almost annihilated, during his boyhood . . . The art of Andrei Tarkovsky . . . points simultaneously toward the Orthodox Christian 'millennium' of Russian history and toward the dark pagan enchantment from which Vladimir of Kiev extracted the country in the tenth century.[9]

Tarkovsky's films were ambiguous and their dense imagery made them difficult to understand at first, but the censors, who waged a constant, but ultimately unsuccessful, battle with him, realised that here was a major figure dealing with man's central spiritual concerns in a totally non-communist way. *Andrei Rublyov* (1969) is one of the most complex historical films ever made, in which Tarkovsky attempts to recreate the religious and artistic atmosphere of the late fourteenth and early fifteenth centuries in a completely authentic and unprettified way. *Solaris* (1972) brings the themes of conscience and atonement into the unexpected context of science fiction. *The Mirror* and *Stalker*, both intricate films full of imagery containing both Christian and pagan elements, were made only under the greatest difficulties. Eventually Tarkovsky emigrated in 1984 and openly declared his Orthodox faith, while making his last two films in exile. He died of cancer in 1986 at the age of fifty-four, without experiencing the fruits of *perestroika*, the acceptance of his films in the Soviet Union, or the opportunity to return to his native land, as other artists in conflict, such as Rostropovich, Ashkenazy the pianist, and Lyubimov, the theatrical producer, were able to do.

Tengiz Abuladze's anti-Stalinist film, *Repentance*, took Moscow by storm when it was released in 1987. It tells the story of an artist, Sandro Baratelli, who is persecuted by the despotic Varlam, the mayor of a small Georgian town. The two characters come into conflict over a church which Varlam has turned into a science laboratory; Baratelli wants to preserve it as an essential part of the town's cultural and spiritual heritage. The church is later destroyed. For any Soviet citizen, the film is evocative of the Stalinist era, with the subsequent arrest and disappearance of Baratelli and the persecution of his relatives. The common theme of 'artist as prophet' or truth seeker, which crops up often in Russian literature, is here used to point to the need for repentance, the central idea of the film. The last scenes show an elderly lady asking Baratelli's daughter if the street she is on leads to the church. 'This street is named after Varlam: it cannot lead to the church.' 'What use is it if it does not lead to the church?' is the poignant reply, the last words of the film.

Religion has begun to play a prominent part in documentary films as well. For example, in 1988 during the celebration of the Millennium of Christianity cinemas all over the country were showing the highly artistic and beautiful study of the spiritual life of the Orthodox Church, *Khram* ('Church'), and it was also screened on television.

More recently there has been an amazing documentary, showing how the great monastic complex on the Solovki Islands in the White Sea was converted into one of Lenin's first prison camps. The film interviewed former inmates and included extracts from a Soviet prison documentary made before such enterprises became impossible.

The key moment for the emergence of a public debate on the reinstatement of Christian values was 10 December 1986, when the youth newspaper, *Komsomolskaya pravda*, printed two opposing views on the value of religion in cultural life. A conservative critic, Kryvelyov, had earlier attacked the religious and mystical leanings of such writers as Chingiz Aitmatov and Victor Astafiev, who were 'flirting with the gods'.

The reply came from Yevgeni Yevtushenko, angry young poet of the 1960s, who had become a kind of 'official dissident', often sent abroad to help the regime to prove how 'tolerant' it was. He was often under fire from those suffering for their non-conformist views. From this time on, however, Yevtushenko became a spokesman for the Gorbachev reforms. He stated that it was a weakness of Soviet culture that it felt obliged to put on counter-attractions at Easter to entice young people away from something genuinely beautiful, the ageless rituals of the Orthodox Church in their finest expression. 'The countenances of saints,' he wrote, 'painted by geniuses of the people, have more popular appeal than the stony frozen faces of those on boards of honour' (this is a reference to the Soviet practice of depicting heroes of labour and other such characters on notice boards outside the public enterprises where they work).

Throughout history, Yevtushenko continued, religion has at times played a positive role, which is not to deny that its influence has also sometimes been negative – but surely an objective assessment should now be possible? The Bible was a book which, in cultural terms, had immense value:

> I cannot understand why state presses have printed the Koran and not the Bible. Without Biblical knowledge young people are unable to understand much of Pushkin, Gogol, Dostoevsky and Tolstoy. The early Mayakovsky is full of Biblical imagery. The Bible fetches a huge sum in second-hand bookshops and on the black market. If Kryvelyov wants everybody to become convinced atheists, how can they be without a knowledge of the Bible? 'Forbidden fruit is sweet.' The socialist world-view cannot exist in a vacuum: you cannot adopt a theory without measuring it against other theories . . . Atheism in and of itself is not a source of morality; the source of morality is culture – culture in terms of human behaviour, conscience, knowledge of what is true and what is false . . . The source of morality is, in fact, life itself, people, creativity. Total unbelief is worse than false belief. There are universal, immutable values based on the struggle of humanity for justice.[10]

Published alongside his article is a rebuttal by a philosopher, Suren Kaltakhchian, who quoted Lenin's argument that the only true culture was one which furthered the development of society – and religion did not: 'Religion did not enrich culture, but extracted everything possible from it that could be used to increase its own influence.' It was necessary, he concluded, to stick to Marxist-Leninist ideology at all costs, as this teaching was all-sufficient for an understanding of the world.

This debate has developed in various ways. For example, Andrei Nuikin wrote in the influential literary journal *Novy mir* ('New World') in April 1987 that it was a poor kind of atheism which rejected religion out of hand or tackled it in a superficial or biased way. He fiercely attacked the kind of mindless hard-line dogmatism which was still finding a home in the Soviet press and contended that it was essential for any writer who tackled religion to be well versed in the subject.

True atheism must have a sound philosophical basis and unless mature creative thinking was encouraged and crude indoctrination avoided, Soviet society would produce not atheists, but 'mere godless men'.[11]

This argument seems now to have gained the upper hand since the Millennium celebrations of June 1988. Atheism in the Soviet media is clearly beating a fast retreat. In March 1989 a letter appeared in *Sovetskaya kultura* ('Soviet Culture') from a 'convinced atheist', who lamented the moral state of society, which was now manifesting all the social evils attributed for so long to its bourgeois equivalent. It was difficult to live without faith. Atheists believed in man, his high moral qualities and potential, in the attainment of communism – but what now? Religion had its own system of beliefs and offered a key to the human soul. The more churches were destroyed, the more the positive values relative to them disappeared. Now the time was past for communism to be afraid of religion and to treat believers as ignorant and fanatical. The Bible should be as easy to obtain as an ideological pamphlet and society would gain immeasurably from this.[12]

Even the main newspapers, such as *Izvestia*, reflected such a view. Two women wrote a letter published in the same month as the above:

> So many times we have heard our grandmothers' stories about their youth. We have been struck by the culture prevalent in those times . . . And now? Now we are persecuted by sex. Time and again we hear: prostitution! A normal, decent girl is simply afraid to go outdoors in the evening. Many people now think that truly pure and unclouded love has died . . . Why all this? It's because we have gone away from religion.[13]

The Christian Academician, Dimitri Sergeyevich Likhachev, talked at length to a correspondent of the magazine *Semya* ('Family') in the summer of 1988 on the essential contribution of Russian Orthodoxy to the whole origin of national culture.[14]

The overall impact of the rehabilitation of Christian and spiritual themes in every aspect of the media is penetrating to the general public. People are rapidly regaining part of their heritage which they believed they had lost for ever. Of course, the ban on religion over three generations, combined with the enforced atheist teaching at all levels from kindergarten to university, has left an immense void which it will take much more than a few novels and films to fill. The limitless hunger for the spiritual is a fact of life for tens of millions of people, but it is unfocused and undirected. Uncontrolled access to the media of proponents of any and every philosophy and paranormal experimentation holds out its own peculiar set of dangers which will need to be tackled in some concerted way.

One disturbing instance illustrating this very point was the televising of faith-healing sessions by A. Kashpirovsky in the autumn of 1989. He has gained a considerable reputation in the Soviet Union for his powers of hypnosis. These sessions were televised as part of a new slot in Sunday television: there is now a Sunday Moral Sermon, where church leaders such as Metropolitan Pitirim have give fifteen-minute talks; on other Sundays the programme has been devoted to Kashpirovsky's healing sessions which were over an hour long. These caused great controversy in the USSR and were the subject of a full page spread in the weekly newspaper *Literaturnaya gazeta* in December. Academic specialists asked if Kashpirovsky was a latter-day Rasputin with a similar corrupting influence in society. The paper also printed an extract from the *Journal of the Moscow Patriarchate* which briefly outlined Christian teaching on exorcism and the occult. The sessions are no longer televised, but the incident merely serves to illustrate how easily people who have been deprived of spiritual food for so long can be led into practices that are incompatible with church teaching.

'The Rehabilitation of Christian Ethical Values in the Soviet Media', as Dr William van den Bercken, of Utrecht University, calls a recent study of religious *glasnost* in the media, is one of the most significant and profound changes of the Gorbachev era, one which most of our radio and newspaper correspondents have lost sight of amid the welter of daily developments in the political field. He notes evidence of this everywhere and concludes:

> To Soviet man the problem of Stalinism and the Brezhnev-lie transcends party politics and historiography. Neither legal rehabilitation of the victims nor revision of history will be enough to overcome the legacy of the past. The Soviet Union under Gorbachev is undergoing a basic change of mentality. The significance of traditional Christian values in this reassessment process is that they arise not out of church involvement, but out of the independent search by Soviet intellectuals for ethical guarantees against the past repeating itself.[15]

The Christian Gospel, in the age of Mr Gorbachev's *glasnost*, is now reflected in the Soviet media in a way which, considering the previous seventy years of Soviet atheism, is little less than miraculous. The policies instituted by Gorbachev, as we shall see, have had a special role to play in the development of the life of the churches in the USSR over the past two to three years. Events such as his accession to power in March 1985 and the Orthodox Millennium three years later will surely go down in history as key factors in the turning of the tide for religious liberty.

2 Gorbachev and His Times

A New Man for New Times

In Rome, 1978 became known as the 'year of the three Popes'. The election and sudden death of yet another Italian Pope (John Paul I) seemed to many a divine intervention conveying the strongest possible message that it was time for a complete change of direction. The conclave of Cardinals looked to where the church was strongest and elected a Pole.

Soon afterwards, the Soviet Union saw a similar process. The time-lapse was a little longer – Brezhnev died on 10 November 1982; Gorbachev was elected on 11 March 1985 – but it included no fewer than three deaths and four leaders. History will judge whether or not divine intervention operated in the Kremlin: Andropov was soon seen to be deteriorating physically; the election of the obviously ailing Chernenko to succeed him was a stop-gap measure. The Presidium was left no alternative but to choose a man young enough to withstand the physical demands of the job and flexible enough to overhaul the complicated and archaic system with decisive and innovative policies.

Nearly twenty years under Brezhnev had led the Soviet Union to the brink of economic catastrophe. But the successive appointment of two men who were visibly – and in the case of Chernenko, frequently and embarrassingly before the eyes of the world on television – unable to perform even the simplest offices of state must also have had a psychological effect on the Soviet people. Andropov, to be sure, had a decisive personality, as one would expect of a man who had risen through the toughest of systems to become head of the state security (KGB), but he was sixty-eight years old on his appointment and it rapidly became obvious that his best years were behind him. The world's press, with more optimism than soundness of judgment, dubbed him an 'intellectual' and an 'innovator', but his plans did not amount to much more than a drive against corruption, and even this was cut short by his ill health. One noteworthy action was his promotion of Gorbachev within the Politburo – indeed some commentators believe that it was he who paved the way for Gorbachev's reforms. Chernenko, who could scarcely speak, achieved nothing of note.

By this time there was a generation of young people who could not remember even the era of Khrushchev's reforms, which had ended twenty years before. For a long time most citizens accepted the threat of foreign invasion as a justification for the massive military build-up, without recognising that this was a major factor in the general economic deprivation. Most sharply of all, the gradual penetration of images from the West, through foreign broadcasts and contacts with visitors, began to prove that beyond those impassable frontiers there was a different mode of existence where people did not live six to a room. The facts of underdeveloped Soviet economic life were not the only realities in the world. Change was long overdue; a leader of vigour and vision was needed.

Mikhail Sergeyevich Gorbachev was born in 1931 in the remote village of Privolnoye, Stavropol Region, in the south of Russia. He needed physical endurance even to survive to the point where his mental toughness could begin to set him on his way towards a special career.[1] Of the millions who died in the famines in the Ukraine and southern Russia during the 1930s, possibly as many as 30,000 came from his own region. When he was eleven, the invading Nazi army penetrated just far enough east to occupy his home village and this hostile influx must have had a profound influence on him. Nearly fifty years later, however, this would not prevent him from tacitly approving the reforms occurring in the German Democratic Republic; his policy of non-intervention over the destruction of the Berlin Wall being a decisive factor in the rush towards democracy in Eastern Europe.

Many neighbouring families suffered far worse than the Gorbachevs, not only from the famine, but from the enforced collectivisation. Gorbachev's grandfather was not a dispossessed land-owner, but a peasant who benefited from the new system to become director of the local collective farm. After the war he played a key role in rebuilding the economy of the area. His father, wounded on the Polish front in the war, became a tractor driver on the *kolkhoz*. He died in 1976.

It was a normal enough background for a boy growing up in the Soviet Union in the 1930s. There was nothing unusual, either, in having a parent or a grandparent who was a believer. Gorbachev's mother was a practising Orthodox Christian and he was baptised. She still lives in the same village and, apparently, is a believer to this day. The young Mikhail probably went to church and would have heard from his mother at an early age, well before starting school, something of the persecution of religion during these times of great hardship.

His early education at the local primary school, later at secondary school, then finally at Moscow State University (1950–55), included not only the standard lessons on Marxism-Leninism, but a compulsory course on 'scientific atheism'. A pass was necessary in this for acceptance at any university, not least Moscow, which attracted the intellectual elite of the Soviet Union, but which was barred to all but the most ideologically reliable.

It seems likely that the enforced dogma predominated over the 'vestiges of the past' (to use the standard phrase of the propaganda of the time) which Gorbachev would have experienced at his mother's knee. This was in contrast to many other families, where children sincerely wanting to be Christians were thrown into constant conflict with teachers at school.

Gorbachev was in Moscow as a law student when Stalin died in 1953. The nation was psychologically unprepared for this event and many feared for the future. Only a few could see that a new age was dawning, offering openings within the system for young people with ambition. A certain subdued anticipation of the future may have tempered the grief Gorbachev shared with his fellow-students, including Raisa Maximovna, whom he met and married during his student years. Without the necessary contacts in Moscow, he was unable to get a job in the capital on completion of his degree and was forced to return to Stavropol to begin an arduous climb up the Party ladder.

Gorbachev's law degree from Moscow University gave him local status, even at an early age. As a dedicated Party man, he was not afraid to criticise, but first of all he always observed. He began to take note of the many defects in the system. Given his background, he was particularly interested in agriculture. He saw it falling massively short of its potential, even in an area of high production like his own, where good soil and a warmer climate gave it an advantage over the harsher north. He must have asked himself whether collectivisation could ever provide the plenty it was supposed to do. Mechanisation simply failed to happen according to the five-year plans. Even where there were tractors, spare parts were woefully short, often keeping the machines out of the fields for weeks at a time. Here, as in many branches of industry, a kind of barter system grew up, in which only material inducements could be sure of making the wheels of production turn. It was only a short step from this to the corruption which was to become endemic.

He saw the toll of days lost to drunkenness, so that when he was finally in a position of supreme authority one of his first edicts curbed the massive sale of alcohol and banned it from Kremlin functions – a brave attempt at reform which failed through popular resistance and complaints at the loss of income from the taxes.

In the meantime, Raisa worked on her doctoral thesis, entitled 'The Emergence of New Characteristics in the Daily Lives of the Collective Farm Peasantry'[2], which was based on sociological investigations in the region. In many respects this was a pioneering work, which undoubtedly had an influence on her husband's later reform programme.

Gorbachev became Stavropol First Secretary at the age of thirty-nine. He was an energetic and popular Party chief with a reputation for getting results. He also had the advantage of presiding over an area of spa towns patronised by members of the Kremlin leadership: it was at the town of Kislovodsk that he first met Andropov and was able assiduously to cultivate good relations with the future General Secretary, himself from the Stavropol region. Gorbachev followed in the footsteps of another ambitious Party man, Kulakov, who had been responsible for Gorbachev's appointment as Party chief following his own promotion to Moscow. Suslov, the chief Party ideologist, also a former Stavropol Party First Secretary, is similarly believed to have promoted Gorbachev. Thus it was that Gorbachev found himself back in Moscow, promoted to the position of Secretary of the Central Committee responsible for agriculture in December 1978.[3]

Gorbachev in Moscow

In 1980 Gorbachev was promoted to be a full member of the Politburo, although he was still virtually unknown to the world at large. He made his mark quickly, travelling abroad energetically and impressing those he met. On his first visit to Britain he met Mrs Thatcher, establishing a good relationship on which he was later to build. It was she who coined the phrase that Gorbachev was a 'man you can do business with'.

On his election as General Secretary of the Communist Party of the Soviet Union on 11 March 1985, Gorbachev appeared as a figure who had spent most of his life in the provinces, far away from the intrigues of the Kremlin and apparently uncorrupted by them. During his first months in office, he showed himself to be his own man, ready to take decisive action particularly in restructuring the top of the *apparat* around him, but in no sense stepping beyond the boundaries within which any good Marxist-Leninist could have been expected to move. He must, however, have been deeply troubled to realise the full depth of the economic crisis which he had inherited and the massive commitment he faced in the arms race, which deflected into sterile confrontation untold billions of roubles which were sorely needed for economic development. He had also inherited international opprobrium for his country's invasion of Afghanistan six years earlier, whilst thousands of grieving families believed they had lost their sons to a useless cause. Led by a well-organised Jewish lobby, world criticism confronted him with the shameful Soviet human rights record of recent years.

In the autumn of 1985 Gorbachev visited France. In an interview for French television broadcast on 30 September, he showed his willingness to debate human rights issues, but without making any dramatic departure from established policies:

> Let us in the Soviet Union manage our own affairs . . . The question of human rights presents no difficulties for us. We are prepared to debate this question anywhere . . . Of course, we have people who follow their own logic, clash with Soviet power and with socialism and profess a different ideology. Problems arise here in those cases in which an individual comes into conflict with the law. That was what happened to Shcharansky . . . When questions of the reunification of families arise, we agree to this, except in cases where people know state secrets.[4]

Four months later, again addressing a French public, but this time through the communist newspaper, *L'Humanité*, Gorbachev stated:

> Soviet Jewry have become the cause of psychological warfare waged against the USSR . . . I believe that in a civilised society there must be no room at all for anti-semitism, Zionism or any other manifestations of nationalism, chauvinism or racism. Now for political prisoners. We have none, just as we do not persecute people for their convictions. But any state must protect itself against those who try to subvert it.[5]

It was obviously extremely difficult then for Gorbachev to take more than a single step at a time. One can discern an attempt to placate the old guard in his painful repetition of tarnished propaganda in the immediate continuation of the interview in *L'Humanité* quoted above: 'Now Sakharov. Measures were taken regarding him in accordance with our legislation . . . Sakharov lives in Gorky in normal conditions, conducts research and remains an Academician. He is in normal health, as far as I know.'

Within three days Anatoli Shcharansky walked free. He was one of the outstanding Soviet human rights activists, whose marriage to Avital and her long years of campaigning during his subsequent imprisonment turned him into one of the world's best-known political detainees. On 11 February 1986 his diminutive figure, striding alone across the Glienicke Bridge between East and West Berlin, hands holding up trousers many sizes too big for him, was an unmistakable signal that something new was happening in the Soviet Union. A factor in this must have been the continual demonstrations suffered by any Soviet statesman making a foray outside the Eastern bloc. But here already were the first stirrings of desire to establish what Mr Gorbachev was later to call a 'law-governed state'.

Between the release of Shcharansky and the Reykjavik summit in the autumn of 1986 an event occurred which shook Gorbachev and all the Kremlin leaders to the core: Chernobyl. The week-long silence of the leadership following the explosion at the nuclear reactor indicates the magnitude of the shock. There was a clear policy break at this point. Everyone could see that the system was totally unprepared to deal with any major crisis; basic improvements were imperative. The pace of change began to accelerate. Chernobyl is in Ukraine and some saw that republic as a victim of Moscow's policies. Demands began to be heard that the republics should have greater control over their own affairs. Now opposition to environmental pollution, which not so long ago had been treated as virtually treasonable, was gaining momentum. The Chernobyl disaster put huge areas of good agricultural land out of production and therefore placed an immense strain on already overstretched economic resources. Internationally, this was the moment at which it became evident that atomic energy, whether for offensive or peaceful uses, was not a panacea for mankind; the stage was set for the first offer of wide-ranging concessions in the armaments race.

By the time of the Reykjavik summit, begun at short notice and with little preparation less than six months after Chernobyl, on 10 October 1986, it was obvious that Mr Gorbachev was determined to present a new face to President Reagan and to the world. In the few hours of hiatus between the departure of the leaders from their capitals and the opening of the conference itself the world received dramatic news. It could not have come at a more advantageous time, with the media anxious to report on something substantial from inside the Soviet Union.

One of the most notorious unresolved human rights cases was the imprisonment and treatment of the young poet Irina Ratushinskaya. Her 'crime' had been to write poetry of a personal and Christian nature, containing clear elements of protest against oppression; for this she had been sentenced as recently as 1983, at the age of twenty-eight, to seven years' imprisonment in a strict regime labour camp followed by five years of exile. Keston College had passed on to the world urgent messages about her deteriorating health, along with new poems smuggled out of the prison. Dick Rodgers, an Anglican minister who had spearheaded a number of campaigns for religious liberty in the Soviet Union, spent the whole of Lent 1986 in a cage in his home city of Birmingham subjecting himself to conditions and a diet which as nearly as possible reproduced those Irina was simultaneously undergoing. His initiative may well have saved her life.

Early on the morning the summit was due to begin, Keston College received a telephone call from Irina herself, back in her home city of Kiev, announcing that she had been released unconditionally the previous day and was now expecting to emigrate with her husband. For a few hours this became the lead story in the world's press.

It would be easy to describe this move as a cynical attempt by Mr Gorbachev to win a major propaganda victory and seize an unexpected advantage at a key time. His move certainly won him the credit he sought, but it turned out to be no mere ploy to gain favour, for it paved the way for another dramatic move, which turned out to be much more than a gesture. Two months later Gorbachev telephoned Academician Andrei Sakharov in exile in the city of Gorky, whither Brezhnev had sent him with no pretence of a trial. Gorky was closed to foreigners, so the aim had been to sever his overseas contacts, but his wife, Yelena Bonner, by coming periodically to Moscow, had managed nevertheless to keep some lines of communication open. As he was by far the best-known democratic reformer in the USSR, his recall to Moscow sent to the Soviet people and to the world the strongest possible signal that there were to be far-reaching changes in the ordering of society. There were some who believed Sakharov was by now a broken man who had compromised himself.

Gorbachev can scarcely have envisaged that just two years later Sakharov would be elected to the new Congress of People's Deputies, that its debates would rivet the nation to its TV sets and that one of the most memorable transmitted images would be the elected deputy, Sakharov, challenging him face to face over the Communist Party's right to supremacy. Gorbachev's evident grief at the sudden death of Sakharov just after this on 14 December 1989 illustrates the respect he undoubtedly feels for intellectuals, even those who do not share his beliefs, such as another deputy, Academician Dimitri Likhachev (not to be confused with the conservative politician Ligachev), an outstanding layman of the Russian Orthodox Church. Indeed, it is true to say that, unlike his predecessors, Gorbachev is himself one of the intelligentsia, as is his wife.

Sakharov's return inaugurated the process, which lasted right through the next year, of releasing nearly all the four hundred or so religious prisoners and the much larger number of political detainees.

However, the Soviet human rights record was not always displaying such positive signs at this stage. Barely three weeks before Sakharov's return from exile – and perhaps also influencing Gorbachev's decision – another veteran Soviet human rights campaigner, Anatoli Marchenko, died in the notorious Chistopol prison. He had spent twenty of his forty-eight years in Soviet prison camps. Arrested originally on charges of alleged hooliganism after a brawl, he discovered the full brutality of the Soviet penal system. His observations evolved into a book, *My Testimony*, which circulated in *samizdat* and was published in the West in 1968. He was serving a fifteen-year sentence for anti-Soviet agitation and propaganda when he died as a result of KGB brutality.

The Jewish community continued, with considerable justification, to complain that the emigration laws had not been relaxed to the extent needed to clear the huge backlog of people waiting to leave the Soviet Union. But the reception Mr Gorbachev subsequently received in Washington and Bonn showed him that at least one aspect of his policy had succeeded, for rarely has a visiting foreign statesman received such an ecstatic welcome in either city.

While these events were taking place, the thankless grind of trying to activate the economy was beginning. The world embraced *glasnost* and *perestroika*, which became household words. The first is usually translated as 'openness', but its root is *golos* (voice) and long before this the word had existed in a human rights context with the connotation of 'giving voice (or publicity)' to injustice. It was an emotive concept and it became the watchword of a new age. Gorbachev probably thinks of *perestroika* ('restructuring') as more important; scarcely a day passes without his criticising those who resist it. At times he seems to try to give it a persona of its own, but one can sense his frustration as he fails to find enough people at middle or lower levels able and willing to implement the vision he proclaims from above. Everywhere now in Soviet society one sees *glasnost* in abundance, so much so that some are growing tired of the superabundance of information previously shrouded from view. By contrast, the progress of *perestroika* is negligible in the very economic sphere into which Gorbachev launched it. In some areas, however, especially the arts, religion and now nationalism, *perestroika* has moved ahead with shattering speed – so much so that the political map of Europe had to be torn up and replaced by a new one in the three months between October and December 1989. Another of Mr Gorbachev's key concepts, *demokratizatsia*, played a major role here.

There was a clear distinction in Gorbachev's mind between 'democratisation' and 'democracy'. The former represented a process designed to galvanise the supine political processes into activity and provide some real leadership in the republics. The latter, under the scrutiny of even the most elementary logic, would mean the disintegration of the Soviet system. This is indeed happening, but he certainly did not intend to precipitate it. *Demokratizatsia* was intended to be some kind of halfway house, a limbo in which the Communist Party could always blow the whistle and remind the contestants of the ground rules. The concept was not a sham, as demonstrated by the setting up of elections to the new Congress of People's Deputies at the end of March 1989. The process was controlled from the top to produce the inevitable communist majority, but the process had invigorated some Party members, such as Yuri Afanasiev and Boris Yeltsin, who led a most outspoken campaign of dissent. There were also genuine lists of non-Party candidates, many of whom were successful in the first legal exercise of the democratic right since 1917. The effect was to produce an enormous burst of self-confidence in the satellite countries of Eastern Europe, and the certainty in the Baltic States that the course on which they were already embarked was not a romantic one leading inevitably to disaster, but a realistic one, in which the statesmanlike approach which they were already so notably demonstrating had a serious chance of achieving the independence they had lost fifty years earlier. The first fragment of masonry from the Berlin Wall in the hand of a demonstrator whose action went unpunished was proof to every nationalist and democrat, and even to millions who had not dared to think that way before, that resolute action could now sound the death-knell of a massive system of oppression and overthrow Soviet communism once and for all.

Opposition to Gorbachev

The advent of *glasnost* has illuminated the secret deliberations of the Kremlin leadership hardly at all (though even in a democracy such as Britain Cabinet discussions cannot come into the public domain for thirty years after they have taken place). Therefore we know little about the real nature of the opposition to Mr Gorbachev at this time. No explanation is yet forthcoming as to why the Red Army stood by in apparent impotence while the basic prop of their policy, the Warsaw Pact, disintegrated in the three months between October and Christmas 1989; or why the KGB acquiesced as central control over the republics collapsed and the whole Soviet system appeared to be tottering towards a rapid end. The old logic would have demanded the hardening of opposition and the overthrow of Gorbachev at a dozen different points, but he has shown statesmanship of unprecedented calibre in dominating the public debates, staying one jump ahead of his opponents and even turning to his advantage the endless contradictions, where what he has dismissed as impossible one week is implemented the next.

In these astonishing days extraordinary explanations abound of how these events have taken such a course. Before we come to our central discussion of the effect all this would have on religious life, perhaps it is worth quoting the most exotic theory on offer: even this is not entirely without credibility. It goes something like this.

In the developing arms race and with the stagnant Soviet economy, disaster seemed to be looming ever closer. Soviet military might could maintain its lead only by draining more and more from the economy, but this could not move forward because of the huge gap between Soviet and American technology. Far from 'overtaking America' (the watchword of the Khrushchev era), the Soviet Union was destined to fall further and further behind. In the USA the simplest processes were computerised, while the Soviet Union kept its insufficient photocopiers under lock and key. That disparity was growing daily and the Soviet Union was degenerating to the economic status of a third-world country. The 'Star Wars' programme of President Reagan gave the uncomfortable feeling that this technology gap would before long annihilate even the capability of the Soviets to deliver a nuclear strike beyond their own territory. The refined espionage techniques of the KGB, especially in the industrial sphere, were producing the message that current Soviet development had reached an impasse; only the most dramatic solution could now offer any hope.

Someone trustworthy and decisive had to be found who would lead the Soviet Union along a new path. It was the KGB, it is argued, who held the real power in the Soviet Union; they discovered Gorbachev virtually within their own ranks, a protégé of their former head, Yuri Andropov, to whom he owed his rapid rise to the Politburo. Therefore, according to this theory, Gorbachev owes the apparent unassailability of his position to the direct protection of the KGB, which gave him *carte blanche* to implement a dramatic programme, though doubtless without their seeing that the logical end of that road would be the disintegration of the system.

A counter-argument to this is the fact that Chebrikov, head of the KGB on Gorbachev's accession, apparently turned against him when his programme became more radical, but the highest Party organs were strong enough, first to move him sideways, then to retire him.

That there was still considerable opposition along the way, even if this theory should prove correct, is demonstrated by the occasional rallies of the counter forces. A non-democratic leader is always particularly vulnerable while absent abroad, as Mr Ceausescu found to his cost during his visit to Iran in December 1989. While Mr Gorbachev was absent in Cuba and then in London in April 1989 there were two separate assaults on his authority. The first was the sending-in of the troops to quell a peaceful nationalist demonstration in Tbilisi, Georgia, with the subsequent massacre, an action which Gorbachev could never have sanctioned. The second was a legal event which was quite out of keeping with his policy before and since.

On the very day after his return to Moscow from London – a Saturday, incidentally – Gorbachev signed a decree which seemed to negate some of the very advances he had been fighting for over the past three years. It consisted of amendments to the old law on crimes against the state, under which so many people had been imprisoned over the last thirty years. It proclaimed a punishment of between three and ten years for acquiring 'material assets or technical means from organisations abroad or their representatives' for 'undermining the political and economic system of the USSR'.[6] Such catch-all phrases threatened all who had contact with foreigners, warning them against receiving even such essential items as photocopying machines. While the decree did not specifically mention religious believers, these

groups felt seriously at risk, because often in the past the demand for
religious reform had been quoted in the courts as an act prejudicial to
the state. The decree went on to designate a three-year sentence for
those who called for 'betrayal of the homeland'. Which homeland?
Clearly, the decree meant the 'Soviet homeland', but this was at
a time when the very concept was disintegrating and nationalist
movements in Georgia and the Baltic States were already operating
openly.

The only other signature on the document beside Gorbachev's was
that of the Georgian, T. Menteshashvili, Secretary of the Presidium of
the Supreme Soviet (Gorbachev was its chairman). The only plausible
explanation for such a blow against *perestroika* is that a group of
hard-liners must have used the Georgian demonstration as the cue
for saying 'enough is enough', put the document together in haste
and presented Gorbachev with a 'sign or else' ultimatum virtually
as he stepped off the aeroplane. A further spur to action must have
been the elections to the new Congress of People's Deputies just a
week earlier, as a result of which a number of the old guard received
their marching orders. Ironically, it was precisely this body which
was now designated to see through any new legislation, and here
was its authority undermined before it had even met. The end of
this episode was nevertheless a victory for Gorbachev's real plans:
when the new body did meet, it repealed the act, which had never
reached the stage of implementation.

Human Rights

There can be no doubt that, in general terms, Mr Gorbachev is well
disposed to the safeguarding of human rights in the new society he
wishes to build. A concrete sign of this was the setting up at the
end of 1987 of a 'Public Commission for Humanitarian Questions
and Human Rights', known as the Burlatsky Commission, after its
chairman. This was a direct response to worldwide criticisms of the
Soviet record on human rights.

Fyodor Burlatsky himself is a man to note. In *Literaturnaya gazeta*
on 1 October 1986 he opened the door to a major debate on human
rights by publishing an article in which he constructed an imaginary
dialogue between an opponent and a supporter of *perestroika*. The
opponent says it will all come to nothing, just as happened in the
period after Stalin. The advocate claims that this time it will be
different, for now there is sufficient 'political will and courage'. In

an interview which he gave to an American Christian journalist in
September 1988, he talks of his career to date:

> I was educated in law. During the late 1950s I tried to push for the
> creation of political science as an academic discipline. I was interested
> in the relationship between the state, democracy and human rights.
> For example, in 1957 I published an article about the process of
> democratization after the Twentieth Party Congress, which included
> human rights problems. I practised law for about three years, then I
> became a journalist . . . I was chairman of the so-called 'scientific' political
> advisory group during the Khrushchev era, and was his speech-writer.
> After he was purged, I returned to my scientific and journalistic
> activities. Then, at the beginning of the Gorbachev era, I realized
> that there were new possibilities for activities with some progressive
> and 'radical' intellectuals. It was my idea to create this commission on
> human rights.[7]

Mr Burlatsky backed up his words with his deeds as soon as his
Commission was in place. He proved that this would not be mainly a
propaganda exercise by calling for the release of Soviet political and
religious prisoners, entering into well-publicised negotiations with a
group set up by Mrs Rosalyn Carter, wife of the former American
President, about individual names remaining on the list of detainees.
He also promoted the legalisation of the Ukrainian Catholic Church,
in the interview quoted above, more than a year before this came
about, and criticised Soviet bureaucracy in 1989 when many of the
projected new laws seemed to be disappearing into limbo between
the promise and the drafting.

The Burlatsky Commission moved ahead of international agreements, but in the spirit of the negotiations going on at the time. During
1988 a lengthy conference in Vienna reviewed and reformulated the
Helsinki Accords of 1975. Here, for the first time, the subject of
human rights was singled out as demanding its own special series
of conferences. Press freedom, the right to emigrate and environmental issues received similar attention from the thirty-five original
signatories to the 1975 agreement (all the countries of Europe except
Albania, plus the USA and Canada). Given the tensions between
Eastern and Western Europe at the time, it was a triumph of patient
diplomacy that all these signatories, who fourteen years earlier had
been concerned mainly with security and the guaranteeing of existing
borders, should now be prepared to sharpen the focus and agree to
a systematic examination of human rights abuses and restrictions on
religious liberty over the whole of their diffuse territory.

The holding of a human rights conference in Moscow had now

become official Soviet policy, since Gorbachev had requested it, virtually off the cuff, at the Reykjavik summit. Some observers interpreted the establishment of the Burlatsky Commission as deliberately preparing the way for this goal; others saw in it an attempt to short-circuit the activities of the various rival independent human rights groups which were now proliferating in Moscow and other cities.

With the conclusion of the Vienna conference in January 1989, the Soviets did indeed secure assent to their conference proposal, but only as the culmination of a series of three meetings to be held in Paris in June 1989, Copenhagen a year later and Moscow in October 1991. The British Government made it clear that it would attend the final one only if there was a significant improvement in Soviet human rights performance, not least in the area of religious liberty; the preceding two conferences would monitor carefully the progress of the Soviet Union and the other countries of the Eastern bloc. As one of the six official British delegates to the Paris conference, three from the Foreign and Commonwealth Office, three from independent monitoring groups known as NGOs (Non-Governmental Organisations), I was able to observe for myself that the process began in a satisfactory way. Though the discussions were so formal as to preclude any cut-and-thrust debate, delegates raised and therefore put on record all the major issues. Representatives from Eastern Europe, not least Romania, were prepared to listen to detailed accounts of their shortcomings. In the past, sharp criticisms of individual nations in various international forums have sometimes led to a walk-out, but there was no suggestion of this in the Paris meeting.

From now on, then, the governments of Western Europe and North America (but the Soviet Government, too, in the shape of the Burlatsky Commission) were prepared to set up modest departments and to put money into the promotion of human rights, a very real contribution to the development of international law and one which must set a standard for other troubled areas of the world.

Whatever the outcome of the series of conferences in a 'Helsinki area' vastly different from the one in which the original agreements were signed, the interim conclusion must be that the Soviet authorities were taking their commitment to human rights seriously at a time when the central authority of a Kremlin directive still meant something. Although the political upheavals of 1990 have meant that the Burlatsky Commission now receives less attention than formerly, it is still an important symbol as a pressure group during Gorbachev's struggle to achieve a law-governed society.

Religious Liberty

From the time of Mr Gorbachev's accession in 1985, it became probable that there would be a softer line on religion, though no one could have foreseen the dramatic initiatives that the new leader would take three years later. During the first six months the press was virtually silent on religion, with the exception of a conventional article in *Pravda* on 13 September 1985. Just over a month later the draft of the new Communist Party programme appeared in the same newspaper. What it said on religion was brief and relatively mild – obviously the ideologues had been too busy on more pressing subjects to pay much attention to believers: 'The right way to overcome religious prejudices is to heighten people's labour and social activity, educating them and devising and widely adopting new Soviet rituals.'[8]

The draft of the revised Party rules a week later did no more than instruct members to continue on the old path of 'resolute struggle' against religion.

Mr Gorbachev had been in power almost a year before he made his own first public pronouncement on the subject. This was at the 27th Party Congress on 25 February 1986. His meaning was far from clear: 'Stagnation is simply intolerable . . . in the entire sphere of ideological, political, labour, moral and atheistic upbringing . . . It is inadmissible to depict in idyllic terms reactionary, national and religious survivals contrary to our ideology.'[9]

When the Congress closed two weeks later, it added a caution regarding believers' feelings, one which had been uttered many times in the past, even though scant regard had been paid to it: 'The Party will use all forms of ideological influence for the wider propagation of a scientific understanding of the world, for the overcoming of religious prejudices without permitting any violation of believers' feelings.'[10]

Six months later *Pravda* published an editorial entitled 'To educate convinced atheists'. Again, the line was not strong, even though at that time, under its conservative editor, Viktor Afanasiev, it often lagged behind the pace of reform set by Mr Gorbachev. It touched upon recent debates in the Soviet press on the place of religion in literature and attacked 'flirting with god'. The hints that young people were still showing an interest in religion and the call for an intensification of atheist education were entirely conventional, merely repeating what had already been said a thousand times in the Soviet press over many years.

As was to be expected from a man who would become known as
the arch reactionary in Mr Gorbachev's administration, when Yegor
Ligachev came into the attack on 1 October 1986, addressing a
conference of social scientists, he was much more specific:

> Sometimes when certain people encounter violations of socialist morality
> they begin to talk about the advisability of showing tolerance for religious
> ideas and of returning to religious morality. In doing so they forget the
> Marxist truism that religion can never be the source of man's moral
> principles. It was not religion that gave mankind the moral norms that
> are now shared by the human race . . . but by its content communist
> morality has significantly enriched the norms common to all mankind
> . . . Sometimes nationalism disguises itself in religious garb. This
> is clearly apparent, for example, in the reactionary element of the
> Islamic, Uniate and Catholic clergy. We must continue to search for
> new approaches, for new ways and means of atheist propaganda and
> work with believers.[11]

No words could make clearer the opposition that there would be
in high places to the new deal which Mr Gorbachev would offer to
believers eighteen months later. But before that offer, Gorbachev
himself would take up Ligachev's challenge in what seems to have
been his only major anti-religious statement. This came in an unexpected place, almost as a throw-away. On his way to India he stopped
briefly in Tashkent on 24 November. Before a predominantly Muslim
audience, he criticised the tendency of many writers to idealise the
past and went on to attack many local officials, doubtless meaning
those present, for compromising with religion by participating in
religious rites. He continued with familiar and tired old phrases,
saying there should be a 'decisive and uncompromising struggle'
with religion and an improvement of atheist work in the republic.
It is significant that the central press did not publish these remarks
and they came to light only through a local newspaper. Was there
some positive censorship in operation which deliberately excluded
these anti-religious sentiments from gaining nationwide currency?
Or was Mr Gorbachev pushed beyond what he had intended to
say and himself attempted to limit the effect of his words after
he had spoken them? The simplest and most likely explanation is
to be found in the context. These words addressed militant Islam.
They were never intended to be an attack against Christianity and
therefore it would have been misleading to publish them in European
Russia.

An article in *Izvestia* just a week later hinted that there might be a debate in the upper echelons of the Party, fuelled by the developments in Poland, where it was clear that the forces of atheism were gaining no ground whatsoever against the church.[12] The attack was against the role of the clergy in political life and its usurping of the role of guardian of and spokesman for the conscience of the nation. The clergy were seizing on the forthcoming Eucharistic Congress and visit of the Pope as a way of strengthening their influence on young people. The article quoted General Jaruzelski's views on the incompatibility of religion and communism.

Yevgeny Yevtushenko's article in *Komsomolskaya pravda*, the youth newspaper, struck a truly new note (see Chapter 1). He wrote of the aesthetic attraction of religious art and ritual and attacked the tendency to depict all discussion of religion as 'flirting with god'. Despite black spots in history, he continued, there were many instances of the church playing a progressive role. Finally, the adoption of atheism in no way guaranteed high standards of personal morality. These were much more likely to come from the general cultural standards in one's life.

This was the first salvo in a debate which began to go in a very interesting, not to say subversive, direction. Could it be that the promotion of atheism in itself was harmful to personal morality? A growing number of people seemed to think so and reflections of the debate began to appear in the Soviet press. If it were true, this would be another blow to the heartland of communism. After all, 'communist morality' had been a slogan of the system since the outset; the concept explicitly implied embracing Leninist atheism, so if it had set society on the wrong course, this was a condemnation of Lenin himself. Set beside the undoubted fact that a genuine religious revival was occurring in many different places, through which young people could see that conversion to Christianity did in reality bring in a new moral code, this article encouraged the beginning of a re-evaluation of attitudes which had become entrenched over seventy years.

New Role for the Church

Mr Gorbachev has always been an energetic traveller. He has, of course, wanted to meet and negotiate with influential foreign leaders, but he has also wanted to see other societies, including communist ones, for himself. This was much easier to arrange once he became leader. As an astute man, he can only have been forcibly struck by the immense difference between those countries which he had been brought up to think of as 'progressive' and those where 'man exploited man', in the phrase of the old dogma. He witnessed how not only was there no comparison between the standard of living of the two systems, but that the latter did, for all its defects and injustices, contribute overall to the dignity of mankind and to the establishment of prosperous social norms and an organised society. Even a tiny country like Iceland, with virtually no resources except fish in the sea and warm water flooding out of volcanic faults, and a climate no less harsh than many parts of the Soviet Union, could build up a prosperous and orderly people.

Increasingly, too, he saw with his own eyes the discontent which ordinary people living in socialist societies were beginning to express at the very time when, at last, they should have been enjoying some fruit from forty years of deprivation and rigorous control. What Gorbachev saw on Tienanmen Square in the summer of 1989 and then on the streets of East Berlin soon after must have contributed directly to his seeking an entirely new solution in the months immediately following.

One feature of his travels, almost entirely ignored by the world of secular journalism, was particularly significant. Almost everywhere he went, at least in the 'capitalist' world, he met church leaders. In Reykjavik Raisa Gorbachev visited a Lutheran church while her husband conferred. In Washington he met a circle of church leaders. In London, even during a visit lasting less than forty-eight hours, he met the Archbishop of Canterbury over a private lunch with the Queen. He also visited Westminster Abbey, where he heard the choir sing, a neat follow-up to his visit before he became leader, when he went to St Paul's Cathedral; his wife went to Christ Church Cathedral during their side trip to Oxford. At the state banquet at No.10 Downing Street I had the privilege of meeting him face to face. On 1 December 1989 came the most significant meeting of all, with the Pope at the Vatican (see Chapter 8), which led to the establishment of diplomatic relations between the Kremlin and the Vatican, a development whose speed no commentator could have predicted. The overall effect of visiting France, West Germany, Finland and other places must have been to demonstrate to Gorbachev that the church played a positive and dignified role within the very fabric of those societies.

At some stage in 1987, or more likely early in 1988, Mr Gorbachev came to a momentous decision: it was time to abandon the old dogma that religion was a retrogressive force, a relic of the past which could have no place in the future ideal communist society. When Karl

Marx had called it the 'opium of the people', he had not intended to damn it as a poison, but in the culture of the day, was using an image which represented temporary relief from pain. It seems unlikely that Mr Gorbachev was echoing Marx at this point and suggesting that, once again, religion could provide temporary relief from pain. His subsequent conduct showed a much more positive approach to religion than that and the effect of the new policies would be to develop the Yevtushenko debate and show religion to be a force for good in society.

As he looked around his vast and disparate agglomeration of republics, Mr Gorbachev could see that religion was alive and well. Believers were building within rather than tearing down the social fabric around them. The combination of religion and nationalism in such a vociferous form in Lithuania must have made him nervous, but even here there were signs of a society on the move, of people who originally wanted to make *perestroika* work. However, events moved so fast that by 1990 they were clearly intent only on immediate secession, not on helping the Soviet Union solve its other problems.

The Soviet system now desperately needed to find ways of turning words about 'restructuring' into deeds. The bureaucracy was as entrenched as ever and Mr Gorbachev could see resistance at all levels. After trying, with almost no success, to impose *perestroika* from above, could he find ways of inserting it into the system from below? It was too early to play the final card of inciting popular discontent against the system, but believers must have seemed to him a huge mass of neutral people who might be moved. There were tens of millions of them – figures are still unreliable, but it could be as many as 100 million, including Muslims, or more than one in three of the whole population. Because of the deliberate government policy of discriminating against the believer by blocking normal career opportunities, they occupied the most menial positions (though Christian workers, frequently loyal and conscientious, were not everywhere barred from exercising leadership on the shop floor and collective farm). If challenged in the right way, Mr Gorbachev must have reasoned, could they not be persuaded to move *perestroika* in at the bottom rung and start reforms at the local level, while above people still deliberated or even actively resisted?

If this was to happen, serious and genuine reforms in favour of religious liberty must come first. Somehow, trust and goodwill between individuals and groups must be re-established. There would have to be serious and deep concessions, not only an entirely new legislation, but, more difficult, the introduction of a new way of thinking among the ideologues of communism and the bureaucrats who maintained the system.

By a happy chance the timing was just right: the Millennium of the Orthodox Church was imminent. Already the state had given permission for the holding of a major international gathering in June 1988 to celebrate a thousand years of Christianity. The Danilov Monastery, returned to its rightful owners some five years previously, was beginning to look resplendent as the backcloth for an unprecedented drama.

Such must have been Mr Gorbachev's thinking as he considered what precise initiative he should take to implement his plan. He considered it was time to prepare new legislation and to make a promise to the leaders of the Orthodox Church.

At the same time as taking these steps, he had to find a formula which would, at least temporarily, satisfy the old guard. One was ready to hand – 'back to Lenin'. It is indeed true that on paper Lenin's legislation on religion looks much more liberal than the manifesto for persecution with which Stalin replaced it in 1929. Nevertheless, in practice the treatment believers received just after the Revolution was more than a foretaste of violence to come: by the time of Lenin's death in 1924 a full-scale persecution of Christians was under way.

While 'back to Lenin' was good enough for the conservatives, at least until they began to see drafts of the new legislation which made provision for the teaching of religion to children, it should not logically have satisfied believers. One suspects, however, that they were by this time so exhausted by the struggle for religious liberty that they took more notice of the tone of voice and the symbolism of the promotion of the Millennium celebrations on television and in the press than of the letter of Lenin's laws (not easily available for examination anyway). Early in 1988 the stage was set for the most portentous breakthrough for the church in Soviet history.

3 Orthodox Millennium

Mr Gorbachev and Patriarch Pimen

He never answered my letter. Instead, he did something better.
Mr Gorbachev began, in 1988, to act as though he really did
need believers to be in partnership with him in the massive task
of rebuilding the moral basis of Soviet society.

I wrote to Mr Gorbachev, privately, in April 1987 and only when
I received no reply did I publish the text. The central section of my
letter challenged him to build a new relationship with believers:

> After seventy years of state atheism, constant pressure and even per-
> secution, believers are still both a dynamic and a growing force in Soviet
> society. They are a major sector of the workforce. They do not want to
> overthrow: they want to construct something better from within. They
> have immense potential, given encouragement, to transform the social
> face of the land. They care intensely for their fellow human beings; they
> care for the values of society. They were of course grieved when, last
> year in Tashkent, you called for renewed and more effective measures
> to combat religion. However, were you to give a lead in a new direction,
> doubtless they would be ready to support you as Academician Sakharov
> has already done.
>
> If you give such a lead, you will be in a position to create a society
> such as the world has never known. But you would do more. If religious
> believers are free to play a genuine and positive role in your society,
> world peace will come a few steps closer, because your aims would be
> shared by millions of believers throughout the world – indeed, by the
> majority of the human race. There will be an entirely new dynamic in
> the struggle by the great powers to build a better world where resources
> go into third-world development and not into the arms race.[1]

Over thirty years I have become used to conducting a dialogue
of the deaf with Soviet officialdom, but this time there was a reply,

not in word but in deed. A year after my letter, church–state relations were transformed in the course of about eight weeks from April to June 1988. No one, least of all Soviet believers themselves, foresaw the drama that would unfold before the eyes of the world.

On 29 April 1988 a meeting unprecedented in post-war years took place. The setting was the grandiose Catherine Hall in the Kremlin. All official statements claim that Patriarch Pimen requested to see Mr Gorbachev to discuss the imminent Millennium celebrations. If indeed he acted so boldly, risking a rebuff, this would have been the most decisive action in his eighteen years of office, a period of passivity on the part of the Orthodox leadership remarkable even by comparison with the past. After all, Stalin had been dead nearly twenty years by the time of Pimen's election and other sectors of society were finding their voice as the terror receded into the past. For the church, memories of persecution were more recent, but they had only accentuated the will of believers to resist. The firm belief among the Orthodox intelligentsia in Moscow is that the Kremlin instigated the meeting, certainly to the extent of suggesting to the Patriarch that he should make a 'request' for it. The published information about it shows clearly that Mr Gorbachev was setting the agenda.

The only precedent for this event was when Stalin summoned Metropolitan Sergi to the Kremlin on 4 September 1943. Conditions, at least superficially, were then very different. It was in the darkest days of the war, when the Soviet Union, after a series of massive defeats at the hands of the Germans, was desperate to muster whatever resources it could. In return for loyalty and support in the war effort, both moral and financial (which indeed had already been forthcoming), Stalin would offer the church a reward if his forces achieved victory. He was as good as his word. The one-time seminarian who had devastated the church in the 1930s encouraged its material revival in the next decade.

Perhaps the moral mountain which Mr Gorbachev had to begin to climb in 1988 was no less precipitous and forbidding than the physical one which confronted Stalin in 1943. It is still, so close to the events, impossible to tell whether Mr Gorbachev's approach was in part prompted by some genuine sympathy for the church – a residual respect from his home background – or whether he acted as he did out of pure pragmatism. Whatever the truth, the decisiveness of his words matched the splendour of the setting and he probably had in mind the transformation which Stalin's meeting had achieved. The Patriarch and five attendant Metropolitans must have realised that history was about to unfold before their eyes.

Gorbachev's speech was statesmanlike, challenging and, within certain limitations, open and honest. He began by admitting the mistakes of the past:

> Not everything has been easy and simple in the sphere of church–state relations. Religious organisations were not free from being affected by the tragic developments that occurred in the period of the cult of personality. Mistakes made with regard to the church and believers in the 1930s and the years that followed are being rectified.[2]

The last sentence implied that unrectified mistakes had continued right up to the present, thus preparing the six church leaders for a decisive offer. According to Konstantin Kharchev, Chairman of the Council for Religious Affairs, who was present on the government side, Mr Gorbachev stated that 'the overwhelming majority of believers accept the policy of *perestroika*' and are contributing to economic improvements, to 'promoting democracy and *glasnost*'. There would be a tangible reward for this: 'A new law on freedom of conscience . . . will reflect the interests of religious organisations.' He continued:

> Believers are Soviet people, workers, patriots, and they have the full right to express their convictions with dignity. *Perestroika*, democratisation and openness concern them as well – in full measure and without any restrictions. This is especially true of ethics and morals, a domain where universal norms and customs are so helpful for our common cause.[3]

To hear the leader of the world's first atheist state, where the law restrained religious activity on all fronts, talk about 'our common cause' must have stunned these men who had themselves long been intimidated into political passivity and self-censorship. A more lapidary phrase was to follow, promising to dislodge a founding principle of Marxism-Leninism: 'We have a common history, a common motherland and a common future.' Unequivocally, Mr Gorbachev was abolishing the dogma of seventy years, which not even Stalin's concessions had permanently revised: that there would be no religious belief in the ideal socialist society of the future. The forthcoming Millennium celebrations, he continued, would cement believers with the whole population in supporting 'the great common cause of *perestroika* and the renewal of socialism'.

In a country which has no democracy there can be no real evidence to sustain or refute the claim that believers 'support the renewal of socialism'. A year later the elections to the Congress of People's Deputies of March 1989, and even more the local elections of 1990, would indicate widespread discontent at the dominance of the Communist Party, but one could not expect the church leaders to open up such a discussion at that point. Mr Gorbachev came now to the only palpably dishonest claim in the whole speech: that Lenin's decree on the separation of church and state of January 1918 allowed the church for the first time to conduct its activities 'without any outside interference'. We have seen that the exact opposite was true. Where the church is concerned, as with many other sectors of society, to insist on a return to 'Leninist norms' would compound, not solve, the problem. *Glasnost* has not yet approached the stage where it is possible openly to admit this, or even to re-examine the whole of historical evidence objectively, though there are signs that this is beginning to happen. Tactics, however, demanded that Mr Gorbachev should express some of the old principles with conviction, in order to allay the worst fears of his conservative opponents.

The Patriarch's reply put more emphasis on *perestroika* than on God. Indeed, He was not mentioned. Pimen pledged the unconditional support of believers for 'the architect of *perestroika*'. He would pray for the forthcoming summit meeting with President Reagan in Moscow. Already monasteries and churches were reopening and the 'pressing problems of church life' were being eased. For this he gave credit to the Council for Religious Affairs, which until recently had interfered daily in every aspect of church life and broken the constitutional edict that church and state must be separate. The Patriarch did not make a single request of the government or of Mr Gorbachev personally, though in discussion afterwards, according to the church's own account, they 'raised a number of specific questions associated with the guaranteeing of normal performance of the Orthodox Church'. There was no indication of what those questions were, but in formal speeches to Soviet officials during the Millennium celebrations the Patriarch, with evident emotion, twice referred to the profound impression the meeting with Mr Gorbachev had made on him.

The next month saw the Orthodox Church move centre stage in Russia and the world for the first time in the Soviet period. In May, the world's cameras followed President Reagan's footsteps as he met Christian and Jewish activists and when he visited the Danilov Monastery. The audience included millions of Soviet citizens themselves. In June the Soviet media reported every detail of the official Millennium celebrations. The famine of positive information

about religion in the Soviet media suddenly became a glut: seventy
lean years succeeded by something less than seventy fat days. When
in my hotel room in Leningrad I switched on the TV, one channel
was reporting the day's religious events; the other was relaying the
recent film about Orthodox life, *Khram* ('Church'), which caught the
atmosphere of worship with compelling beauty and a great reverence
for Christian spirituality.

By visiting the Danilov Monastery on 30 May 1988, President
Reagan turned his attention away from summitry to embrace publicly,
as Mrs Thatcher had done at Zagorsk a year before him, the cause of
religious liberty in the Soviet Union. There, in March 1987, she had lit
a candle as a symbol of hope for those who were still being oppressed
for their faith. Now there was an open monastery in Moscow for the
first time since the 1920s. Curiously, it was Mr Andropov, former
head of the KGB, or his staff who took the decision in 1983 to
present the church with a dignified Moscow headquarters, where
it could both host the Millennium celebrations five years later and
gather within one complex all the main administrative divisions of
the Moscow Patriarchate.

The monastery is enclosed within a massive wall. 'About right for
a prison,' I mused in 1959 as I viewed its forbidding exterior while
I was charting the open churches of Moscow. Entrance was barred
then. Little did I know that inside was a Soviet borstal for young male
offenders. Even less would I have guessed that thirty years later I
would step inside to see it magnificently restored and awaiting the
closing ceremony of the Millennium celebrations.

Due to a typical Soviet administrative error the first monks arrived
before the young criminals had moved out. The two groups formed an
immediate bond. Suffering from the standard treatment of offenders
in the Soviet Union, the boys had never experienced any hint of love
or care for them as individuals. The clergy, long before 'charity'
was to become legal, spontaneously began to show their Christian
compassion to a group who surely needed it.

When the boys moved out and restoration work began, the task was
massive. Officially it cost 30 million roubles (£30m at the exchange
rate then operating), but many believers in the Soviet Union think
that the real figure was 50 million. Even this is a subsidised total,
because Christian volunteers helped in the massive task of clearing
and reconstructing the site.

The magnificence of the restored monastery provided a foretaste
of the imminent jubilee celebrations. While the timing of the Moscow
summit cannot have been set to precede them by only a few days, the

way events unfolded did seem to form part of some greater plan: the Russian Orthodox Church, having survived persecution, was poised to play a visible role on the world stage during its second millennium.

The Millennium Celebrations

The choice of Moscow as the focal point of the celebrations, before the guests departed to attend subsidiary events in other cities, was in itself controversial. After all, the city-state of Kiev had been the eye of medieval civilisation long before the foundation of Moscow and it was here that Prince Vladimir had descended the steep slope of the River Dnieper, ordering his courtiers and subjects to be baptised after him and to embrace the new faith. The river bore away the jettisoned idols and the images of paganism.

These events of 988 (though the date is a contested one among scholars) are considerably more than a folk memory. Partly as a result of the devastation of Kiev by the Golden Horde, the Asiatic invasion from the East, the focus of Russian civilisation shifted north; after the rise of Muscovy, Kiev declined in status and paid tribute to a new master. In time Kiev, restored to reflect the glory of its past, diverged in custom and language, eventually to become the capital of the emergent nation of Ukraine. Though part of the Russian and then, after a briefest spell of independence, of the Soviet empire, this vast region, with enormous economic resources, came to nurture a variety of anti-Moscow sentiments which were exacerbated by the growing insensitivity of the central government.

The choice of Moscow for the whole first week of celebrations (5–12 June) reminded Ukrainian believers that it was the Russian Orthodox Church which played the dominant role. It had even justified and benefited from the liquidation of the Ukrainian Catholic Church in Western Ukraine over forty years earlier (see Chapter 8), and it was now going to ensure that the focus was on Moscow. The rumblings about this below the surface – and they were not confined to Ukrainian nationalists – were an aspect of *glasnost* not aired in the Soviet press at the time. Certainly none of the 1,500 official guests from around the world and from other Soviet churches broke diplomatic protocol to raise such a sensitive issue publicly.

Sunday 5 June saw the opening liturgy in the Cathedral of the Epiphany, a building which had become the Patriarchal Cathedral after the eviction of the church from the Kremlin in 1917 and the destruction of the Cathedral of Christ the Saviour in 1934. For the second time in a week the world's television cameras recorded the splendour of Russian Orthodoxy at its most solemn and imposing. Christian leaders from many parts of the world joined in this ceremony, though ordinary believers would later complain at their exclusion from the main events.

The centre-piece of the whole event was the *sobor* (Council) which took place at the Holy Trinity Monastery at Zagorsk, to which we shall return later in the chapter.

I was due to arrive in Moscow on 7 June, not as an official guest, but as leader of a group of forty pilgrims coming to the Soviet Union under the auspices of Inter-Church Travel to join with Russians, Ukrainians and Belorussians in prayer and celebration of this most solemn event. In the few days before my departure I was a most unwilling participant in a personal drama which echoed around the British media.

All of our group received their visas well ahead of departure, with the exception of my wife and me. Mr Gorbachev and his *perestroika* had received very positive coverage in the world press as a result of the Moscow summit. Newsmen were only too ready afterwards to give prominence to any story which would make a negative point. In truth, the refusal of a visa to an individual was neither new (it had happened so often in the past) nor particularly newsworthy outside church circles. However, the way it was put made it sound more dramatic than it was. The 8 a.m. news on Radio 4 on 5 June introduced its leading item with the words: 'The Archbishop of Canterbury is in Moscow for the opening of the Millennium celebrations of the Russian Orthodox Church. However, one churchman who will not be accompanying him is . . .' Dr Runcie, furthermore, criticised the Soviet authorities for their refusal, which occasioned another wave of publicity a day later.

By the evening of Monday 6 June, the day before our scheduled departure, I had given up all hope and concluded that the combined efforts of the media, the travel agency (which threatened to cancel all future tours to the Soviet Union), the Foreign Office, the Archbishop and, not least, the prayers of many sympathisers had all failed.

But at 8.15 p.m. the phone rang to announce that our visas were ready and waiting for us at the Soviet Consulate. Our two-year-old son not only in the wrong bed, but in the wrong house, visas to be collected an hour's journey away, suitcases to be packed, departure at four next morning for a five-thirty check-in at Heathrow: all this domestic drama was soon forgotten in the joy of finally landing in Moscow and hearing our Intourist guide turn to an obstinate customs official with the words, 'These people are guests of the Patriarch; please let them through quickly.' What she said might not have been quite accurate, but the doors did spring open and we even spent part of the next day at the Holy Trinity Monastery, where the *sobor* itself was taking place.

On 7 June, the day I arrived in the Soviet Union, the Ukrainian Council of Ministers made a conciliatory gesture of major symbolic significance. In 1961 the authorities had expelled the monks from the great Monastery of the Caves in Kiev, a magnificent complex of buildings which linked the conversion of St Vladimir to the present. Nikita Khrushchev was surely aware that this would be one of the most brutally symbolic acts in his campaign to eradicate religion in the 'era of advanced communism' for which he believed he was preparing. History has a way with those who make extravagant claims. Khrushchev's decisive step towards the formulation of a religion-free society was reversed less than thirty years later. No single event of the Millennium could have been more pregnant with symbolism than the return of part of the Monastery of the Caves. A televised ceremony, during which the title deed was returned to Metropolitan Filaret of Kiev, gave it full publicity. If the state had not made this concession, the entire proceedings of the Millennium would have been tainted with hypocrisy.

The central drama of the week was hidden from the eyes of ordinary Russian believers and invited guests. The closed sessions of the *sobor* will go down in history as far more important than the combined weight of all the ceremonial occasions. *Sobor* is the Russian word for a gathering of people (a council) or for the building in which large numbers of worshippers meet (a cathedral). In practice a *sobor* meets only irregularly to transact business of extraordinary importance, especially the election of a new patriarch upon the death of the incumbent. Each diocese should send three representatives: the bishop, an elected priest and an elected layman.

The *sobor* of June 1988, which ran for four days (6–9 June) within the period of the Moscow Millennium celebrations, was the fourth in the Soviet period (counting the one already in session at the time of the 1917 Revolution), but the first which was not meeting for the election of a patriarch. When asked what was his single most abiding memory of an unforgettable occasion, Professor Sir Dimitri Obolensky replied in a single word, 'Laughter.' Far from being a flippant observation, this reveals the unimaginable change of atmosphere which had come about within the Russian Orthodox Church in so short a time.

The build-up which we have already described led to an expectancy in the air, a sense of quiet joy that something had so visibly changed in favour of the church. Walking around the Holy Trinity Monastery as I did on the day of the closed session (8 June), one could sense this among those whom we met and who were on the fringes of this great event. There could have been no greater contrast than the atmosphere of the previous *sobor* of 1971, which elected Patriarch Pimen. Here the aim of the Soviet authorities had been to dominate the proceedings by the silent presence of the representatives of the Council for Religious Affairs. Would-be dissenting bishops had been prevented from attending by physical attacks on their persons; regulations restricting the participation of clergy in the administrative and financial affairs of their own parishes had been illegitimately in place for a decade and this assembly of 1971 had to formalise the status of these; the *sobor* had to 'elect' a quiescent patriarch whose unopposed candidature was virtually signed and sealed before the event.

By 1988 it was time for the *sobor* to regain its dignity and self-respect. That it went so far towards achieving this is a milestone in the history of the Russian Church. The laughter was only one sign of a spontaneity about the proceedings which was something new under Soviet conditions. The best illustration of this came with two acts of 'charity' which, even at that time, were still technically illegal.

On the Saturday immediately before the opening of the Millennium celebrations (4 June) there had been a rail crash and the detonation of a truck of high explosives at Arzamas, near Gorky. In accordance with the new policy of open reporting in the press, the news immediately went round that sixty-eight people had died in the explosion and several hundred others were injured. Someone organised a collection at the *sobor* for the victims, which realised no less than 50,000 roubles. If, say, there were 500 people in the room (there were probably fewer), the average contribution was £100 sterling per person at the official rate of exchange. At the very end of the *sobor* there was a requiem for the dead in the Afghan War, in itself an unprecedented event, as the churches had always been barred from publicly praying for any victims of Soviet adventurism. The collection at this service amounted to no less than four times the contribution for the rail disaster.

The opening and closing days of the *sobor* were largely ceremonial and the foreign guests were present. The closed sessions contained much more of significance and it has become possible to reconstruct the main events, as the press office made available the texts of the most important speeches. There are no transcripts of the ensuing discussions, so one is dependent on hearsay evidence for some of what took place, but the émigré newspaper *Russkaya mysl* ('Russian Thought'), of Paris, did publish an account which appears to have been compiled from interviews made by the participants from France.

The centre-piece of the whole proceedings, which could do no other than raise the most controversial issues of church–state relations, was the discussion of the new *ustav* (statute) on the third day (8 June).

The statutes under discussion were internal church regulations, not state laws, though under Soviet conditions one would expect the two to be in harmony with each other. In fact, in some particulars the old statutes were even more restrictive than the operative law demanded. For example, no published law had ever excluded the priest from the administration of his own parish. There is a discussion of the subsequent drafting of a new state law in the following chapter.

The architect of the new church statute was one of the youngest of the hierarchy and unquestionably one of the most intellectually gifted, Archbishop Kirill of Smolensk and Kaliningrad. Kirill Gundyaev, a protégé of the late and influential Metropolitan Nikodim, under his tutelage became Rector of the Leningrad Theological Academy at the extraordinarily early age of twenty-eight. However, after Nikodim's early death in 1978, Kirill's brilliant and innovative ideas fell out of favour and in 1984 he was transferred to the provincial city of Smolensk where, presumably, the state authorities, leaning on the church, felt that he could do less harm. However, from there he developed an energetic ministry and it took someone of his integrity and determination, perhaps slightly removed from the more intense scrutiny which his activities would have attracted in Moscow or Leningrad, to draft a statute which was new and bold. When the text began to circulate two months before the opening of the *sobor*, there were those who doubted whether it would be possible to move so far ahead in one step.

It was. Archbishop Kirill, in his introductory speech, noted that the body of the present regulations evolved in wartime, when the Orthodox Church could once again establish the bare bones of an administrative system after two decades of chaos. The expectation of that time was that when peace came there would be a reconsideration of the whole system and the drawing up of a permanent statute, but this had never happened. These shortcomings laid the church open to the abuses it suffered during Khrushchev's anti-religious campaign of the early 1960s (Kirill did not mention this specifically, but the implication would have been plain to all his listeners). His point was to deny the validity of the 1945 and 1961 regulations and to state that what he was asking the *sobor* to pass today should be taken as the direct successor of the *ustav* of 1918.

Kirill naturally highlighted the most controversial article of the 1961 amendment, an issue which had at the time occasioned bitter controversy and which had caused opponents of the new measures to forfeit their careers, some perhaps even their liberty. Clearly under the most intense state pressure, a hastily-convened and irregular 'Synod of Bishops' in 1961 excluded the priest from the executive body of three people in his own parish, itself open to infiltration by the forces of atheism. This was an opportunity which the local authorities were quick to exploit and it was one of the most significant contributory factors to the mass closure of churches which ensued. Kirill did not go over all this detail because he did not need to and because he wanted to focus all eyes on the present document and the future.

The new draft was elaborate and detailed: thirty-four pages of type-script, divided into fifteen sections, further subdivided into numerous clauses. In presenting it, Archbishop Kirill already knew by this time that he was on firm ground, at least as far as the church was concerned, because the bishops had met in March to consider the draft of the *ustav* (interestingly, a month before the Gorbachev and Pimen meeting in the Kremlin). Therefore he moved confidently into his proposal to sweep away the ban on the parish priest and instate him as chairman of the parish assembly (though not necessarily immediately, as some parishes had satisfactory lay chairmen). The acceptance of this proposal puts the local church, from the organisational point of view, in a far stronger position, should there ever be another wave of persecution.

Several of the proposals related to the office of patriarch. There were many reservations about Patriarch Pimen, a man without theo-logical education and with a passive record over eighteen years (he died on 3 May 1990). However, it would be unwise to interpret the new proposals as a direct attack on him. Rather, the current problems gave rise to mature reflection and new guidelines came out of this. Now there would be provision for a patriarch to retire, there would be an election of a *locum tenens* during any interregnum and, quite naturally in the new age, there was an emphasis on the importance of theological education.

Even more important was a series of regulations upgrading and regularising church meetings at all levels. In practice, as we have seen, the state had restricted Christian activity to worship at set times within a registered church building. Meetings to discuss church affairs, either administrative or spiritual, had been well-nigh impossible to summon; even the *sobor* had had to wait until the death of a patriarch to be convened. Now the church was to have a voice in the regulation of its own affairs. Parish and diocesan assemblies would meet regularly. The Council of Bishops would have a regular status and convene every two years. Even the *sobor* itself would meet every five years, thus shifting the absurd backlog of essential business which inevitably built up. Clearly these high-level meetings would keep a close check on the work of the Synod, a very small and self-perpetuating body (the ecclesiastical equivalent of the Politburo) which hitherto had been solely – and with no hint of accountability – in control of church administration. At the same time, it would be more difficult for the Council for Religious Affairs to interfere in church life if these assemblies could regularly monitor events at local and national level.

Among a wealth of other administrative details of importance to the future well-being of the church there is a feature which stands out: three of the new provisions contradicted state law as it existed at that time. Even though Archbishop Kirill could hardly have inserted these without reference to the secular authorities, nevertheless the boldness with which he framed and presented them signified an entirely new departure in the development of church–state relations and marked the archbishop as a man of outstanding leadership qualities. Subsequently, when draft revisions of the state law began to circulate in 1989, it could be seen that they were in harmony with the church's own proposals.

For the first time parishes, theological seminaries and monasteries should receive church buildings and other (previously confiscated) property free of charge from the state. Where these were not available, they could build, rent or buy premises according to their needs. Previously all buildings had belonged to the state from the time when they had been nationalised under Lenin's 1918 decree and the religious association could rent them back only upon a successful application for registration. The new regulation adds immense new strength to the local Christian community.

The members of the *sobor* retrospectively regularised (though not of course technically legalised) the collection they had taken up for the alleviation of the rail disaster. Having been banned from participation in any charitable activity over the decades, parishes could now, according to the new regulation, spend money on 'general church, diocesan, patriotic, internal parish and other charitable aims' (not defined). In the past, the straitjacket had yielded only to

allow donations to the Soviet Peace Fund, which the Christian intelligentsia had naturally come to resent. While the new proposals
did not exactly exclude a continuation of this, it was clear that the
emphasis would be elsewhere. We shall resume discussion of this in
Chapter 9.

Now for the first time the church could be represented in court as a
legal entity, which in practice had never been possible. The new *ustav*
stated unambiguously that the parish council or executive committee
'takes on the obligations of representing the parish in court', or the
assembly of the whole parish could appoint a person to represent all
of them at law.

Here was a massive body of complicated new legislation vitally
affecting the life of the church at all levels: and yet no in-depth
discussion of it was possible. Some speakers rose to suggest that
some clauses should have gone further; others were uncertain as
to how they should treat those which contravened existing state law.
The whole document did not exactly go through on the nod, but
there were no split votes and applause accompanied the unanimous
acceptance of even the most controversial proposals.

Even under optimum circumstances, such a large assembly could
not have redrafted a document of great complexity and adequate
discussion would have entailed clause-by-clause consideration over
a number of days. Therefore all depended on the initial drafting and
presentation; surely in the person of Archbishop Kirill the Russian
Orthodox Church, in its top leadership, had at last found the man
for the hour.

The aspect of the *sobor* which achieved the most international
publicity was the canonisation of nine new saints at a special service
in the shrine of St Sergius. The most ancient was the icon painter
Andrei Rublyov, born in the middle of the fourteenth century. A new
saint of especial interest was Amvrosi of the Optina Pustyn Monastery,
whom Dostoevsky knew in person and whose life spanned virtually
the whole of the nineteenth century. His tradition of promoting
spirituality through individual counselling is influential in the church
today.

The *sobor* did not address the issue of modern martyrs. Already the
Soviet press was beginning to publish a spate of articles revealing the
crimes of Stalin. It would, therefore, have been neither inappropriate
nor politically impossible for church leaders to have referred more
openly to the need to honour the Christian martyrs of the twentieth century, even if it would not have been feasible in the time
available to single out candidates for possible future canonisation.

Naturally, there were many Christian activists not represented at the *sobor* who considered it an essential matter of public conscience to begin the process, but this did not happen and the *sobor* was the poorer for it. The nearest any church leader came to it in public was a declaration by Metropolitan Yuvenali of Krutitsy and Kolomna (the Moscow archdiocese) in his speech at the Bolshoi Theatre at the end of the week that the time was 'not yet ripe' for this.

The most significant business at the other sessions of the *sobor* was a series of eight reports, mostly concentrating on events since 1971, from members of the Holy Synod. They were of uneven quality and value, so we will confine ourselves here to picking out some of the highlights.

Metropolitan Vladimir of Rostov and Novocherkassk took the stage. These double titles, as with English country parishes today, often designate an administrative merging of what were once separate entities. Metropolitan Vladimir had become a permanent member of the Holy Synod and its administrator only six months previously. He gave the most precise statistical account of the institutions of the Russian Orthodox Church ever to become available. He did not compare his figures either with those at the time of the Revolution or with those at the death of Stalin, but it is worth setting out his statistics for 1988 alongside these two,[4] for they provide a clear picture of the massive devastation the church has suffered over the past thirty-five years and of the ground to be recouped in the age of *perestroika* (see Table 1). One should remember that the territory of the Russian Empire just before the Revolution was less extensive than it became by the end of the Second World War, as a result of military conquest.

Metropolitan Vladimir stated that more than sixty new parishes had begun to function in the past year and hoped that the rate would increase (see Table 2). The whole assembly would have hoped the same, because at the speed he quoted it would take well over two hundred years to bring the number back to what it was on the day Stalin died, whereas it took only five years for Khrushchev to wreak this devastation across the face of the whole nation. *Glasnost* among the church hierarchy was still some way from being able to make such a point explicitly and it is curious that some articles in the secular – and still technically atheist – press now go much further, while activists such as Deacon Rusak, who tried to tell the full story in a history which he wrote but could not publish, were imprisoned as recently as 1986. (In April 1989, still

TABLE 1: INSTITUTIONS OF THE RUSSIAN ORTHODOX CHURCH

	1914	1939	c1945	1988	1989
DIOCESES	73	?	73	67	70
BISHOPS IN OFFICE	163	4	74	70	70
CLERGY	51,105	some 100s	about 20,000	6,674	8,100
(DEACONS)				(724)	
CHURCHES	54,174	some 100s	about 18,000 (possibly fewer)	6,893	9,374
MONASTERIES AND CONVENTS	1,025	NIL	67	21	35
MONKS AND NUNS	94,629	?	about 10,000	1,190	
THEOLOGICAL ACADEMIES	4	NIL	2	2	} 19*
SEMINARIES	57	NIL	8	3	
STUDENTS	?	?	?	1,999	3,948
PRE-THEOLOGICAL SCHOOLS	185	forbidden by law			
PAROCHIAL SCHOOLS	37,528				
HOMES FOR THE AGED	1,113				
PARISH LIBRARIES	34,497				
HOSPITALS	291				

* Church 'teaching establishments' (number probably includes newly opened pre-theological schools). New seminaries in Minsk, Kiev, Tobolsk.

TABLE 2: OPENING OF PARISHES

Statistics given by Metropolitan Vladimir
at Bishops Council, 11 October 1989:

1985	3
1986	10
1987	16
1988	80
1989 (first 9 months)	2,815

under a cloud, he emigrated after an early release.) However, Metropolitan Vladimir did strongly underline that such a programme of expansion would be possible only with the opening of new theological seminaries and greatly improved facilities, particularly in the provision of adequate textbooks. He might have added that the church had been barred from the production of these for seventy years.

Archbishop Alexander of Dmitrov would later take up this point more forcibly. He stated that the increase in student numbers had led to deterioration in conditions in the seminaries, so it was urgent to open new ones, especially in Siberia. Every diocese should set up its own local facilities for training choir masters, singers, psalm readers and altar-boys. Monasteries would be especially appropriate for this purpose. The establishment of a central school for training icon painters was also long overdue.

Metropolitan Vladimir then riveted the attention of his audience by making a pointed criticism of the work of the Publishing Department and, by implication, of his fellow-Metropolitan, Pitirim of Volokolamsk [original English text]:

But today the church still feels the need to increase the number of printed copies of the New Testament and the prayerbooks. We are entitled to expect more in-depth reflection of the church life with its real problems on the pages of church periodicals. The Department's contribution to the development of our theological scholarship and to catechisation of the faithful and familiarising them with the spiritual heritage of the church should be greater.[5]

The Metropolitan then passed on to the question of the personal spiritual formation and conduct of the parish priest. This is clearly an example of the sort of vital question which should be discussed in the pages of the *Journal of the Moscow Patriarchate*, but about which there have been over forty years of silence, since it resumed publication at the end of the Second World War. He said:

More attention should be paid to the spiritual profile of the pastor on whom the spiritual state of the community of faithful is dependent. Behaviour by a member of the clergy that does not correspond to the demands of pastoral ethics has an extremely negative influence on parish life. A most important obligation of the clergy is pious and fervent celebration of liturgical services. Arbitrary abridgment of service formularies is inadmissible. A pastor's bounden duty is preaching the word of God. The sermon must be preached at each Sunday and festal service. Together with his faithful, a pastor must implement the Gospel principles of love for God and one's neighbour.[6]

One of the most encouraging aspects of this speech, and therefore of the *sobor* itself, was that Metropolitan Vladimir may at this point have been consciously counteracting the secular authorities, for Mr Kharchev had earlier in the year made a claim that atheism had cut deep inroads precisely in this area of the moral stature of the parish priest. While not published in the Soviet Union, the transcript of this speech to the Higher Party School in Moscow (see the next chapter for its content) was circulating and was eventually published abroad three weeks before the Metropolitan spoke. Mr Kharchev had said:

The Party has an interest in the new type of priest. At the moment the priest is often not at all involved in his parish. He has been born in another area, often he is even of a different nationality. A priest like this comes in his car once a week, takes a service, and doesn't want to know any more about it . . . We have gained the most success in control of religion and our influence over it through the priests and bishops of the Russian Orthodox Church.[7]

For the first time since Patriarch Tikhon's defence of the church in the face of Lenin's decrees, Metropolitan Vladimir's speech at the *sobor* began to stake out the public ground for a new defence of the faith. Thereby he put himself, albeit modestly, in the very forefront of the Orthodox movement for reform, along with Archbishop Kirill.

Metropolitan Pitirim was not unresponsive to the criticism made of his department, which, he said, was at a disadvantage because of the poor financial support it had received and because it had no printing press of its own. All books went out to state presses, which frequently failed to meet deadlines and produced work of a lower technical standard than required by the contract. This had happened even with a key publication for the Millennium celebrations, a monograph by Archpriest Lev Lebedev which had only just come off the press, ten months late. However, to go on to state that this was compelling his department 'to consider establishing a printing base of its own' was a mild enough and somewhat tardy reaction against the exigencies of the period of Brezhnev's 'stagnation', when nothing of the sort was possible.

It is significant that the Publishing Department had already made at least a token gesture to forestall these criticisms. The number of the *Journal of the Moscow Patriarchate* then current had gone to press a full two months earlier, but it excluded many of the usual interminable and repetitive articles on peace and also the dull, conventional section, 'Life in the Dioceses'. In their place there was more on theology, history and, in the light of the current debate on canonisation, hagiography.

Metropolitan Pitirim made no mention of the English-language version of this journal, the regular publication of which, parallel to the Russian, was an expensive undertaking and of value to probably no more than a few dozen people abroad: perhaps even of negative worth, because most Russian émigrés would prefer to read the original and English speakers could have access to superior (though less extensive) information.

Participants said that this report provoked strong adverse reaction, but no detailed information of what was said has become available. Nevertheless, the very fact that there was such controversy has to be a positive sign for the future.

Another plain speaker, and one who was to sharpen his criticisms of several aspects of church life in the period after the *sobor*, was Metropolitan Mefodi of Voronezh. He was then responsible for the 'economic activity' of the church, a side of its life which for decades the state had managed to suppress almost totally. However, in 1980, while Brezhnev was still alive, and counter to the trend of the period, the authorities gave permission for the opening of a workshop at Sofrino (near Moscow) for the production of all kinds of articles needed for the normal maintenance of church life: crosses, chalices, vestments, icons and especially candles. The response of Orthodox churches overseas had swollen the order book, so now there was employment for a thousand people, ten per cent of whom were skilled craftsmen.

Though the enterprise was a non-profit-making one, in the sense that any profits were ploughed back into the church and the products are not accessible to the public at large, the state imposed punitive taxation. Metropolitan Mefodi stated:

Though this report is of, so to say, jubilee character, it would be a vain attempt to hold back a number of serious problems which the Economic Department has faced until now. In spite of the fact that the whole production of the Economic Department is not meant for marketing or for sale to the population at large but is only for religious purposes to be used only in churches during services, the whole production is taxed as if it were produced for marketing. We believe that this principle should be revised and considerably corrected.[8]

From here Metropolitan Mefodi went on to launch an even stronger attack against state taxation. The essence of his case was that the state had expropriated all the church's buildings after the Revolution, but such 'so-called protection as it provided is usually reduced to hanging a protection board on a dilapidating [sic] building'. Now, however, when the church undertook its own restoration work, the state immediately stepped in and began to tax all the materials, when they should have been subsidising them, because of past neglect and because such enterprise was restoring the nation's cultural heritage for the benefit of the whole population. It was imperative, he continued, to evade bureaucracy and massive unnecessary expense by establishing the church's own restoration department, instead of having to rely on the inferior calibre of work provided through state institutions. Restoring the Danilov Monastery had been enormously expensive, but this precedent would enable work to go ahead much more satisfactorily at the great monastic centres of Optina and Tolga. New laws should make it possible for contributions in hard currency to be used to best advantage (he was implying that the state was illegitimately benefiting from its handling of these donations from abroad).

These outspoken statements were brave even under the more favourable conditions of June 1988: Metropolitan Mefodi was the first to bring these issues forcibly to the attention of the church. He was, however, dismissed from the Economic Department the following November under suspicion of mismanagement of funds. The exact nature of the accusations and the attendant circumstances remain, at best, contradictory.

No observer of Russian church life, whether present at the *sobor* or merely reading these texts subsequently, could fail to be stirred by the tone of the best of the speeches. It is clear that decades of failing morale among the hierarchy, even the deliberate pro-motion and appointment to senior positions of less able and less worthy men, have failed to eradicate its sense of values. While the tasks ahead are immense in human terms, these days witnessed a new phase in the reconstruction of the life of the Orthodox Church.

A Symphony of Church and State

At the end of this astonishing week the Bolshoi Theatre, in the centre of Moscow, became the scene of another unprecedented series of events. The 'solemn act', as it was called, opened at 10 a.m. on Friday 10 June and continued with a succession of speeches which lasted many hours, including congratulations from seventeen world church leaders. Metropolitan Yuvenali gave the address, which contained evidence of a new openness in the public posture of the church leadership. Never before had it talked in any official context so freely about past persecution. In earlier days it had been impossible to speak this openly about the Stalin era:

> After the Revolution, at various times which were so difficult for the people and which now go under a terminology well understood by all, the church fully shared the fate of all other citizens. Now it is openly stated that many thousands of communists and non-Party members, agricultural and military brigades, scientists and representatives of the arts were subjected to mass repressions. Among their number there were both priests and laity.[9]

After a reference to the new deal resulting from Mr Gorbachev's reception of the church leaders six weeks earlier, the Metropolitan continued with some statistics, the first two of which brought home as much to state officials as to the ecumenical visitors that the Orthodox Church had overcome persecution, that young people were joining its ranks and that it would have a guaranteed role in the society of the future:

> The Russian Orthodox Church now comprises many millions of believers. It is sufficient to observe that between the last *sobor* (1971) and the present more than 30 million individuals have been baptised. The average age of the clergy is now forty-seven and in round figures two thousand young people are now receiving a Christian education in our theological schools.

The day ended with a jubilee concert in the presence of dignitaries representing both church and state (Raisa Gorbachev and President Gromyko were the most notable secular figures present). I am able to describe it in detail, because it took place also the previous evening, in the presence of a slightly less official audience. My wife and I were there, the Moscow Patriarchate having provided us with tickets. We sat in the second row of the stalls to witness yet another revelation. No fewer than seven choirs, six orchestras and some of the stars of Soviet screen and concert platform combined in a joint celebration of the Millennium by church and state. To witness the best choirs of the Russian Orthodox Church alternating with the finest secular choruses was to see a new era in microcosm. There have been thousands of evenings when the Bolshoi atmosphere has sparked electricity: rarely can it have been more charged than it was then. Nuns from Riga and Kiev, with whom I talked, were given the opportunity to see and hear something which would remain with them for the rest of their days.

The great Soviet actor Sergei Bondarchuk has a resonant voice and even more stage presence than one might expect from his films. He generated as much emotion, I felt, among his atheist as his Christian listeners. He read the account of Prince Vladimir, as described in the *Chronicle* of the historian Monk Nestor (himself of the Monastery of the Caves). The Prince, feeling his pagan religion was outmoded in the increasingly civilised Europe of the tenth century, sent envoys to witness and report back on the splendours of the Catholic Church in Western Christendom, on Islam and on Orthodoxy in Constantinople. It was the magnificence of the liturgy underneath the soaring dome of St Sofia which impressed him most. The envoys advised Prince Vladimir that 'We did not know whether we were in heaven or on earth.' There were undoubtedly Communist Party officials in the Bolshoi that night who felt the same.

Nowhere in the whole celebration did the Russians – church and state – better employ their sense of drama and their feeling for symbolism than at the close of this concert. The Bolshoi Chorus and Orchestra combined first to sing to the church the traditional Russian paean *Mnogoye leto* ('long life'). Televised throughout the Soviet Union, this conveyed an astonishing message of hope to those who were, until very recently, being told that there was no future for them under the Soviet system; equally, the atheist cohorts must have felt on the retreat as never before. Even this was not the climax. The heavens – literally – were about to open to reveal a Christian future. The final scene of Glinka's opera, *A Life for the Tsar*, makes just such a promise. As the final cries of *slava* ('praise') resounded through the theatre, the blue sky above the stage set opened to reveal a carillon of real church bells which engulfed the Bolshoi in a peal of thunder. Before any audience this would have been a *coup de théâtre.* In a country where the ringing of church bells had been outlawed for decades, this was more than symbolism: it was a pledge of a new beginning, presaging and, on the second day, reinforcing Metropolitan Yuvenali's words of confidence.

It is true that some of the Christian intelligentsia whom we subsequently met said that this was 'vulgar drama without substance' and claimed that the secular artists appeared only because the church hired them at enormous expense. It is true also that, while foreign guests could witness everything at first hand, Soviet believers found not only that admission even to church services was strictly by ticket, but that they could not even approach the venues to stand and offer prayers outside because the authorities had put barriers right round them. The counter argument is, however, that the nationwide and two-week-long exposure of all the major events on radio and television administered a psychological boost to believers even in the most remote corners of the country. The effect on a Christian in a Siberian village where, perhaps, the church had been closed for half a century and from which the nearest formal worship was now two hundred miles removed can only be imagined.

President Gromyko was near the end, as it turned out, of his long life. He must have felt that the church was beginning to weave a spell around him, for he was host in the Kremlin to no fewer than two receptions the day after the second concert. Unusually for such a ceremonial occasion, the first included a public dialogue with selected participants. They had received beforehand an invitation to submit questions in writing and Gromyko answered ten of them, mostly from among those already to hand. At this point the topic of new legislation was looming large in the minds of many people, but he was defensive in his response. He stated that Lenin's decree on the separation of church from state and church from school would continue to be operative, no discrimination against believers in their jobs was possible under the Soviet system and registration of religious communities in no way reduced believers' rights. The more perceptive foreign guests felt that, while the occasion demonstrated a certain new openness at the very top of the government structure, the words themselves did not advance the frontiers of religious liberty. The second reception, much larger, was a buffet lunch for some 700 participants, Soviet and foreign, but this occasion included no dialogue.

For the concluding liturgy on the Sunday morning (12 June), the gates of the Danilov Monastery swung open in cold and windy weather to receive a more representative congregation of Soviet believers than had been able to attend any previous event. This was because it took place in the open air, in the vast enclosure between the two main churches of the monastery on the right and left of the main gate. Six Orthodox patriarchs and an archbishop representing seven different nationalities concelebrated. At the conclusion one of the most prominent Roman Catholic guests present, Cardinal Glemp of Poland, spoke. He commanded the rapt attention of the huge congregation as he pointed out that this past week had provided incontrovertible proof that God was renewing the faith of His people by sending spiritual strength from above and that the Russian Church could look towards the future with faith, hope and love. These may have been conventional sentiments – until one considers the age-old rivalry between Catholicism and Orthodoxy and the traditional hostility between Russians and Poles.

Following this, Patriarch Pimen received his guests of honour in the Praga restaurant. He again referred to his meeting with Mr Gorbachev and the guests began to disperse to the provincial centres where the celebrations would continue for a further week.

There was still one more ceremony to be held in Moscow. Monday was a beautiful day on which some foreign guests witnessed the laying of a foundation stone of a new church designated to commemorate the Millennium of St Vladimir's baptism. The site of the new church falls just inside the Moscow boundary, as circumscribed by the outer ring road, and is just off the Kashira highway to the south of the city in the region known as Tsaritsyno Ponds. An optimistic speech by the Patriarch, in which he called on believers to build their faith from the same materials as would be used in this church, contrasted with one from Mr Kharchev, of the Council for Religious Affairs, in which he curiously declared that 'the laying of this foundation stone is the incarnation of Leninist principles'. Nine days of solemnity were to end on a quizzical note, but this was not the final impression the media conveyed. The regional ceremonies continued to proclaim the good name of the church and to underline the inauguration of a new era in church–state relations.

Now the focus would shift away from the church and on to the state, particularly to the question of whether it could deliver its promises on new legislation, while believers asked themselves whether the events of the last few weeks had been an elaborate sham or a pledge that a new era was about to begin.

4 New Laws and Old Institutions

New Laws

One of Lenin's earliest laws concerned religion. In January 1918 he emended in his own hand a decree which confiscated all church property, monastic lands, church buildings and schools. From that moment the public rights of the church were reduced almost to nil. The proclamation that henceforth the church would be separated from the state created the fiction of a separate domain within which the church operated and in which the state had no right to interfere. That turned out to be almost exclusively inside barbed wire for the next quarter of a century, though even there any open practice of religion usually led to the punishment cell and even death. Lenin removed juridical status from the church so that, as a corporate body, it could not defend itself before the law, nor even be represented in court – something of enormous consequence at a time when the whole place of the church in society was being reappraised.

Lenin's constitution provided the right both to religious and anti-religious propaganda, but Stalin's new law of April 1929 underlined the spuriousness of this proclamation and killed any lingering idea that the separation of church and state might become a reality. The only recognised unit was to be the 'religious association' consisting of a minimum of twenty people which must apply for and be granted registration by the state before it could meet at all. This blatant abnegation of the constitutional guarantee of the separation of church and state made a mockery of the whole concept of justice for believers, but worse was to come. Those bodies which were successful in their applications for registration must supply lists of members' names to the local authorities, which provided a tool for use in direct acts of persecution. The legislation afforded the local authorities the right of surveillance over religious activities and of 'removing individual members from the executive body'.[1] In practice, this right often extended to the appointment of atheists to church bodies, which put in place a devastating mechanism for the destruction of church life. As the legislation recognised the existence of no national or central religious bodies, there was no one to defend believers from the attacks of the atheist authorities. The 1929 law banned religious education of children in every form, as well as every single parish activity which would normally take place outside the strict context of worship in a registered church. Stalin's constitution even removed that single right guaranteed by Lenin to 'religious propaganda', balancing this by the sole right the church enjoyed of establishing 'religious worship' in a building registered for the purpose – but it was the state alone which could grant such registration.

With such a blueprint for eliminating religion altogether from Soviet society, Stalin did not originally consider it necessary to establish any bureaucratic entity to mediate between church and state. However, after his meeting with the leaders of the Russian Orthodox Church in the Kremlin in 1943, the concessions he granted necessitated the setting up of two bodies: one for the Russian Orthodox Church, another for all the rest. However, there was no change in the law, nor was there to be for nearly fifty years, so the new bodies had no legally-defined existence, no statutes, and for many years no public role, except in the occasional speeches of their representatives, who tried to pretend they were some kind of benevolent intermediary between church and state.

The two bodies merged in 1966 to become the Council for Religious Affairs under the control of Vladimir Kuroyedov, who had been instrumental in the persecution of the Khrushchev period as head of the council concerned with the Orthodox Church. He remained in office until he was replaced by Konstantin Kharchev in November 1984 – and while the old guard was in control there was never a question about revamping an outdated law. Keeping the *status quo* in this way was a typical Brezhnev contribution to 'stagnation'.

Even in the new conditions, the controversial – it would be safe to say bitterly disputed – projected new law on religion has received only relative *glasnost* in the Soviet media. Opinions and arguments from believers and atheists have been reported, but so far a first draft for public discussion has not been published. This silence (apart from one article in a law journal, which would have reached only a tiny proportion of those whom it mainly affects) can indicate

only that there has been high-level disagreement. Instead, there have
been countless promises of a new law, starting with Mr Gorbachev
himself when he received the church leaders in April 1988. He
assured his guests that the law was well into the drafting process, but two years later not even a timetable had been fixed.
Undoubtedly, the Party die-hards hoped in this, as in everything
else, that it would be possible to confine the debate to points of
detail, but as *glasnost* has bitten deeper, this is obviously going to
be impossible.

A further problem has been the mass of new legislation jostling for
attention, which led Fyodor Burlatsky to state in October 1989 that
several draft decrees on human rights seemed to be disappearing
down the plug hole.

The elements in place at the time of Mr Gorbachev's accession
were Lenin's Decree on the Separation of Church from State and
School from Church of 1918 and the subsequent constitutional
articles, Stalin's Law on Religious Associations of 1929, the Penal
Code of the Russian Republic of 1962 and various unpublished laws,
never known to believers, except when they came to be punished
under them.

The debate on the proposed new laws began in January 1986, less
than a year into Gorbachev's period of office, in a most unexpected
place, *The Journal of the Moscow Patriarchate*, the most heavily censored
of all Soviet publications. Through a fog of ambiguous wording,
the anonymous writer stated that 'religious associations' (parishes)
were now to be bodies in law, thus overturning Lenin's denial of
this right of nearly seventy years earlier. While no other major
changes were mentioned, the general tone was positive, stressing
what the clergy could do, in contrast to the negative approach of
state legislation which carefully listed the dozens of unacceptable
activities. Now clergy could 'perform religious rituals in hospitals,
old people's and invalids' homes and in penal institutions', which
had always been difficult and usually impossible, even though not
outside the provisions of the law. Stating this so clearly would
obviously encourage clergy in general to make a stronger stand
for their rights. No information has ever come to light on exactly
who or what caused this article to appear, but it was a foretaste of
the bolder initiative that the church would take at the *sobor* two
years later.

Metropolitan Alexi of Leningrad and Novgorod, an Estonian and
one of the 'safest' spokesmen for the *status quo*, followed this with a
more personal initiative in 1987:

It is particularly sad when, sometimes, at a local level, and running counter
to the basic principles of our socialist state of the people, [believers] are
treated as 'second-rate' people, and looked at with a certain suspicion and
watchfulness. Quite often, local bodies violate the existing legislation on
cults to the detriment of believers. The more there are such cases, the
easier it is for Western propaganda 'to get hold' of them and use them
in their interests.[2]

This went well beyond the normal limits of criticism, despite
the side-swipe at those agencies outside the Soviet Union who
were attempting to help fellow-believers inside the country. By the
end of 1987, there was talk of 'upgrading' legislation affecting the
churches.[3]

Six months later came Mr Gorbachev's meeting with the church
leaders, then immediately afterwards, on 4 May 1988, Metropolitan
Yuvenali, another defender of the system, illustrated the new mood
of self-confidence in bringing the authorities to book when he spoke
some sharp words in a television broadcast (access to the media was
now to become normal for church leaders):

> A priest . . . does not have the right to visit a baptismal or marriage
> candidate at home. Worship buildings cannot even have libraries attached
> to them . . . The further from Moscow the more complicated the situation.
> For example, the law states very simply that twenty believers collectively
> can request a building for worship. And it happens that hundreds and
> thousands of believers are making these [requests] but without response.
> I could even give you specific examples from my own diocese in the
> Moscow region. But I have more hopes here – the diocese is close
> to Moscow. So we should like our legislation to be observed, even the
> outdated legislation.[4]

During the Millennium celebrations, when Moscow was flooded
with foreign Christian visitors, Mr Kharchev and his associates
went out of their way to state daily, especially in interviews with
foreign radio and TV stations, that the old law was no longer
operative and the drafting of a new one was now a matter of
urgency. The usual suggestion was that it would come into being
by the end of the year. There were assurances that there would
be consultations with believers in the process, though never a firm
promise that any church leader would be a full member of the drafting
committee.

However, by the end of the year the public debate was only just
beginning. In December *Nauka i religia* gave Dr M. P. Kulakov, a
leading Seventh Day Adventist, a platform for his views, though he

was stronger in pointing out the discriminatory effects of the old law than in proclaiming what needed to be done now.

Much more significant, and in the same publication, was an article the next month by a 'special correspondent', V. Kharazov, who had investigated a specific local complaint relating to the Ukrainian town of Drogomyshl. His findings clearly disturbed him. On 10 December 1962, at the height of Khrushchev's campaign, the Orthodox parish there lost its registration and the priest was ousted. For twenty-six years the local believers had campaigned for their rights. In studying the archival material the correspondent discovered that the authorities had closed 880 churches in the second half of 1961 alone. Was there some kind of competition among local authorities, Kharazov asked, to see who could close the most churches? It was hypocritical of officials of the Council for Religious Affairs now to talk blandly about past mistakes when they themselves were so largely responsible.

Nauka i religia had now clearly become the main vehicle for the public discussion of the new law and the editors solicited views, published in February 1989, from various public figures, such as the Catholicos (Patriarch) of the Armenian Apostolic Church, an Orthodox priest, a Buddhist, the leading rabbi and an imam, as well as various secular figures. T. G. Rabdanov, a member of the Buddhist 'spiritual directorate', said that parents must have the right to teach religion to their children, but the most challenging intervention came from the priest, Fr V. V. Suslin, who said that, as no believers were represented in the Supreme Soviet, there should be a referendum on the provisions of the new law. *Moscow News* quoted a similar range of opinions in April (No.15), where several men (no women!) put the emphasis on the right to teach the faith to young people.

A more solid contribution to *Nauka i religia* came from Archbishop Kirill of Smolensk in June 1989, in a close-packed three-page article entitled 'Laws and Principles'. Unlike Metropolitan Alexi, he did not claim that all those who confronted him abroad with awkward questions were motivated by anti-Sovietism. There was genuine and legitimate concern and it was high time to do something about it. He cited the teaching profession as an example where there was severe discrimination because of religious views. Young believers still often found it impossible to enjoy their full rights. No new law could be effective without a change in the ideological perspectives of society: the marginalisation of believers must cease and they must be accepted into every sector of public activity, not just the peace movement. He continued by making the most open denunciation of

Khrushchev's campaign ever to come from a bishop of the Russian Orthodox Church.

While still waiting for the new legislation to appear, a psalm-reader in the Orthodox Church was offered major space in the influential weekly, *Literaturnaya gazeta*, on 10 January 1990, to put the case for freedom of worship. After arguing that the obligation to register a religious community was a flagrant violation of the basic principle of separation of church and state, Sergei Bogdanovsky exposed the typical atheist tactic of forcing the church leadership itself to take decisions detrimental to the life of the church, such as ensuring that 'troublesome' priests were put into remote parishes where they would be able to exercise very little influence. Heavy taxation of the clergy continued even in the days of *perestroika*; this was a relic of the days when the priest was considered to be an 'enemy of the people'.

Some new laws affecting religious life are already operating. Going against the general trend of liberalisation, the Council of Ministers issued a decree in December 1988 banning the new co-operatives from manufacturing religious goods. It forbids 'the production and restoration of icons, objects used in religious worship, articles with religious symbolism and attribution', as well as the manufacture of candles, unless for 'decorative' (that is, secular) use.[5]

The new draft law on publishing, which made its first appearance in a regional newspaper in the autumn of 1988, implied that state censorship should now be abolished, with the safeguards of the penal code being sufficient to curb any impropriety. This would open the way to Christian publishing houses, and Estonia was quick to lead the way.

The new property law of March 1990 states that religious communities should have the right to own property, a dramatic departure from one of the most serious forms of discrimination, in place ever since Lenin's decree of January 1918:

> Religious organizations may own buildings, religious objects, production and social facilities and charitable operations, money and other assets essential to their activities. Religious organizations are entitled to own assets purchased, built, created or produced by them using their own resources, donated by believers, or handed over by the state or other persons or acquired in other ways stated in legislation.[6]

This new law pre-empts what would seem to be one of the most controversial sections of the new general law on religion and overturns one of Lenin's key decrees. It leaves open the question of reparation for the untold billions of roubles stolen from the church in the form of land, buildings and valuables in the early days of the Revolution and the rent communities subsequently had to pay to the state for the right to reoccupy just a selected number of their own churches.

A further concrete gain has been the repeal in April 1989 of the secret laws. The published laws never mentioned any individual denomination by name, which meant that there could be no discrimination against any. However, it is certain that the secret laws did ban a variety of sects, such as Pentecostals (except when merged with Baptists) and Jehovah's Witnesses, as well as the mainstream Ukrainian Catholic Church. By extension, they were interpreted as a ban on the Hare Krishna when they came into existence in the 1970s. When the Council for Religious Affairs annulled these laws, the way was opened to legalise these groups and sects and, with the exception of the Ukrainian Catholic Church, their position gradually eased.

All these, however, are piecemeal changes and they leave open the question of a new general law on religion. The first unambiguous statement about the existence of a draft of this appeared in *New Times* in September 1988. A prominent jurist, Yuri Rozenbaum, stated:

> As far as I know, the initial draft of the law has already been prepared. A group of experts has been working on it . . . Late in 1987 the Council for Religious Affairs officially requested the Institute of State and Law of the USSR Academy of Sciences, where I work, to prepare a draft of the law. The draft was prepared accordingly, discussed in the Institute and then forwarded to the CRA. I do not know what happened to it subsequently.[7]

It seems that there were no believers on this commission, which later occasioned criticism from Fyodor Burlatsky, who rightly questioned what confidence the religious communities could have in such a process, even though some consultation had apparently taken place.

Three drafts have so far reached the West. The first was published in *samizdat* by *Express khronika*, an unofficial human rights journal, in July 1988, but Kharchev subsequently confirmed its authenticity. Rozenbaum published his personal version of what the new law should be, together with a commentary, in a legal journal in February 1989, while *Izvestia* reported in the same month that there had been a meeting at the Council for Religious Affairs where church leaders had seen another draft, the text of which reached the West soon after. In the year since then, believers have had to make do with repeated assurances that a draft would soon be published, which seems to make it certain that the process has run into severe difficulties behind the scenes. If, however, an amalgamation of the three very similar drafts becomes the working text, there will be some basic changes, though they will not be radical enough to satisfy many believers.

Religious communities would gain the status of legal entities (so what was the basis of the *Journal of the Moscow Patriarchate*'s statement of three years earlier?). Registration would still be required by law, which would be certain to invalidate the whole proposal, as far as many believers were concerned. This had always been the principal instrument of state control, so there would be no guarantee of freedom from this while such a provision remained in force, even if it was reduced to 'informing' the authorities, as opposed to petitioning for legalisation, though church amendments to the draft they had seen stated that in the event of a refusal by the authorities to register a community its members should have recourse to a court of law. Charitable activities would become permissible, as would the printing of religious literature in any language.

Taking the third draft, seen by church leaders at the Council for Religious Affairs, as the most likely basis for future discussion, believers will not be generally satisfied with the restrictions on religious education. Article 7 states that 'citizens may teach or study religion privately as individuals or with others, at home or in the religious society', whereas previously no group activity was permissible. However, the more controversial issue of teaching children was left ambiguous. Parents would have the right to 'ensure the religious and moral education and teaching of their children in accordance with their own convictions', so Sunday schools on church premises and private teaching should become possible, though church schools offering a general curriculum are specifically banned. Will it be possible to secure the proper teaching of religion on the curriculum of existing schools? The question remains open, though some schools are opening their doors to clergy in order to counterbalance the decades of misinformation to which pupils have been subjected. Permission is still theoretically required for the holding of services in hospital, old people's homes and prisons, but now they sometimes take the initiative by inviting Christians in. Finally, conscientious objection may become legally possible. One very important clause at the end of the state draft is the affirmation that the new law would be brought into line with existing international human rights agreements ratified by the Soviet Union.

As one would expect, the public participation of believers in the debate on the new law represents only one side of their aspirations. There have been numerous pleas in *samizdat* and in documents sent to émigré publications. Many ask the question why the new law should be so clearly a revision of the old law. Surely it is time for a totally new approach?

However, anyone expecting direction and challenging proposals from the Holy Synod of the Russian Orthodox Church was looking in the wrong place. According to reports, its discussion of the new law early in 1989 missed a major opportunity. Instead of seizing the chance to stake out a claim for the church and a demand for the return of its lost patrimony, it meekly compared two versions of the draft supplied to it and said, without adding to or subtracting from either document, 'We prefer the first version to the second.'

Unofficially, however, Christians of all denominations and from various republics have been signing a variety of documents to request major changes in the law. Alexander Ogorodnikov has been among the most active here and in March 1989, in consultation with others, including a monk from the Danilov Monastery, he produced his own version of a law on freedom of conscience. Most importantly, he said, there should be a total separation of religion and atheism from the state, especially the ending of any form of compulsory atheist education, and all property confiscated since 1917 should be returned (as, indeed, the Lithuanian Government decreed immediately after its independence declaration in March 1990).

It is highly likely that there are many other such documents in existence, but they have not reached the West. The new Baptist journal *Protestant* produced a short but succinct criticism of the draft in April 1989. Later that year, the editorial board set up a conference on 'problems of freedom of conscience and the law', with participants from all denominations, as well as Mr Kharchev.

This debate did not continue with the same intensity during the last half of 1989 and the first part of 1990. The most substantial official contribution to it came in the new programme which the Central Committee of the CPSU adopted in February. It devoted a brief, though important, section to religion, guaranteeing:

> Man's free self-determination in the spiritual sphere, freedom of conscience and religion without abandoning an atheist world outlook. The Party will step up the dialogue between atheists and believers and pursue a policy that offers all churches the opportunity freely to operate within the law, contributing to mutual understanding between people.[8]

If the Party is thinking in terms of a philosophical dialogue, it is probably too late, seeing that the days are long since past where zeal exists to propagate Marxism as an ideological system. Following its failure, the new thinking is in practice coming from the Christian side, as believers begin to make good the social shortcomings of the system. In general terms, however, believers welcome the invitation to dialogue.

Meanwhile the question of a new law is still very much on the agenda. I recently asked the leader of a Russian Orthodox delegation to the UK whether he was apprehensive about the long delay in the publication even of a definitive draft. Was it not unsettling, I asked, to be living in a kind of limbo where clearly the old laws were not operative, even though the main ones were still on the statute book? Did he not fear a return to the old ways and a crackdown on all the 'illegal' activities which the church was so publicly promoting? His reply surprised me. 'No,' he said, 'long may the uncertainty continue. The greater the delay, the more liberal the new laws are likely to be. Meanwhile, our fledgling institutions are growing up and becoming more secure in the role they are playing. It will become very difficult for any new law to curtail them. Perhaps if this goes on long enough the state will see we don't need a new law at all, then we shall all be happy.'

Parallel to these rather grey and impersonal discussions of the new law, an extended high drama was developing around the personality and role of one individual: Konstantin Kharchev, Chairman of the Council for Religious Affairs. His own attitude to the need for new laws changed while he was in office and that is part of his story.

The Council for Religious Affairs

Kharchev was an appointee of Chernenko and his initial mandate was to maintain the *status quo*. The transformation of one hard and orthodox Marxist into a key figure in the liberalisation of the state's attitude to religion is one of the most fascinating stories in recent Soviet history.

Kharchev was brought up in an orphanage in Gorky. He became an engineer and later took a higher degree in the economic sciences. He went to the Soviet Far East and eventually became Party Secretary in Vladivostok, where he built up enough trust to be sent to Guyana as Soviet Ambassador. When he was recalled it was to become head of the Council for Religious Affairs.

At first Kharchev gave no hint that he would be any different from the faceless and unyielding Kuroyedov whom he replaced. In May 1986 the British Council of Churches sent a delegation to the Soviet

Union, some of whose members secured an interview with him. He did not produce a favourable impression. One delegate, linguistically able to pick up the nuances of the conversation, reported that he was a man of vacillating words, alternately bullying and trying to charm. Having no background for his work, he pretended to know more than he did and could ill conceal his insecurity at being confronted with a group of articulate foreign church leaders, probably better informed than any others he was likely to meet in the course of his duties.[9]

At this juncture, Kharchev was vigorous in his defence of existing Soviet legislation and harshly critical of Keston College, which was by this time being widely used as a reliable resource on religion in the USSR and whose staff had extensively briefed this delegation.

A year later his attitude was noticeably changing. On 7 April 1987 the influential government newspaper *Izvestia* printed an interview with Kharchev in which, while restating some traditional positions, he announced that Pentecostals had the full right to register just like any other religious community. This was indeed a step forward, because their existence had been marginal at best, with registration under the Baptist banner being the only recognised way of becoming legal. There had been a few recent independent registrations as Pentecostals, but never before a public statement that this was now the way forward for a group which had been among the worst persecuted of all Soviet believers.

Six months later the watchword of *perestroika* was taking over the Soviet scene. Kharchev made his contribution with an article in *Nauka i religia* ('Science and Religion'), the state's flagship of atheism which had proclaimed the official view since its founding as a tool of Khrushchev's anti-religious campaign nearly thirty years earlier. Kharchev was not the first to call for respect for believers' rights, but in the new climate this meant something, especially when he went on to say that the authorities acted illegally when, for example, they denied Christian prisoners the right to a Bible or stopped a clergyman visiting a dying parishioner. He ended by hinting that it was time for a revision of the laws on religion.[10]

The British group who met Kharchev in 1986 noted a series of inconsistencies in his presentation and nowhere did these appear in sharper outline than in statements he made in the few months leading up to the Orthodox jubilee.

The first of these was very official indeed, appearing in *Izvestia* on 27 January 1988. One has the feeling that in it he was trying to move backwards and forwards at the same time. He justified Lenin's 1918 decree in detail, even the removal of the right of the church to juridical status. At the same time, he noted that in the previous year he had received no fewer than 3,000 complaints from believers, mainly stating that they were still denied church buildings. These were due, he continued, to subsequent malpractice, not to the nature of the legislation itself.

In March and May he addressed two different audiences. The first occasion was a speech to a private hard-line gathering at the Higher Party School, taken down in note form by a listener who passed it on for publication abroad. Little did Kharchev know that just one year later, Metropolitan Pitirim would address the same audience.[11] Speaking in a more open and less guarded way, Kharchev said that there was popular unrest resulting from demands to reopen churches; the 1929 law needed revision in line with current Party policy. He admitted that the Party was responsible for carrying out 'administrative measures' against the churches, for example in the demand that priests should baptise children only upon the production of passports (that is, identity documents) by the parents. He continued:

> We, the Party, have fallen into the trap of our own anti-church policy of prohibitions and persecution . . . The Party and the state are increasingly losing control over believers . . . The choice and appointment of priests is a Party matter, given that the Party must retain control over all spheres of citizens' lives . . . The Party is interested in promoting a new type of Orthodox priest.[12]

It is scarcely surprising that, in the process of church *perestroika*, these words were to prove highly controversial. They were not likely to endear him to the church at a time when the Millennium celebrations were imminent and all aspects of church–state relations were due for immediate revision.

Then in May *Ogonyok*, a popular illustrated journal, printed Kharchev's interview with Alexander Nezhny (the same man who had published the lament for the churches of Kirov). He spoke of 70 million believers in the Soviet Union. This contrasted with the astonishing figure he had given in his private speech: 115 million believers (70 per cent of the population) for the 1950s. He did not say why he did not give a more up-to-date statistic, but he did state that the authorities falsified the figure and quoted it as 20 per cent. Even the figure of 70 million was perhaps the most amazing admission of the failure of atheism yet to be published in the Soviet press. From now on the growth of the churches under Soviet rule became a matter of public record. Kharchev was speaking just after Gorbachev's reception of the Russian Orthodox leaders

NEW LAWS AND OLD INSTITUTIONS 77

in the Kremlin. He therefore stated with confidence that a new policy of co-operation and toleration was a matter of urgency to prevent believers from becoming hostile to the state. In *Ogonyok* he emphasised that Lenin supported the private teaching of religion to children (always permissible in law, but treated as a punishable offence in practice). The Bible should be more freely available and the church should now play a more active role in charitable work, not just in making a financial contribution.[13] In this interview Kharchev was therefore clearly inviting the church to act beyond the restrictions of the existing law.

Just after this I met him in Moscow on the last day of my visit for the Millennium celebrations. He received my wife and me in his large office in an old building on the inner ring road. As others had before reported, I found him domineering and inconsistent. It was impossible to discuss anything properly because he insisted we should hold rigidly to the informal agenda I had jotted down, barking short answers before commanding me to ask the next question. I reported to him a conversation I had had the previous day in Kiev, where a group of Baptists from Dneprodzerzhinsk had approached me and asked me to help them in their efforts to build a new church, which had been frustrated for years. He said: 'Tell your friends to go ahead and build their church. We'll sort out the permission afterwards' – which perhaps typified Kharchev's brusque but not ineffective way of doing business. When I challenged him on the fact that in June 1988 some 200 Christian prisoners were still detained for doing just this and committing similar 'crimes', he refused to follow up the argument and said it was a diversion. Kharchev then took us in his chauffeur-driven limousine to his next appointment, a press conference for the foreign dignitaries who had also been attending the celebrations.

As someone who had chronicled the misdeeds of the Council for Religious Affairs and the bodies which preceded it for nearly thirty years, I found this encounter an assurance that *glasnost* applied to me, too, but that *perestroika* was not yet effective. I ended by inviting Kharchev to come to Keston College during the visit to the United Kingdom which he planned for later in the year.

A few weeks later T. K. Belokobylskaya, head of the legal section of the Council for Religious Affairs, gave an interview to *Argumenty i fakty* ('Arguments and Facts'), another beacon of *glasnost*, in which she claimed that her organisation was now frequently intervening on behalf of believers to correct acts of injustice against them by the local authorities. In this sense, she answered affirmatively the question posed as the headline of the interview, which was apparently being raised by a number of readers, 'Is the Council for Religious Affairs necessary?'

In the autumn of 1988 Kharchev undertook journeys first to the World Council of Churches in Geneva, then to Britain at the invitation of the Mayor of Coventry. For the first journey he had five senior churchmen in his entourage, but he made the second in the company of a single young interpreter. His deputy, Yuri Smirnov, whom I also met in Moscow, visited Vienna in September. Kharchev's objective was to proclaim to the world that *perestroika* for believers was now a reality and that new laws on religion were about to be passed. However, in private meetings in Switzerland people who talked to him noted that he was still behaving in an unpredictable and blustering way, a far cry from the diplomatic approach which would have been more readily convincing of Soviet good intentions.

Kharchev had a busy few days in England in mid-November. He stayed privately in the home of a residentiary canon of Westminster Abbey, where the buildings and atmosphere around him can hardly fail to have produced an impression, as did the fact that on his first full day (13 November) the Foreign Office put him on the same balcony as the Queen when she attended the Remembrance Day ceremony at the Cenotaph. Later that day he went to Lambeth Palace to meet the Archbishop of Canterbury, by which time he was probably more fully aware of the grandeur of British official religion than any other Soviet atheist.

The formal occasion in Coventry's Guildhall the next evening underlined yet again Kharchev's unpredictability. His address was in the line of mild *perestroika*, but when Dick Rodgers, the defender of Irina Ratushinskaya and other former prisoners, gently raised the question of eighty-three remaining Christian prisoners (an accurate figure at the time: it had gone down since the summer) Kharchev became aggressive:

> It's profitable for certain organizations to list prisoners without saying why they have been sentenced. We now have only six on our records, and a further fifteen who are doing corrective labour while living comfortably with their families. The rest on these lists are criminals. You in Britain put drug peddlers in prison, even if they claim to be Christians. Tomorrow I'm going to visit Keston College and I will continue discussion of the question with Michael Bourdeaux, who is here in the audience tonight.[14]

He did continue after a fashion, seeing the current Keston College prisoner list not for the first time. However, his mood at the college was defensive and he was not willing to pursue any agenda item in a spirit of dialogue. Indeed, he rather seemed to object to the idea of there being an agenda at all when he came as a 'guest', and we deferred to his unwillingness to allow anything to be recorded on tape. It would be more correct to describe the event as a series of monologues by Kharchev which went in the direction he wished to follow, but he stayed beyond his allotted time and had tea in a reasonably convivial mood at the end of it. The willingness of Keston College to receive Kharchev had been controversial from the first – was not this an act of compromise with the Soviet authorities and would believers understand our motives? – but the event justified itself and demonstrated unequivocally to the Soviets that Keston College was open to dialogue.

Another remarkable development in November was the transfer of some of the archives of the Council for Religious Affairs to the Central State Archive of the October Revolution, the main historical repository in the Soviet Union. This included information on the closure of churches in the Khrushchev period. At first it was open only to those with special permission from the Council, but it soon became more generally available and it is said that private citizens may now have access to it.

In December Alexander Nezhny and Konstantin Kharchev continued their public dialogue in the pages of *Ogonyok* (No.50). Whatever inconsistencies and aggression Kharchev had shown during his recent travels, he now made statements which went well beyond anything to date in their demand for a new relationship between church and state, declaring himself in favour of all sorts of progress towards religious liberty and forecasting a diminishing role for the Council for Religious Affairs as Soviet society acquired more equitable laws. Later he would suggest its abolition.

There had, he claimed, been a breakthrough in the opening of new churches, sixteen for the Orthodox in 1987 and 'more than 500' in 1988. This was far from being sufficient, however, and it was disgraceful, he said, that there were still many instances where believers were having to travel to Moscow in an attempt to seek justice. He continued with the surprising question, which cannot have endeared him to his superiors: 'And what if here too he comes up against a bureaucrat, an indifferent executive, a cold functionary? All this happens! Then he'll return and say to the people at home: there's no justice, don't look for it.'[15]

His office, he went on, did reverse eighty-three wrong decisions in 1988 by various local authorities who refused to open churches.

Alexander Nezhny then cited some of the more horrific examples of persecution in the Lenin period, thus breaking the taboo that one could criticise Stalin but not the father of the Revolution. Kharchev's slightly evasive reply to this was that the most urgent matter was to revise the 1929 law.

Nezhny claimed the full right for Christians to proclaim the Gospel without hindrance and stated that believers, through taxation, were in effect helping to pay for anti-religious propaganda. Kharchev said that state printing presses should now be producing serious works of theology. Even more unexpectedly, he said that the whole principle of registration, so hated by believers and so divisive among them, should be abandoned. Truly democratic local Councils of People's Deputies should regulate any difficulties, which in turn would relieve the Council for Religious Affairs of one of its main responsibilities.

The photographs alongside this article displayed various scenes from Orthodox life. This reflected the increasing public profile of the Russian Orthodox Church in Soviet society. The government newspaper *Izvestia* started to report regularly on its official activities and the media began to perceive religion, following the lead from Mr Gorbachev, as an ally in the moral and spiritual regeneration of society. Alongside the interview *Ogonyok* printed an appeal from four prominent reformers for complete equality of believers and unbelievers before the law. They were S. Averintsev, an Orthodox Christian and a corresponding member of the Academy of Sciences, subsequently a People's Deputy, S. Zalygin, a writer, and Tatyana Zaslavskaya, a founding figure in the drive for economic reform. Amazingly, alongside these appeared the signature of Fr Gleb Yakunin, the first time that a recent political prisoner had appeared in such a context.

Kharchev furthered his relations with Orthodox activists by receiving a group of them on 12 January 1989, one of whom was Fr Gleb. Again, the tone was constructive, though nothing really new emerged from it. However, March saw a new development. One of Kharchev's deputies, Z. Sharipov, joined in a debate in *Izvestia* on 8 March to say there was no ban on believers who wished to become schoolteachers.

However, while all seemed to be going well on the *perestroika* front, rumours started that in the life of Konstantin Kharchev himself it was not. In early April Kirill Kasyanov, his interpreter when he came to London, said he had had major surgery; Alexander Ogorodnikov said he was on the way out of office. His information proved reliable, as usual. On 3 May the *Frankfurter Allgemeine Zeitung* reported that

Kharchev had been appointed ambassador to Mauretania. Another source said Ghana. In either case, this would have been a return to the sphere from which he had come. But neither was to be. A subsequent rumour said the posting was to the United Arab Emirates (perhaps to use his experience of Islam?) and later he himself said he was to be an 'ambassador at large'.

Why the move? Some said the conservatives in the Kremlin had ousted him because his ideas on religious liberty were clearly at variance with Marxist orthodoxy. Other sources said he had been removed for criticising the leadership of the Russian Orthodox Church for its unwillingness to move ahead with the times, in an unpublished interview with *Izvestia*. He had claimed that not only was the leadership slow to implement *perestroika*, but it was also financially corrupt: it was time to start publishing audited accounts for the benefit of believers. Later another rumour would emerge from Orthodox circles: that Kharchev was too sympathetic to the Ukrainian Catholics and wanted to legalise them.

In the days of *perestroika*, unlike earlier times, when the pointing of a finger led to a person's immediate disappearance from the scene, it is now a common sight to see someone who has suffered official disapproval immediately come bouncing back, even able to propagate his ideas abroad and then return to the Soviet Union. This happened with Konstantin Kharchev.

Whatever illness he had suffered in the spring, by midsummer he was in London to give a speech at the assembly of the International Religious Liberty Association (a Seventh Day Adventist group). Some of the awards this association has given in the past have been astonishing, regularly honouring representatives of repressive governments who have ultimately come to adopt a more liberal stance, rather than supporting those who, under dire persecution, have formulated new concepts which have eventually revolutionised perceptions.

His citation, signed by Carl Mau (President) and B. B. Beach (General Secretary) 'honours Konstantin Kharchev as spokesman for human rights, promoter of religious freedom, builder of bridges between peoples, contributor to the trust that weaves peace'. By the time he came for his award it seemed that if there had ever been any trust, it had dissipated some months since.

In his acceptance speech he spoke of 'routine and sensible transfer of cadres, as in any government, to somewhere that I'm more needed'. He went on to say nothing new for the initiated, but for the third-world delegates present it was a good basic lesson in religious *perestroika*. He ended by proposing that Mr Gorbachev's 'common European home' should contain icons and an altar.

Kharchev gave no subsequent indication that he was about to subside into silence. If indeed he is an ambassador at large, he sees his role as that of a Yeltsin-type maverick in religious affairs, criticising government policies and extending his links with Western public opinion. There had been signs that he wished to do this over the previous three years. In October 1989 *Ogonyok* published round three of his ongoing dialogue with Alexander Nezhny. In it Kharchev admitted that although he had been an upholder of the 'total subjugation of church to state', he had quickly seen that this position was untenable in the days of *perestroika*. However, two or three members of the Ideology Commission (not previously publicly identified as playing a leading role in the formulation of religious policy) had opposed his views, while Gorbachev alone had upheld them. (The censors forced *Ogonyok* to remove the names of his opponents from the original article, but they have subsequently become known.) It was he, he boasted, who had convinced Gorbachev of the opportunity the Millennium celebrations would afford, leading to the meeting of April 1988 with church leaders in the Kremlin.

The strangest and boldest assertion in the interview was the reason for his dismissal he was allegedly given by a member of the Politburo (sources later claimed that this was Anatoli Lukyanov, Deputy President of the Council of Ministers of the USSR): he 'had not found a common language with the ideological *apparat*, the "neighbours" [the KGB] and the leadership of the Russian Orthodox Church'. If this statement is true, it is astonishing. Binding the Orthodox hierarchy into an unholy trinity with two of its greatest enemies might have been dismissed as sensationalism, but it does confirm rumours which had been rife since the news of his dismissal. An alliance between the KGB and the church leadership over one specific matter would tend to suggest they worked together on others, raising more serious doubts about the integrity of that leadership – doubts one would never expect to read in a published Soviet source. If one faction of the Holy Synod visited the Supreme Soviet to complain about Kharchev, that would confirm that there was now a growing power struggle within the church. It was, after all, a time when the patriarch was old and ailing and endemic attitudes of compromise were audibly clashing with the aspirations of a new generation. Kharchev said: 'I suspect that some members of the Synod, from force of habit, have counted more on the support of the authorities than on their own authority in the church.'[16] On a more intimate note, Kharchev states that he remains a communist and a convinced materialist, but he now reads the Bible and the Koran and they have both given him 'an exceptionally great deal'.

This interview opened up a fascinating public debate in the Soviet press and elsewhere, which continues at the time of writing. In an article in an émigré journal Victor Popkov, an unofficial Orthodox lay commentator on church affairs, affirmed that the KGB was indeed exerting influence over the Holy Synod, which was one of the reasons why so much secrecy surrounded its deliberations. A group of hierarchs, he claimed, went twice to the Central Committee of the Communist Party complaining about Kharchev's 'interference' in church affairs. The second time they saw Lukyanov, who obtained the removal of Kharchev. This perhaps supports the claim that Kharchev was trying to make the Holy Synod more accountable, particularly in financial matters. Popkov went on to say that the Council for Religious Affairs and the KGB were still exerting an influence on the appointment of priests.

Sovetskaya Rossia, a newspaper known for its conservative tendencies, published an article by Professor A. Ipatov on 22 November, in which he both accused Kharchev of cashing in on changes already under way to enhance his own reputation and also defended the hierarchy of the Russian Orthodox Church. Ipatov began, astonishingly enough, by quoting Jane Ellis, researcher on the Orthodox Church at Keston College, although without naming her. She had written a sardonic article in the *Church Times* about Kharchev's award, in which she wondered whether he would go down in history as 'Saint Constantine' – a quote which provided *Sovetskaya Rossia* with a banner headline dominating an inside page.

Ipatov went on to counter Kharchev's claim that he had played a major role in upgrading the Millennium celebrations. He also said it was quite right that the Orthodox hierarchy should have complained about him, because he had indeed been interfering in the internal running of their affairs. The main reason for the *Ogonyok* article was that Kharchev now suspected he was to become an ex-ambassador designate, as well as ex-Chairman of the Council for Religious Affairs, and was desperately looking round for support.

Whatever the rights and wrongs of Kharchev's conduct, Ipatov did not do full justice to his criticisms of the Orthodox Church, ignoring, for example, what he said about financial mismanagement.

Immediately after this *Ogonyok* opened its pages to another reply to Kharchev. It came from Alexander Degtaryov, first deputy director of the Ideological Department of the Central Committee of the

Communist Party. This senior functionary accused Kharchev of 'insufficient competence and lightweight irresponsibility decked out in the vocabulary of *perestroika*'[17] and pointed out that he had had no interest in religion before his appointment. His assertion in his speech to the Higher Party School in March 1988, where he said that the Party had a major role in the selection and placement of the priesthood, was a disgrace. After such remarks it was inevitable that the Orthodox hierarchy should complain about him – but the Lithuanian Catholic bishops and two Muslim leaders had done so before them (the latter over a plan to divert Muslim funds to the setting up of an information and analysis department within the Council for Religious Affairs). From this he went on to accuse Kharchev of diverting church funds designated for other purposes into his organisation.

The judgment of history on Kharchev's brief though dramatic tenure of office may well contain some of the phrases used by Degtaryov in his conclusion: 'lack of theoretical preparedness, of sufficiently deep understanding of the processes taking place in the religious sphere, of know-how in organizing the work of the Council for Religious Affairs . . . impulsiveness, inconsistency, ambition'. It is too early, however, to accept his verdict as final. No one has ever before said that the church leadership was strong enough to succeed in removing an official where two departments of the Central Committee had failed. Can it be true? Kharchev did identify correctly many of the problems in church–state relations, including the resistance to change undoubtedly found among some church leaders, but he was unable to carry many people with him because of his rudeness and unpredictability, a tendency to make sweeping promises with little chance of implementing them. The financial accusations, coming at this late stage, cannot be substantiated, because Kharchev told Nezhny that the Party had earlier been seeking ways to compromise him financially.

It would not necessarily be accurate to seek to portray Kharchev as the unfortunate victim of manipulative forces jockeying for supremacy in the ideological struggle. It is interesting none the less to see the whole saga as a reflection, in personal terms, of the wider conflict on ideological issues between the Ideology Commission, the Institute of State and Law, the CRA, the Procuracy, the KGB and the Ministry for Internal Affairs – all of which are known to have had some finger in the pie of religious affairs in the Soviet Union.

Kharchev's successor was Yuri Nikolaevich Khristoradnov, who, like Kharchev, came from Gorky. If one had to choose a background from which not to pick someone to implement religious *perestroika*, it would probably be the bureaucracy in the city of Gorky and it provided two men in succession. Khristoradnov had spent virtually his whole working life there, from 1949 (aged twenty) to 1988. For the previous fourteen years he had been First Secretary of the Regional Committee, from which post he was reportedly sacked after severe criticism from Gorbachev in person. If this is true, then his new appointment was a consequent demotion, though it is odd to give an official on the way down such a sensitive post, particularly to follow a man who had been in trouble partly because of his complete inexperience in religious affairs. As First Secretary in Gorky he had been Sakharov's jailer and would have been ultimately responsible for his abominable living conditions and the restriction of access to him up to the time of his recall to Moscow by Gorbachev. Further, over the past twenty years the Orthodox community there had been among the most vocal and least successful petitioners for the opening of new churches, latterly to Kharchev in person, as he himself reported in his first Nezhny interview.

It is certain that Khristoradnov had had no more experience of church affairs before he took up his new post than Kharchev had done five years earlier. In his first interview he struck a note of understandable caution, but what he said did not give ground for any new worries among the religious communities:

> There can be no return to the primitive scheme under which religion was regarded as opium and believers as an insignificant part of the population . . . What has been going on until now cannot be called anything other than infringement of believers' rights . . . They are not admitted to institutes of higher education, they are not taken on for work, they are given negative references, they are not allocated flats . . . Sometimes it becomes quite absurd . . . As for religion as such, then the attitude to it has not essentially altered. However, the struggle of opinions, we now realise, must be conducted on the basis of equality, with the two sides respecting each other.[18]

Only the last sentence gives cause for concern, because the 'struggle of opinions', with the state having all the resources, now seems something of a relic of the past. In a subsequent interview with *Nauka i religia* (January 1990) he took issue with Kharchev's view (unattributed) that the Council for Religious Affairs was no longer needed. He said that it still had much work to do in overcoming the stereotyped way in which many people looked at religion: it needed to continue working on the new draft law and it must help to resolve any new conflicts which should arise after it was passed.

Will Mr Khristoradnov emerge as a new protagonist in a long struggle, or will he oversee a real improvement in church–state relations? Many questions remain unresolved, but meanwhile we shall examine how *perestroika* has so far affected the lives of the main Christian bodies in the Soviet Union. Has his organisation had a hand in the selection of a new patriarch, or has the age of such interference passed?

On 10 June 1990 Patriarch Alexi was enthroned in great splendour – though without the presence of the usual galaxy of foreign guests, absent, reportedly, because the church is bankrupt after the Millennium celebrations, the continuing financial demands of church restoration and the drop in income because of the loss of so many Ukrainian parishes (see Chapter 8). The new patriarch comes from an Estonian noble family of German origin (surname Ridiger). Though he has never been allied with the national cause of the Baltic states, it is nevertheless a curious choice. Alexi, formerly Bishop of Tallinn and then Metropolitan of Leningrad, owed his rise to his espousal of Brezhnev's negative church policies. He is now 61 and was only 35 when Krushchev's persecution ended. He has gained himself a considerable reputation internationally, having been chairman of the Conference of European Churches for several years. In this and other forums he has followed a safe political line and, even under *perestroika*, has failed to speak openly of the persecution to which the church was subjected until recently. Furthermore, his election complicates the most important aspect of ecumenical relations – with the Vatican. As an elected member of the Congress of People's Deputies, he has publicly criticised the Ukrainian Catholics and given credence to the falsehoods spread about the violence they were accused of initiating against the Orthodox. The election can give rise only to further internal dissension.

5 The Orthodox Church and the People

Pre-Millennium Expectations

The excitement of the Millennium celebrations of the Orthodox Church, the church's continuing high profile in the media and the promise of a new law have transformed perceptions of the present and expectations for the future. For the previous twenty years the church had seemed on the one hand a timid adjunct of Soviet foreign policy in its public pronouncements and a voiceless mass of disadvantaged worshippers on the other. This was always too simplistic a view, but it is broadly true to say that the hierarchy failed to provide the leadership for which people yearned. For three decades only a handful of activists had challenged both the state on the essential issues, especially religious liberty, and the hierarchy on their duty to invigorate the dormant social structures of Orthodoxy.

In those towns and rare villages where there was an open church, the liturgy began to exert its age-old power in a new way. That strength came, in total contrast to the febrile desire in the West to make worship 'relevant' at all costs, precisely from the refusal to modernise in any way. Not only was the colour and beauty of the ceremonial and the singing in marked contrast to the dismal, grey surroundings of everyday life; the voice of the past seemed to have more and more to say about the condition of man in a society where moral standards were collapsing and active support for the Party was found mainly among people who embraced it for career purposes. So people came to church. The days had passed when scarcely a young face was seen among the ranks of *babushki* – the old women in head scarves who formed the backbone of the congregation.

In the early 1970s a *starets* (the term applies to a monk or holy man who acquires special spiritual authority) began a new ministry in a country area not far from the city of Jelgava in Latvia. Tavrion, after many years of prison and harassment, became a focus for spiritual revival. He was one of many such men, but we know him specially well from a *samizdat* document of the time:

> Drawn by tales of this extraordinary *starets*, they flocked from the spiritual desert of modern life as to a fount of living water; the sick, the old, intellectuals from the big cities, peasants, engineers, hippies, all who were suffering in any way . . . Today in summer you will find about two hundred people every day . . . Very early in the morning, just before five when the city is still asleep, there is such beauty here when we sing the Gloria and gather at the banquet of the Lamb of God . . . Nowhere have I seen the liturgy celebrated with such conviction and authority, such paschal joy. One can really feel the strength of the prayers of the *starets*, the fire of the Spirit in them.[1]

There was a new spiritual life outside the immediate confines of the Orthodox liturgy as well. In the late 1960s Fr Alexander Men used to hold open house on certain days of the week in his village of Semkhoz, near Zagorsk in the Moscow region. They were known in Russian by the French name of *jours fixes*. They began totally informally – on the platform of Moscow's Yaroslavsky railway station, where a group would assemble waiting to board the 3.15 train. The two-hour journey to the home of Fr Alexander would be a sort of seminar in itself. Conversation would be animated and unbroken from that moment until they returned home late at night. Fr Alexander would come out into the garden to greet his guests and bless them. In the summer they would sit on the verandah, and their discussions ranged over the fields of literature, art, politics and the Christian faith. I wrote of him several years ago:

> His library was open to all, a collection of philosophy and religious literature such as could not be found in a single public library anywhere in the country. Despite the rarity of his books, he would lend them freely and sometimes they would pass from hand to hand for a year before they came back.[2]

In the worsening climate subsequently, Fr Alexander had to become more circumspect in his work with young people. During the later Brezhnev years, the time of 'stagnation', as the Russians now officially call it, the atheist authorities attempted to suppress every form of initiative, whether inside or outside the official structure of the church. Jane Ellis's comprehensive book, *The Russian Orthodox Church: A Contemporary History*,[3] appeared as recently as 1986. It could have

been written in a different age. The final fifty pages lament the
suppressed voice of renewal, and list dozens of activists either forced
into a humiliating public renunciation of their activities, or silenced
by imprisonment and exile. She could not even mention the name
of Mr Gorbachev, as there was no indication that he would become
leader at the time.

Four years later the picture has changed out of all recognition.
Fr Alexander has been able to resume his work with full publicity
and increased vigour. Archbishops challenge the church to change.
Former so-called 'dissident' clergy bid for position in the new elected
political forums. Lay Christians sometimes have their say in the
press.

As early as November 1986, a document appeared in *samizdat* which
carried a sober and far-reaching analysis of the changes promised by
Mr Gorbachev's appointment to the post of General Secretary of the
CPSU in March 1985. Entitled *The Day is Coming*, by Kirill Golovin,
it gives an extensive commentary not only on the situation as he saw
it then, but an overview of church and society during the last few
decades. Golovin warns against accepting everything at face value in
the initial euphoria generated by *perestroika* and goes on to analyse
the history of the movement for renewal amongst the Orthodox
intelligentsia.

The Brezhnev years saw large-scale 'administrative persecution'
but, far from being suppressed, Golovin says, the religious revival
among the intelligentsia gathered momentum along with the developing human rights movement in the Soviet Union. Alexander
Ogorodnikov's seminar and Fr Dimitri Dudko's question and answer
sessions were among the activities which flourished for a time during
the 1970s, before their abolition under the new repression.

Years of inculcation of atheism, he continues, have had a paradoxical effect: there are many 'nominal atheists', who, despite the
effects of propaganda directed against the church, have continued to
experience a naive sense of nostalgia and a vague romantic sympathy
for the faith of their forefathers. It is partly due to this feeling of
having lost touch with the past that there has been a general revival
of interest in Russia's national heritage, in itself inextricably linked
with Orthodoxy. As a result, attitudes towards Orthodoxy have been
increasingly sympathetic.

However, warns Golovin, it would be premature to assume that
because of these trends social opinion is ready to accept the idea
that churches should not only be preserved but open for worship.
Professional atheists are working out their own response by seeking

to pass off Russian culture as the product of some vague neo-pagan elements. State atheism may have lost its fervour, but it has immense resources to fall back on as the prevailing, state-funded ideology. The Orthodox Church may well have been making its own preparations for the jubilee, but so have the forces of atheist propaganda, Golovin maintained. Spring 1986 saw the start of a monthly television programme, 'Religion and Society', intended to dispel the 'myth' about persecution and create the impression that the church was some kind of political organisation of considerable usefulness when it comes to the politics of peace-making. The Party needed a submissive and ignorant church to suit its own purpose, said Golovin, and successfully achieved this, but the church should have done more to defend itself in recent years, given increasingly sympathetic attitudes in society. The Soviet authorities would hardly dare unleash an anti-religious campaign on the eve of the Millennium, so now was the time to challenge both church and state, as well as the activists themselves, to press for real changes in the sphere of religious life.

Golovin could not have predicted the wave of prisoner releases during the amnesties of 1987, nor the beginnings of a more positive profile for the church on the pages of the more *glasnost*-minded Soviet press. However, the processes which he had analysed in society and the general revival of interest in Orthodoxy were contributing to change – a thaw in the previously frosty and hostile official attitudes towards believers.

Released activists – the reformers and the democrats – brought the full vigour of their new liberty into the process of church *perestroika*. Alexander Ogorodnikov launched *The Christian Community Bulletin* in July 1987; a few weeks later Victor Aksyuchits brought out the first issue of *Vybor* ('Choice'), which covered a range of issues affecting the church. A host of other journals, not necessarily religious in their primary inspiration, such as *Glasnost*, have also devoted space to religious questions and seek in varying ways to assess current developments in Soviet society.

January 1988 saw a number of more specific declarations issued by Orthodox groups at the beginning of the Millennium year in an attempt to determine priorities for the Orthodox Church and exert pressure on hierarchs and state officials alike. In a document entitled 'Religion and *Perestroika* in the Soviet Union', Ogorodnikov made some definite demands regarding increased religious freedom, acknowledging that positive changes had taken place, but at the same time striking a note of caution:

All the democratic changes to date have merely loosened some of the bonds which tie the church hand and foot, immobilising the whole of religious life. The bonds have been loosened in that there has been a lull in the arrests of those that seek greater religious freedom.[4]

Ogorodnikov, along with many others, recognised the tremendous opportunity offered by the coincidence of *perestroika* and the Millennium. On 31 January 1988, he and a group of Russian Orthodox Christians organised an unofficial Millennium committee to carry out its own events in connection with the jubilee. This declaration set down a seven-point plan for immediate action. This included requests for the release of all prisoners of conscience, the abolition of Stalin's laws on religion, the reopening of the Monastery of the Caves in Kiev (in support of a plea by Archbishop Feodosi of Astrakhan), the right to hold a Christian seminar during the Millennium celebrations, putting on a photographic exhibition to mark the darker side of the church's history, and the canonisation of modern martyrs.

Nothing could mark the progress made more clearly than the fact that all these requests except the last one quickly came about. There was a truly public mounting of the exhibition in Westminster Abbey, following the export of magnificent photographs showing the destruction of the churches. They made a fine atmospheric addition to the premiere of John Tavener's *Akathist of Thanksgiving*, written in honour of the Millennium.

Reactions to the Millennium

The public pomp and ceremony surrounding the Millennium surpassed the expectation of every Orthodox believer. It must have been Mr Gorbachev's reception of the hierarchy in April 1988 which reversed the tide of articles attempting to discredit the forthcoming jubilee. In fact, so dramatic was the change that it was a temptation for all to be carried away by the euphoria generated by such a momentous event in the life of the Orthodox Church.

Despite the impression given by the high media profile accorded the events themselves, however, there was a less positive side to the celebrations. Kirill Golovin makes it clear that, for the ordinary believer, it was extremely difficult to participate in services held to celebrate the jubilee:

> While the Church Council was in session, Zagorsk was almost like a town under siege, entry being restricted to local residents and those with special

passes. Believers wanting access to the Patriarchal Cathedral in Moscow and the Danilov Monastery came up against triple cordons of militia. The numbers of militiamen deployed around the cathedrals exceeded by far the numbers to be seen around football grounds at a cup final. On top of that, there was transport laid on by the militia for guests, the provision of the best banquet halls, theatres and other facilities for meetings and concerts.

This was obviously gratifying for the hierarchs and clergy, accustomed as they are to being denigrated and marginalised. However, the expenditure was immense: Golovin and others estimated that the celebrations cost the Moscow Patriarchate a million roubles a day, all of which was financed from the pockets of ordinary parishioners. Yet they were largely excluded and most of the major events were not intended for them:

> It was impossible not to notice amid all the pomp and ceremony how few ordinary believers were present. In the Patriarchal Cathedral they made up barely a quarter of the congregation, at the Danilov Monastery they crowded around outside, and even half of these were merely curious bystanders who did not even know how to cross themselves. When ordinary church-goers came to St Vladimir's Cathedral in Kiev at 6 a.m., they were unable to enter – only those with special permits were allowed to go inside. This happened in many places because, as it turned out, the main 'participants' of the festivities were numerous foreign guests.[5]

One of Golovin's major concerns was that these guests, having witnessed such magnificent proceedings, would go back to their respective countries proclaiming the 'total well-being' of the Russian Orthodox Church.

Many lay activists were of the opinion that the official celebrations gave an unrealistic and idealised picture of the true nature of Orthodox Church life in the Soviet Union after decades of persecution. These activists were disappointed that there was no open discussion of questions crucial to the future of the church and that not one of them was present at the *sobor*. Such feelings led one group to organise an 'alternative Millennium' in a Moscow flat which would better represent the concerns of ordinary Soviet believers in line with their proposals for action set down in January 1988.

This event, in a large but shabby flat high up in an apartment block in a dismal suburb of Moscow, was something never to be forgotten by those few foreigners, mostly not official visitors, who found their way to it. I attended for a few hours at Alexander Ogorodnikov's invitation and took with me about twenty of the group of British tourists whose leader I was.

After climbing several flights of stairs, we entered another world. All the furniture had been replaced by benches in two rooms with an open door between them. There must have been at least a hundred people in the flat which would normally, probably, have accommodated a family of six. Alexander brought me up to the front and introduced me, with the request to launch straight into a lecture in Russian about the work of Keston College. There was a barrage of questions and enormous interest, but one emotion predominated: gratitude that a group of Western Christians came to offer them fellowship and support.

In conversation we discovered that those present came from almost every republic and represented every facet of the 'Persecuted Church', from Pentecostals to the Orthodox of the 'Catacomb Church'. After my address, I was taken into another room – and there I found a large delegation from the Ukrainian Catholic Church, including two clandestine bishops in full regalia, but now openly petitioning for the restoration of their rights (see Chapter 8). They had come to Moscow to beg the Vatican delegation at the jubilee celebrations to help them in their struggle for self-determination. They had had difficulties on the way – the KGB had originally turned them off the Moscow train – but they were determined to stay until their mission was accomplished. These meetings were perhaps, for me, the most intensive and worthwhile experience of the whole Millennium celebrations.

Among the many concerns voiced by lay activists at this time was the question of the 'new Soviet martyrs'. For them it was perhaps the litmus test of church *perestroika* – would the hierarchy dare open such a discussion under the new conditions? Many felt that it was a matter of conscience for the church to be frank about the persecution of the past at a time when the rest of society was opening up the 'blank pages' of Soviet history (to use the popular phrase of the time).

Ironically, Deacon Vladimir Rusak, sentenced to twelve years for anti-Soviet agitation and propaganda for writing a history of the Russian Orthodox Church in the Soviet period, spent the Millennium languishing in an isolation cell in Perm strict regime camp, though I had a memorable and moving meeting with his wife, who asked my blessing just before setting out on the long journey to visit him. He was released four months later, on 19 October 1988, not because the Soviet authorities now considered him innocent, but because they ruled that the sentence was too harsh. On his release, Deacon

Rusak gave his own commentary on the canonisation of the modern martyrs:

> I am convinced that this is a vital step which the Russian Orthodox church must take. Indeed, I would say that this must be the primary aim of the Moscow Patriarchate, taking precedence over the resolution of any other problems. It is inexcusable to delay any longer. The beatification of the new martyrs is a matter of conscience for the church and the sooner it is done, the better.[6]

Zoya Krakhmalnikova, arrested for her Christian publishing activities in 1982, sentenced to one year of strict regime camp and five years' exile and then released in 1987, expressed similar sentiments, adding that not only did the Russian Orthodox Church still refuse to tell the truth about the persecution of the Soviet period, but had also denied support to those suffering in prison camps for their Christian activities. Writing in 1989, she was scathing in her criticisms of the hierarchy:

> How can believers learn about the history of their church when the only account published by the Moscow Patriarchate for the Millennium of the Christianization of Rus, called *A History of the Russian Orthodox Church 1917–1988*, which is now being sold in our churches, is a pack of untruths and fairy stories?[7]

Such political concessions have led to serious spiritual compromise, she said, undermining the very fabric of the Orthodox Church.

Although in his speech at the Bolshoi Theatre on 10 June Metropolitan Yuvenali referred to the 'new martyrs', he steered his listeners away from what the hierarchy saw as a politically sensitive step. This sentiment met with the condemnation of the activists present at the discussion. Fr Georgi Edelstein argued that 'the Russian Orthodox Church is politicized through and through', while Victor Antonov stated that 'it is the refusal to beatify which is the political act', since it is a clear illustration that the Russian Orthodox Church still does not feel able to decide its internal affairs without the interference of the state. For Gleb Yakunin, like Deacon Rusak and Zoya Krakhmalnikova, the beatification of the new martyrs transcends the political:

> I am deeply persuaded (this is one of my principal religious feelings) that those positive processes which are taking place in our country – what is happening at the political and historical levels and which can in essence be called a miracle – originate from the influence of the new Russian martyrs.[8]

There are many who would have qualified: perhaps principally Patriarch Tikhon, who had stood so bravely for the truth in the first days of Soviet power, and whose death was hastened by the harsh treatment he received; but there were thousands of lesser-known men and women who died in the camps for their witness – for example, more recently, Boris Talantov. The choice would have been impossible to make fairly, but a symbolic two or three would have sufficed.

It is true that at the time of the Millennium celebrations to glorify the new martyrs would have been a courageous move, but Fr Gleb Yakunin felt that the church should at the very least have held a requiem for those who had perished during the period of the Stalinist repressions. This could hardly have been seen as a wildly political act when the Soviet press has been increasingly open about the atrocities committed during the Stalinist era. The church was still, he felt, waiting for directives from above, rather than taking initiatives itself.

Interestingly, a few months after the celebrations the Orthodox Church at last began to respond to these demands. Early in 1989 a TASS report stated that the Russian Orthodox Church was beginning to study materials about the repression of believers during the Soviet period. According to the report, the Holy Synod discussed the rehabilitation of church members during November and December. An article subsequently appeared in *Moscow News*, reporting a meeting held in memory of persecuted Orthodox priests at the Leningrad Theological Academy. This followed a decision taken by the Holy Synod on 10–11 April 1989 to establish a commission, chaired by Metropolitan Vladimir of Rostov and Novocherkassk, to study the relevant materials. Obviously this is a very positive step which will contribute to a general revival of religious life, restoring the credibility of the Russian Orthodox Church as an independent institution.

Attitudes to the Hierarchy

The advent of *glasnost* led to increasing demands from the laity that the Russian Orthodox hierarchy should begin to take advantage of the new opportunities. Such demands were, in the main, ignored by the hierarchs, which led to a growing sense of anger and frustration among the active laity. Activists became more vocal in their demands for reform, sending numerous letters to Mr Gorbachev and to members of the Holy Synod requesting the release of all political and religious prisoners, asking for greater freedom to be granted to the church and for changes in religious legislation. Those who had formulated the demands for religious liberty a quarter of a century earlier, who had seen the beginnings of Christian renewal among the intelligentsia and who had personally suffered arrest and trial at the beginning of the 1980s began to sense they were being vindicated. At last, in their eyes, the time of repressions was past, and the way was now clear for the church to begin to make a much more positive contribution to Soviet society.

There was still a void between the hierarchy and the activists. Fr Gleb Yakunin's criticisms, which, as we have seen, went right back to 1965, continued. In May 1987, recently released after eight years in prison, Fr Gleb and other Orthodox laymen sent an appeal to Gorbachev and the Holy Synod on the release of prisoners of conscience. They then held a press conference for foreign journalists on 27 May in the flat of one of the signatories, Victor Popkov. They were bitterly critical of the church hierarchy for their passivity and inaction: 'Church life is not responding today to the principles of democratisation and glasnost.'[9] It was in this spirit that the appeals had been sent, in an attempt to facilitate the improvement of church–state relations and the development of more active religious life. Among several issues addressed was the question of the new law on religion. Andrei Bessmertny, another prominent activist, stressed the need for democratisation in this sphere and for the inclusion of Christians in the campaign for general renewal in Soviet society.

In a retaliatory measure, Metropolitans Filaret of Kiev and Yuvenali held their own press conference on 5 June 1987, in which the latter expressed his displeasure at Fr Gleb Yakunin's 'negative assessment' of the Russian Orthodox Church and its hierarchy. He claimed that Fr Gleb was raising issues which could be decided only by members of the church hierarchy: responsibility for the life of the church rested with the Patriarch and the Holy Synod. According to Metropolitan Yuvenali, Fr Gleb and others gave a one-sided, even false, representation of the life of the church and, what is more, they had no authority to undertake such activity. Insisting on the absolute authority of the church, Yuvenali stressed that '*glasnost* and *perestroika* should not lead to anarchy within the church'[10] – a revealing statement which perhaps hints at the underlying fear amongst certain of the Orthodox leaders that they would now have to be galvanised into action, under mounting pressure from the 'grass roots'.

Metropolitan Filaret rejected the view that the church had merely 'survived' the past seventy years. He was at pains to stress the favourable relations the Orthodox Church had with the state. As far as he was concerned, '*perestroika* and *glasnost* are not some turning point in the life of the church', thus demonstrating his own unwillingness to recognise what the activists were encouraging the church to do. Both the hierarchs were content that the church was continuing to celebrate the liturgy, perform the rite of baptism and be active in the international Christian arena. Fr Gleb had stepped out of line in his criticism of the church and was reminded of the recent clemency shown him not only by the Soviet authorities, but by the church itself.

This conflict occurred just a few weeks after Fr Gleb's appeal to the Holy Synod on 28 April 1987 to reinstate him to the parochial ministry. He had never left the priesthood, but since 1966 had been denied any pastoral responsibility. A positive decision was taken by the Holy Synod on 12 May on the following terms:

> In view of the mercy and love of God, Gleb Yakunin is to be reinstated as priest, but chastened with the following words: 'Go, your faith has made you whole, sin no more, lest a worse thing happen to you.' (John 5:14).[11]

Fr Gleb was then placed under the authority of his diocesan, Metropolitan Yuvenali. Such words can have done little to build the confidence of believers in the hierarchy. The leadership was still determined to isolate itself from any reforming tendency, but in the age of *perestroika* such conflicts would become much sharper.

No lesson had been learned by the seventieth anniversary of the October Revolution that year. A Patriarchal Communication was sent out to all believers to commemorate this date. It paints an exclusively positive picture of church–state relations in the Soviet period, completely glossing over the repressions suffered by the church during that time, not to mention the numbers of people martyred for their faith. A group of lay people have strong words to say about it:

> The Communication of the Patriarch and the Holy Synod on the seventieth anniversary of the October Revolution caused much bewilderment and bitterness among believers. It depicts the situation of the church in our country and church–state relations as an ideal symphony, in terms characteristic of the Stalin era. This message is a political anachronism from beginning to end, even though, these days, government leaders are saying that 'the time has come to stop misrepresenting history' (Gorbachev, *Pravda*, 5 November 1987) and that 'the truth, unpalatable

as it may be, is still preferable to sweetening by omissions, fantasies and emotions. Lies can only blacken history – the truth enhances it' (Yakovlev, *Izvestia*, 4 November 1987). Is it not strange that while the chairman of the Council for Religious Affairs admits openly that the state has been frequently at fault in its dealings with believers, our church leaders continue to cover up the tragic truth about the fate of the church in past decades?

Positive steps were now being taken to improve the standing of the church in society, the document acknowledges. *Glasnost* and *perestroika* offered the church the chance to secure a 'dignified and free existence', if only its leadership would seize the opportunities presented to it:

> Our country has entered a unique period of history and this places a great obligation on us and on the whole of the Russian Orthodox Church, 'for the time is come that judgement must begin at the house of God' (1 Peter 4:17).[12]

Such was the challenge issued by Orthodox activists at the end of 1987. They must surely have wondered if there were any amongst the hierarchy who would truly defend the interests of the church.

One positive development was the letter sent by Archbishop Feodosi of Astrakhan to Mr Gorbachev on 20 October 1987, requesting the return of the Monastery of the Caves at Kiev to the jurisdiction of the Orthodox Church and detailing the abuses that this shrine has suffered since its closure 'for repairs' in 1961. Lay people welcomed this initiative and issued their own statement in support of this request on 5 January 1988: 'Archbishop Feodosi's call for the return of the Kiev Monastery of the Caves is, for us, a shining example of service to the church.'[13] Calling for the support of all believers, activists saw this as an indication of hope that people who are prepared to defend the rights and interests of believers would remain within the framework of the church.

However, the general lack of positive action from the majority of the hierarchy is tragic at a time when the moral fibre of Soviet society has been seriously undermined. In fact, one is now encountering the paradoxical situation where, as Yevgeni Pazukhin stated at a discussion of the Millennium and the current state of the Russian Orthodox Church, 'The State is encouraging Christian activity: priests are doing all they can to obstruct it.'[14]

It would be a misrepresentation to claim that there are no individuals within the 'institutional' church who are seeking to meet the challenges of *perestroika*, and the proceedings of the *sobor* did give greater grounds for optimism, as a real debate began on the internal life of the church. Meanwhile, lack of information has also been the object of criticism from the activists, who maintain that knowledge of what went on at the Council would enable each and every Christian to play a full part in the renewal of the church.

Another positive development was when at the *sobor* Archbishop Pimen of Saratov spoke of the difficulties he was encountering with the local authorities in his attempts to get a third community registered. Saratov has a population of over 900,000 and only two Orthodox churches. Constant toing and froing between various departments had yielded no results. Nearly a year later, in April 1989, the situation still had not resolved itself and became the subject of a strongly worded article in the Orthodox Church's new weekly publication, *Moscow Church Herald*. This in itself was an indication that the church was beginning to feel sufficiently confident to be able openly to criticise local state authorities.

There have been various pronouncements by state and church officials alike regarding the number of churches returned to the Russian Orthodox Church. At the Council of Bishops held in October 1989, Metropolitan Vladimir stated that a total of 2,185 churches had been returned to the Russian Orthodox Church during the course of 1989. Despite the favourable impression created by this statistic, areas remain where communities have faced opposition exceeding that encountered in Saratov. A case which came to the attention of the Western media during 1989 was that of Ivanovo. Here the local authorities, entrenched in pre-*perestroika* attitudes, refused to return the Church of the Presentation of the Mother of God to believers, despite a decision made in their favour by the Council for Religious Affairs. This led to a long-drawn-out conflict with the authorities, involving hunger strikes and demonstrations in Moscow, resulting in widespread publicity not only abroad, but in the Soviet press as well. *Izvestia* published an article giving the basic facts about the conflict, expressing a favourable attitude towards the believers. This did not prevent the local press from publishing a slanderous article about the four women involved in the hunger strike, as *Moscow News* discovered. *Ogonyok* published a five-page article by Alexander Nezhny on the subject, bitterly criticising the local officials for their handling of the case. The church was eventually returned to believers on 14 August 1989, according to a report in *Izvestia*.

Throughout the Soviet press displayed a uniformly positive attitude towards the believers, which was in itself remarkable. However, it is also an object lesson in caution, illustrating how local authorities do not necessarily respond to the liberalising signals coming from Moscow. The fact that a satisfactory outcome came only after a protracted struggle illustrates the extent of the conflicts lurking beneath the surface. There are continuing problems in Kerch in the south of Ukraine to secure the return of the oldest Russian Orthodox church on Soviet territory. Fr Valeri Lapkovsky, who has spearheaded the campaign, has several times been vilified in the local press for his alleged 'anti-Sovietism' and has written to Keston College asking for help.

While the continuing difficulty over registration of communities remains an important issue, even more crucial is *perestroika* within the church. Archbishop Kirill of Smolensk declared that in no way should the church isolate itself from society, but stressed that change and renewal should not come at the expense of church unity. This was undoubtedly a tacit admission that there has been mounting pressure on the church leadership from the grass roots, as well as that there is considerable opposition to change within the Orthodox Church hierarchy itself.

Archimandrite Alimpi of Voronezh commented on the upsurge of interest in the Russian Orthodox Church expressed by non-believers as a result of the Millennium celebrations and lamented the fact that spiritual matters did not seem to come first on the agendas of the church: at meetings discussions appeared to revolve around finance and material advance, rather than on spiritual renewal within the church and the need to teach. Yevgeni Pazukhin echoed this in a far-reaching evaluation of the spiritual state of the church, in which he placed emphasis on spiritual renewal rather than on outward signs of prosperity and wealth: 'Who will bring restoration not only to destroyed churches but also to the trampled, crippled souls of both ordinary believers and the Russian Orthodox Church hierarchy?'[15]

A debate on the morality of the clergy originated within the *sobor* and its subsequent development is of great importance. If Dr Gareth Bennett, the late chaplain of New College, Oxford, felt it right at about the same time in his preface to *Crockford's Clerical Directory* to open a debate about the role and attitudes of the senior clergy of the Church of England, how much more important was it for the activists, now joined by a growing number of supporters, to pursue the same discussion in a country where the problems were much more acute and the possibilities for establishing an open forum that much more difficult.

Victor Popkov wrote a long analysis in 1989, published unfortunately only abroad so far, which has proved to be one of the most
penetrating discussions of the current problems. 'The Church Today'
covers the whole situation of the Russian Orthodox Church, but it is
the section on the hierarchy which is the most important.

What does a person who has been used all his life to taking orders
do when he suddenly finds the superior authority removed and the
initiative with himself? The members of the Holy Synod, Popkov
argued, had formed their social outlook in an atmosphere of submissiveness. They always knew what was expected of them. Now, with
freedom at their disposal, they suddenly became disorientated when
they needed to stand on their own feet. The automatic response was
to begin following the new political line, even though it was so very
different from what had gone before.

Popkov singled out for especial criticism Archpriest Vladimir
Sorokin, Rector of the Leningrad Theological Seminary and,
incidentally, a bitter critic of the work of Keston College, as I
found out when he visited Britain with a delegation to the British
Council of Churches in 1983. Allegedly he tried to impede the new
charitable work being done by lay people in the diocese, but perhaps
following the philosophy 'if you can't beat them, join them', he took
it over when he found he could not stop what they were doing.

Popkov echoed the severe criticism which Metropolitan Pitirim,
head of the publishing department, had sustained at the *sobor* the
previous year. It was remarkable, the author suggested, that a man
found so seriously wanting could continue in his job. Admittedly, he
had a high social profile and had thrown himself unremittingly into his
public activities. Setting up a rehabilitation centre in Volokolamsk for
soldiers wounded in Afghanistan looked like a bid for the Patriarchate,
but that could not cover up the fact that he employed 270 people in his
publishing division, who could not manage to bring out more than five
or six titles a year between them.

Popkov identified three main groups of senior clergy, though
there were subdivisions within each. There was one around the
Patriarch, looking solely to maintain the *status quo* at all costs and
prepared to move nowhere without the say-so of the KGB. Another
group, having had considerable experience of leadership, was bolder
and took advantage of new opportunities, but within clearly defined
limits (he included Archbishop Kirill among them). A third group
lived in and for their dioceses, faithfully seeking to serve God and
the church wherever they happened to be and at whatever cost.[16]

It is a shock to find that, years into the development of *perestroika*, the author of this document, a man of great culture who was allowed to travel to the Second Lausanne Congress on World Evangelisation in Manila in July 1989 and in March 1990 to Paris to confer with the publishers of his article, should be attacked in the street, almost certainly at the instigation of the KGB. This happened on 30 December 1989. A group of about six assailants hit him over the head with a metal bar and kicked him on the ground. They did not converse, there was no attempt to rob him or to prevent him from doing anything in particular and he was lucky to escape with relatively minor injuries. The incident convinced him that this was the KGB's revenge for his severe criticism of them in the article which was still in the process of being serialised in Paris at the time the attack took place.

The KGB, therefore, is still capable of thuggery. An incident in which I was involved at one remove happened to one of Popkov's close friends earlier in the year. In February 1989 I received my visa at the last possible minute to go to Vilnius for the reconsecration of the Cathedral. There was no time to obtain in London my onward ticket from Moscow to Vilnius and as time for the change of aeroplanes was very short, my old friend Andrei Bessmertny, an Orthodox layman of initiative and courage, promised over the telephone to come to the airport to help. As he was leaving his apartment for Sheremetevo airport, a group of KGB activists bundled him into a car and drove him around Moscow for several hours, releasing him well after the time that my connection had departed. As it happened, this incident, minor in itself, received international press publicity and there was a curious sequel. A week later in Victor Popkov's flat, when I had returned to Moscow, Andrei himself was able to recount to me in detail what had happened. While the KGB clearly cannot persecute the church in the way that it did up to about five years ago, it still has massive numbers of under-directed people on its books who doubtless continue to hold many watching briefs and from time to time engage in acts of violence or obstruction.

Alexander Ogorodnikov would vouch for the truth of this. Not only was the Birmingham priest Dick Rodgers in dialogue for months with the KGB in an attempt to deliver to him printing equipment for his journal, but there was a series of break-ins at Ogorodnikov's flat and offices, when much of his equipment was smashed or stolen.

Archbishop Chrysostom of Irkutsk, one of Popkov's third category, has taken up the issue of the morality of the clergy. The lack of discipline and poor education of priests is a fundamental problem within the church, leading to disorder and division. The adoption of low standards, under the old system of state control, was often a gateway rather than a barrier to high positions within the church. Chrysostom had personally encountered difficulty when trying to exercise his rightful authority as archbishop and discipline unworthy priests, because in his own words at the *sobor*, 'Many people leap to the defence of unworthy priests.' By uttering such statements, Chrysostom was making a very important contribution to church *glasnost* – people were aware that what the archbishop was making clear to the delegates was the appalling effect of KGB influence in the church, which was placing considerable obstacles in the way of genuine renewal of church life. Priests were often guilty, he said, of celebrating the liturgy in a way that was both negligent and unfitting: indeed, as Archbishop Mikhail of Vologda declared, he was sometimes led to question whether such priests were true believers and asked, 'How can we preach and call people to prayer if we ourselves have lost the art of true prayer?'

In an interview with Jim Forest, an American who has much Soviet experience behind him, Archbishop Chrysostom said that he had been sent to Irkutsk as a kind of exile from his European diocese of Kursk, where he had incurred official displeasure for his attempts to ordain more than his share of vigorous and uncompromised young men to the priesthood. Chrysostom was transferred to the diocese of Vilnius in 1990. Even in the pre-*perestroika* days, he had managed to increase the number of clergy in the first diocese by twenty-three and to bring down their average age from seventy to thirty. But better theological education is the highest priority:

> We were not prepared by our theological schools to answer the hard questions that people increasingly bring to those with pastoral responsibility. There is very little purposeful preaching and few pastors can evangelize those who are educated . . . We are suddenly on the stage, face to face with the people. Yet we are not ready for the dialogue we are being offered – a dialogue between believer and non-believer, a dialogue not to convert, but to make contact, to illuminate, to help.[17]

The future priest must be better educated, better equipped for the service of the church in both intellectual and spiritual terms. For this to begin to happen on a satisfactory level, as Metropolitan Vladimir stated in his main presentation at the Council, there must be many more educational establishments. Positive steps in this direction are now being taken: the church plans to open a new seminary in Tobolsk, Siberia, and a new seminary has opened in Minsk following a decision taken by the Holy Synod on 10–11 April 1989.

Archbishop Kirill of Smolensk has been quick to take the initiative in the establishment of diocesan training centres. In an interview published in *Moscow Church Herald*, a publication which began in April 1989, Archbishop Kirill highlighted the desperate shortage of priests in his own diocese, which receives at most two new graduates from the seminaries a year. In addition, out of the forty-eight parishes, thirty-five are without choir directors and psalm-readers, who have an essential role to play in the Orthodox service. Courses for men aiming to go into the priesthood and for choir directors were planned for autumn 1989, with twenty places being made available at the outset. Kirill is anxious that the serious shortcomings in the training and preparation of priests highlighted at the Council are overcome, with less unnecessary duplication of subjects and less time spent on elementary studies, which has seriously detracted from the value of the theological training on offer in the past.

There have been, then, positive responses to the issues raised at the *sobor*. However, as activists are quick to point out, there are more words than actions – and one could say the same of Soviet society as a whole. In a survey conducted after the Millennium by the *samizdat* journal, *The Christian Community Bulletin*, activists expressed their concern in varying degrees: they were united in their demands for more openness and honesty about the past and current state of the church. For them, the problem remained. The church leadership was, in itself, a product of the Soviet system, suffering from the effects of long years of fear and compromise and which now found itself in that most contradictory of situations where even the state was criticising the hierarchs for their passivity and inaction. Criticism of the hierarchy – and of the late Patriarch Pimen in particular – continued. In March 1988 Gleb Yakunin, Andrei Bessmertny and other activists signed a joint appeal calling for the resignation of the Patriarch on the grounds of ill health and his submissiveness to the authorities. Further severe criticism came in a scathing document written by Fr Gleb Yakunin on 11 December 1988, entitled 'Patriarchate or Matriarchate?', in which he alleged that Pimen was completely under the influence of a certain Nadezhda Nikolaevna Dyachenko, his secretary and factotum. He called her 'Nadezhda of Moscow and all Russia' – a play on the title, 'Patriarch of Moscow and all Russia'. Yakunin claimed that access to Pimen was gained only by means of expensive presents given to the aforementioned lady. Such views, though they seem extreme, do have fairly wide currency among Orthodox activists, who believe corruption is rife in the Patriarchate.

What is clear from the varied declarations of activists is that the process of renewal in the church will take a considerable length of time. And yet there is an additional sense of urgency because both the church and society as a whole face an uncertain future. This in itself presents a tremendous challenge to the church, which must raise its voice with more vigour to defend its rights and freedoms. Above all, the church needs to repent of its past tendency to compromise and, thus cleansed, learn to play its part in society with full conviction. There is a danger that, as people get used to reading reports in *Izvestia* about church activity and seeing church representatives visiting prison camps and hospitals, they will lose the initial sense of *glasnost*-inspired euphoria that this has been 'allowed' and look deeper for the spiritual authority and sustenance that is not there.

Orthodoxy in Soviet Society: 'Secularisation' of the Spiritual

Activists soon turned their attention to these more long-term concerns once the excitement of the Millennium had died down. Perhaps because, unlike the beleaguered hierarchy, they did not have to overcome the psychological inhibitions resulting from compromise, they were free to see some sort of vision for the future.

There is a danger in the new climate that the Orthodox faith may become a 'culture-bearer' rather than a 'God-bearer' – to use a Russian formulation – a type of nominalism rather than a development of true Christian commitment. In a discussion of the Millennium in June 1988, Gleb Anishchenko spoke eloquently of the dangers of what he called the secularisation of spiritual values:

> Especially since the secular authorities began to devote a lot of space to religious questions, one can observe an unremitting process: religion is being replaced by culture and history. In earlier times religion was perse-cuted, but it still carried the name of religion, it was still Christianity.[18]

There were real grounds to fear that a vague neo-pagan respect for the past was supplanting Orthodoxy: *glasnost* has led to the proliferation of small groups with an interest in the defence of Russia's heritage, often with strongly nationalist overtones. As Yevgeni Pazukhin put it, the Russian Orthodox Church was in danger of being turned into an 'ethnographic myth . . . where Christ, Mary and the Apostles and their flock look for all the world like ancient Russian peasants'.[19]

Many of these groups had a pseudo-Christian feel to them, Pazukhin continued, but in the absence of a basic knowledge of Christianity and of the practice of the Russian Orthodox Church, any manifestation of 'spirituality' was in danger of becoming an end in itself, emotionalism rather than truth. Should *glasnost* continue, the biggest challenge for the church lay precisely here. There was now an acute spiritual hunger in Soviet society, a fact even the Party admits. People were now unafraid to express this need and approach the church. The church, in turn, had a great responsibility in giving people a firm grounding in the Christian faith: society now expected a 'living word' from the church. While there were individuals, both lay and clerical, who were convinced of this need and prepared to take decisive action, there was as yet no truly co-ordinated effort, no unity of purpose within the hierarchy. Many of them lacked the conviction that the church's mission to society was first and foremost the preaching of the Gospel. Indeed, despite large imports of Bibles and other Christian literature, the Church was ill-equipped to expound Christianity to those who have shown interest.

If the Orthodox Church wants to ensure that the many people who are searching for spiritual reality become fully active members, well grounded in their faith, then it must answer the need for firm teaching. Priests must learn how to preach the Gospel in a way accessible to those who are totally ignorant of the faith after decades of atheist indoctrination. Tentative steps have begun: according to the *Moscow Church Herald*, a regular discussion group with the monks at the Danilov Monastery takes place after the Saturday evening service and some churches are introducing discussions on various aspects of the faith, such as fasting and prayer. There is a need for massive expansion of this. In December 1988 an action group was formed by Orthodox lay people which attempts to meet the needs of those making their first contact with the church. This is a summary of its aims:

1. Missionary activity – the creation of catechetical groups, Sunday schools, groups to study the Scriptures, the liturgy, church history, the works of the church fathers, religious thinkers and theologians.
2. Work with the young people – the church should involve them in the restoration of churches, in pilgrimages to holy places and monasteries and hold literary and musical evenings.
3. The renewal of parish life, taking advantage of the changes announced in the Statute of June 1988 [see Chapter 3]. There is a need for discussion about the organisation of parish meetings, contact with the central church authorities and work with the various social groups of parishioners. More contact with other Orthodox communities could enrich parish life.[20]

The remaining points cover the need for support for communities campaigning for the return of churches, the provision of legal aid for believers, the extension of charitable activity and the revival of all forms of Christian culture such as theology, philosophy and icon-painting. These aims represent a mammoth task, but at least areas of need are being identified so that the church can plan some future action.

There are other initiatives. In Leningrad Yevgeni Pazukhin has begun a venture called the Society for Christian Enlightenment, with the aim of encouraging Christians to meet and discuss the faith. Mikhail Bombin in Riga has set up a society for the free distribution of Christian literature, following the scandal caused by the sale at a very high price of Bibles donated free by Western Christians to the Moscow Patriarchate in 1988. Other activists are engaged in youth work. Energetic and imaginative priests such as Fr Valentin Dronov, who has only just been given a parish after a brush with the authorities in 1984, are keen to develop all aspects of parish life. Perhaps it is on this level that there will be a greater achievement of unity between clergy and laity and together they will be able to influence the upper ranks of the Orthodox Church. It is certainly true that many appeals for unity have been made by laymen such as Golovin, as well as by people such as Archbishop Kirill of Smolensk. There are indeed some signs of convergence between the activists and the hierarchy, but one still looks for the prophetic word from the leaders. How many of them have unambiguously condemned the resurgence of anti-semitism? Nevertheless, a growing number of bishops openly proclaim the real needs of the church and of society. In the eyes of Pazukhin, young people from the intelligentsia who are coming into the church must find that, as well as receiving from the church, they can make a positive contribution to parish life, without being limited in any way – otherwise the church will lose much of its potential.

The challenges facing the church as it enters its second millennium are immense: the foundations have been laid and it is now time to build a truly Christian church equipped to play an apostolic role in society. There has never been an occasion in history when a church has been presented with such a massive literate population which has rejected the prevailing ideology and is looking for a new one. The Orthodox Church encloses spiritual treasures which can inspire the world: at the same time it needs to evolve a whole new approach to society and an openness to such events as the Evangelistic Congress which the Protestants are planning for the autumn of 1990.

The church is not, and cannot be, merely a social or political ally in the campaign for general reform within society, but must regain its evangelistic zeal: 'Both the church and the world need people of an apostolic cast in our times, ardent preachers and fearless instructors. Their time has come, praise be to God!'[21]

Here is a subject of debate among the activists. Kirill Golovin, along with many others, doubts the capacity of the institutional church to rise to the challenge: where were the new Pauls and Andrews, he asked. A 'small remnant' remained by the mercy of God, he said, and a panorama of new opportunities for the church was opening out, with the hope that a time of renewal had at last come to the Suffering Church:

> The time of the church's Calvary and Resurrection is past. It moves now to a time of Pentecost, a time of inspiration by the Holy Spirit and preaching of the Good News in the fields and city squares.

The judgments of activists are a necessary counterbalance to the perhaps superficial impressions of freedom generated by the jubilee celebrations. They are looking ahead and giving a more mature evaluation of what has been termed the 'religious renaissance' which took place among the intelligentsia during the Brezhnev era. Many *samizdat* documents have appealed for maturity rather than emotionalism or, as Pazukhin puts it, Orthodox Christianity rather than Orthodoxy as a purely historico-cultural phenomenon. The Orthodox Church must not change its basic teachings. In the words of Dr Sergei Sazhin, who emigrated to Britain in April 1989, 'It is neither a discussion group nor a philosophical idea; it is the revealed truth.'

exander Men: a gifted Orthodox priest who had a formative influence on young people in the 1960s; he now lectures openly in Soviet schools and factories.

Fr Tavrion, the *starets* (holy man) who attracted many by his spiritual authority and teaching in the 1970s.

'Building for the future' (Pimen, seated), or
'The incarnation of Leninist principles'
(Kharchev, centre, wearing dark glasses)? The
laying of a foundation stone for a new cathedral
dedicated to the Millennium, in the presence of
world church leaders, including Archbishop
Desmond Tutu.

One of the few: Boris Talantov, who wrote a
detailed account of the persecution of the
Russian Orthodox Church in Kirov in 1966,
died in prison in 1971.

rch and State: Millennium press conference held by (left to right) Alexei Buyevsky,
ropolitans Filaret of Kiev and Pitirim of Volokolamsk and Konstantin Kharchev, Chairman of the
ncil for Religious Affairs.

ing worship of the Millennium celebrations at the Danilov Monastery: 'It was impossible not to
e… how few ordinary believers were present'.

Archbishop Kirill of Smolensk, author of the new statute passed at the *sobor* and one of the most gifted of the hierarchs.

Fr Mark (Valeri) Smirnov, correspondent for *Moscow News,* at a service for charity workers in Moscow Baptist Church.

bishop Chrysostom of Irkutsk: 'We are suddenly on the stage, face to face with the people. Yet e not ready for the dialogue we are being offered.'

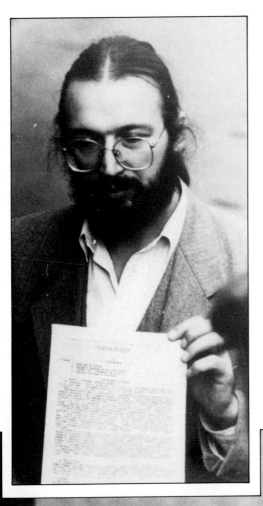

Alexander Ogorodnikov, holding up the *Chronicle*, a bulletin of events published in conjunction with his *samizdat* journal, *The Christian Community Bulletin*.

Metropolitan Filaret of Kiev, April 1987.

r Popkov. In December 1989, following the publication abroad of an article protesting at
ʌuing KGB influence over the senior Orthodox hierarchs, he was attacked in the street by
ɔwn assailants.

Fr Gleb Yakunin at the unofficial Millennium, writing a greeting to the author.

Deacon Vladimir Rusak on his release from Perm strict regime labour camp, 24 October 1988. He spent the Millennium in an isolation cell.

...rchs, priest and laity gathered for the Church Council *(sobor)* at the Holy Trinity Monastery, ...rsk.

One of the photographs in the unofficial exhibition to mark the Millennium. The exhibition did take place and the photographer was not allowed into Moscow.

...sm in River Dnieper, Kiev, marking the Baptist celebration of the Millennium. Unlike the ...odox, they made Kiev the focal point of their celebrations.

...Christian volunteer workers at a special ...ce in Moscow Baptist Church, attended ...by the head doctor of Kashchenko ...hiatric hospital, Valentin Kozyrev, and ...ital workers.

Alexander Semchenko, editorial board member of the unofficial Baptist paper, *Protestant,* which promotes reform within the Baptist Union.

Ivan Fedotov, a leading Pentecostal strongly against the registration of churches. He has spent much of his adult life in prison.

Nijole Sadunaite, a leading member of the Committee for the Defence of the Lithuanian Catholic Church and now active in national revival. The author met her in Vilnius in February 1989.

Celebrations at Odessa unregistered Baptist church on the return of their pastor, Nikolai Boiko, from labour camp. The text reads: 'I will build my church and the gates of hell will not overcome

Barinov in the secret recording studio where he produced *The Trumpet Call.* He now lives in
est.

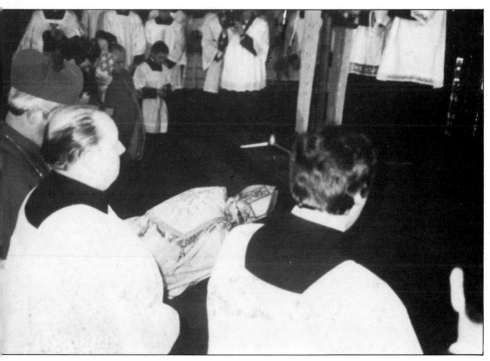

p Julijonas Steponavicius prostrating himself on the altar steps of Vilnius Cathedral at the
e of reconsecration after forty years as a picture gallery.

Bishop Pavlo Vasylyk giving communion at an illegal Ukrainian Catholic service in 1986.
Clandestine worship was, until recently, the only option for these outlawed believers.

Ivan Hel, leader of the campaign for the legalisation of the Ukrainian Catholic Church, heading
demonstration in Lviv. Over 250,000 people took part.

...ssion of bishops at the demonstration in Lviv.

Iosyp Terelya, former leader of the Committee for the Defence of the Ukrainian Catholic Church, meeting the Pope in 1987, following his release from prison and emigration to the West.

The wife and grand-daughter of Ivan Hel at an open air Catholic service.

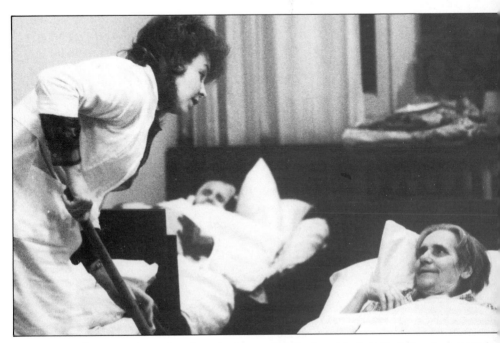

The quality of mercy: a young Baptist volunteer caring for the elderly at Kashchenko hospital, Moscow.

6 The Protestants

Registered Baptists

In the autumn of 1987, just before he emigrated to Britain on 22 November, Valeri Barinov, Baptist rebel extraordinary, challenged Soviet authority head on when he stood on the steps of the Kazan Cathedral in the middle of Leningrad's Nevsky Prospect and preached the Gospel. It is hard to imagine a confrontation more charged with symbolism, as the cathedral had, for more than two generations, been the premier atheist museum of the Soviet Union and the spearhead of its fight against religion. Before his last imprisonment the officials of the registered Baptist Church had expelled Valeri precisely for provoking conflict and employing unconventional evangelistic methods as a Christian rock musician who set out to bring the Word to the youth subculture of Russia's second city.

Less than two years later, on 29 March 1989, the choir of Valeri's former church not only mounted the same steps, but proceeded inside in formal order. They formed a group high up in the desecrated sanctuary, not quite in the middle, but a little to the left, so that they were beside the museum exhibit attacking 'sectarianism'. Underneath the massive dome of the classical cathedral more than 700 people gathered to listen to their proclamation of faith through song. The combination of the emotion in the music and the extraordinary symbolism of the event itself left few of the audience unmoved. In their official account, the church leaders said, 'Many listeners were crying during the singing, which somehow touched the delicate strings of the soul.'[1] The account even went on to claim that this restored the sacred to the desecrated shrines of the Russian people – Baptists talking of a former Orthodox Church and symbol of old Russian imperialism, no less.

Alexander Shebunin, musician and 'art director' of the museum, had organised the event. The emotions he felt when he heard the huge building reverberate to the strains of 'Glory to God in the Highest' by Bortnyansky or Bach's 'I will love you, Lord' remain unrecorded. Pastor Peter Konovalchik spoke about 'charity' (this was one of a series of concerts held in various parts of the Soviet Union on the same theme), but he clearly viewed the occasion as an evangelistic one, for he went on to speak about the longing of each soul for God and for spiritual nourishment. In 1990 the authorities announced the return of the cathedral to the Church.

The Baptists joined with two other choirs in a series continued at no fewer than seven other venues. When the BBC played Valeri Barinov's rock opera on the Russian Service several years earlier, letters had poured in to Valeri from both believers and doubters. Even though there was only a live performance and no broadcast of these more recent concerts, similar letters came to the Baptist Church in considerable numbers.

Christians generally – and not only Baptists – are finding they have the space to do what ten or even five years ago would assuredly have landed them in gaol. Many of what had seemed the most inviolable of Soviet taboos have collapsed in the face of *perestroika*. The dichotomy between the permissible (under strict control) and the illegal has greatly narrowed. In contrast to the Orthodox, Baptists have always made a specific and emphatic point that they are committed to the Christian upbringing of children within their community. When under the severest pressure the official leadership accepted government restrictions on even private religious education, this issue more than any other tore the community apart, causing a schism between the registered and unregistered churches. The Moscow leadership (the All-Union Council of Evangelical Christians and Baptists) appeared to have become a tool of state policies and many communities felt they had been betrayed. This rift, as we shall see, persists even today, despite the swift abolition of the so-called 'New Statute' and the 'Letter of Instructions' of 1960.

Years of persecution followed for those Baptists who called for a church free of atheist interference. The attitude of the state was, 'Register under the Moscow umbrella, or you are outside the law' – even though this clearly entailed breaking the constitutional separation of church and state over, for example, the submission of membership lists to the local representative of the Council for Religious Affairs. Not until nearly twenty years later did the authorities permit the 'autonomous registration' of some of the previously illegal communities without their having to submit to the authority of the official Baptist Union (AUCECB). However, the more rigid representatives of the illegal leadership stated that registration even under these conditions was a concession to the atheist authorities, which led to further internal dissension.

To add a further complication to the picture, the subtleties of which it is virtually impossible for the outsider to comprehend, many churches which have tried to register, some over long periods of time, have met arbitrary refusal to this legal request. In yet other instances, a registered church has had its legal status removed. Some church leaders outside the Soviet Union, under the influence of communist propaganda, have said more than once, 'These unregistered churches bring persecution on themselves: they should legalise their situation' – thereby demonstrating nothing except their own gullibility. It is no wonder that many Russian Christians despair that the outside world will ever understand their unique problems.

Hundreds of Baptist activists have gone to prison over the last thirty years for organising youth activities of various kinds. Yet in July 1988 the municipal authorities at Saran (Kazakhstan) gave permission for a baptism to take place in a horticultural nursery. They went further and offered to set up stalls for the sale of *kvas*, a proposal which was rejected, presumably because this drink is fermented from bread and therefore has a mildly alcoholic content. The compromise was that a thousand ice creams were available for the many children and public buses displaying the destination sign 'Baptism' were kept busy all day transporting 3,000 people.

The distribution of ice cream was a gesture to mark the Millennium, with the authorities presumably judging that Baptists should benefit from the event as well as the Orthodox. Although Baptists regarded the jubilee of midsummer 1988 in a somewhat different light from the Orthodox – in centennial celebrations of twenty years earlier they were emphatic and historically correct in tracing their movement back to the 1860s – that did not impede them from enthusiastic participation in their own way. They even, unlike the Orthodox, designated Kiev as the focal point for their biggest celebration.

Thousands of believers from all over the Soviet Union were present in Kiev on 18 June 1988. The Baptists had printed 4,000 handbills advertising the event, some of which they stuck over posters and signs bearing the face of Lenin and other communist symbols. So many attended the service in the main Baptist church, with a capacity of about a thousand, that the pastors asked believers to leave the building so that non-believers could hear the Gospel. Eventually, cut off from the events inside, those in the courtyard began their own worship service. There were dozens of converts, both inside and out. Together and joined by many more, the company moved off to the monument to St Vladimir on the slope overlooking the river Dnieper at the site of the first baptism.

Five days later (Saturday 23 June) an even larger gathering converged upon the monument. For the time, at least, members of the various Baptist groupings forgot the hostilities of the past and joined together in common celebration. About twenty musicians formed a brass band and sat on the steps of the statue (reminding some foreign onlookers of nothing so much as the Salvation Army, outlawed since the Revolution). An effective amplification system was in place. In the preaching there was more than a strand of denunciation of state atheism, the kind of confrontational approach which the registered Baptists had until now tried their best to avoid. Some observers reckoned that as many as fifty per cent of the vast crowd were unbelievers and believers moved among them to distribute little blue books, produced beforehand on underground printing presses, which explained the Gospel.

The event continued for many hours, undisturbed by any show of hostile authority. Eventually, one senior communist official hesitantly approached the crowd at about 5 p.m. With a handful of policemen behind him, the man demanded that the sermon should stop. The preacher asked the crowd what they wanted. 'We want you to stay!' was the unanimous response, after which the officials abandoned any further attempt to intervene. Dark clouds gathered, but no rain fell, so the meeting continued for a considerable time, after which the crowd reformed into a column and marched into the heart of the city. At October Revolution Square they came to a halt close to the statue of Lenin which dominated this as well as countless other central squares in towns throughout the Soviet Union. Here they prayed and continued to share the Word of God until late into the night. Not a few of those present who were familiar with the Acts of the Apostles felt that they were witnessing a twentieth-century recreation of those biblical events.

This was only the beginning. In Moldavia celebrations began in mid-August with eleven meetings in eight days, one of which took place in a large hall belonging to the state railway. The club of a furniture factory in Orgeyev was host to an evangelistic event, well attended as a consequence of an announcement in the local paper. At the end many non-Christians present were able to put their questions in a lengthy discussion. Iosif Bondarenko, a pastor from Riga who had been hounded by the Soviet authorities for the best part of three decades, was able to preach in a rented cinema in Kishinyov, the Moldavian capital.

No evangelist in the Soviet Union is more popular than Earl Poysti: he is an American originally from Finland, who speaks perfect Russian. His voice has become known to millions through foreign radio stations which broadcast the Gospel message. He not only received a visa to visit the USSR at this crucial time after decades of absence: he preached on 26 June to a massive congregation at Brest (Belorussia), a city which thirty years earlier had witnessed some of the earliest and most severe persecution of the Khrushchev era, resulting in the closure of the Baptist church. Attempts then to continue to worship as a congregation in Brest itself led to immediate persecution: one of the arrested pastors, Vladimir Vilchinsky, was sentenced in 1968 to five years' imprisonment. His family continued to suffer harassment into the second generation: his daughter, Galina, was arrested in 1979 and sentenced to three years' imprisonment for her Christian youth activities; she received a second sentence just three months after completion of the first on a trumped-up drugs charge. To survive at all as a congregation, its members had to find their way to a building in an inaccessible village right out in the countryside. In 1988, with part of this previously persecuted church now registered and in a new building, Earl Poysti had to hold two services, because only a fraction of the 10,000 who sought access could find space the first time. The second service took place outside, with people climbing to the roofs of adjacent buildings and up surrounding trees to come within earshot. Most of the hundred or so new converts who made their first Christian profession that day in the makeshift arena were young people.

Just one year later Earl Poysti received an invitation to return to the USSR to preach in several cities, including Kemerovo, Novosibirsk and Irkutsk. Everywhere he spoke to capacity crowds in churches, public halls, sports arenas and on outdoor platforms.

More subtle, perhaps, but no less important was the emergence of a Christian–atheist dialogue, ongoing, not 'one-off', in Leningrad. In 1989 the atheist club of the Herzen Pedagogical Institute met young members of the Leningrad Baptist Church and their pastor to discuss such topics as the history of the Bible, the person and teaching of Christ, communist and Christian personal morality and the Christian attitude to *perestroika*. The format of the meetings has not yet settled down, but informal question and answer sessions are proving popular. The atmosphere is said to be friendly and good-humoured and Leningrad radio and the local press have reported on them.

Perhaps this is a harbinger of a new era of Christian–communist dialogue, once such a feature of life in Czechoslovakia until the Soviet invasion of 1968. One must state, however, that there are few believers in the Soviet Union who reckon that they have much to learn on morality from their erstwhile persecutors. The main thrust of the process is likely to be in the church's favour, with the communists listening avidly to find out what they can learn about their past mistakes. The collapse of communism in Eastern Europe proves that the vast majority of people do not want dialogue, but an entirely new system.

Alexei Bychkov, then General Secretary of the official Baptist Union, stated with great satisfaction in 1989 that it was now possible to announce their evangelistic meetings in newspapers, on placards and on the radio. He went on to say that after a gap of sixty years there would shortly be a residential Baptist seminary in Moscow. In the field of literature, developments had been dramatic, Bychkov continued. Within the last year the Baptist Union had received over 1,200,000 books from abroad, hymnals as well as Bibles. Nor were the minority languages being ignored. For example, Moldavians had received 18,000 Bibles in their own language. He did not say whether these were in the Cyrillic script which Stalin had imposed on their Latin language, in an attempt to cut them off culturally from fellow-Romanians on the other side of the frontier. There is an unquestionable need for Romanian-language Bibles, as well as Moldavian Cyrillic ones, but supplying them would most likely be viewed by the Kremlin as a semi-political gesture, supporting the would-be self-determination of the local people.

The Baptist Union, Bychkov continued, was exploring the possibility of preparing its own news and evangelistic radio broadcasts, to be sent out officially to Trans-World Radio based in Monte Carlo and then transmitted back via the airwaves. Their own videotape ministry was already beginning to develop, despite the lag in Soviet technology and the tiny number of recorders in private hands outside the main cities, where some people have privileged access to Western imports. New churches were opening in some areas, notably a second one for Leningrad, much more central than the existing building far out in the suburbs. This, in a church confiscated from the Old Believers sixty years ago, would replace the one the Baptists lost in the Khrushchev period. There would be offices for Baptist work in the north-west region, a church to seat a thousand people and a completely separate conference hall for two hundred. The issue of who legitimately owns church property confiscated decades ago is one that needs meticulous legal guidance and it is difficult to see who is competent to provide it, even after the passing of corrective legislation, which has not yet occurred.

Not even the best friends of the Russian Baptists ever claimed that the old *Bratsky vestnik* ('Fraternal Herald') led the world in Christian publishing. Its appearance every two months in a never-changing academic format had the heavy hand of censorship apparent on every page. However, the publishing scene soon changed dramatically. A new *Information Bulletin*, later renamed *Christian Word*, appeared in March 1989. Here, for the first time, is a Christian newspaper. Monthly issues are planned and the intention is to make it relevant to young people, who are well represented on the editorial board. Many of the early photographs were dull, but the reporting contains items which open up unimagined perspectives.

Several Bible study circles for young people meet under the aegis of the Moscow Baptist Church. They are grouped according to age, intellectual ability and maturity in the faith. The regular meetings are on Fridays, but for some the weekend continues with travel to smaller congregations beyond the confines of the city. Here there is much give and take; they offer help in the organising of evangelistic meetings and in the conduct of worship, presenting their own testimonies. In return, they experience a much more free and easy atmosphere away from the formal setting of their parent church. The different experiences of Christians in the countryside can sometimes enrich the visitors, not least in hearing how suffering and imprisonment have strengthened the faith, a topic which has always been taboo in any context connected with the All-Union Council.

Everywhere the question of Christian education is high on the agenda. In the past anyone who openly embraced the faith by being present at public worship was almost inevitably barred from higher education. This meant that any clandestine Christian reaching a position of influence in the professions would have at best a rudimentary knowledge of the faith: even if he had been able to study from foreign-language books concealed among his possessions, there would still be a lack of practical experience. For the first time in Soviet history there was now an opportunity for these men and women, and their younger successors setting out on their careers, to make good this deficiency.

But how can they acquire this firm intellectual grounding even in the improved conditions, given that books are simply unavailable and there are no experienced teachers? The wave of imported Bibles over recent months has meant that the text of scripture is available for study to many of those who showed sufficient determination to acquire it, at least in the larger cities of the European part of the Soviet Union. There are still hardly any Bible commentaries, not to mention books on such topics as Christian family life, marriage, history, culture, personal testimonies and experiences, answers to atheism and materialism, the likes of which anyone in the West can acquire by simply walking into a Christian bookshop, or by borrowing free of charge from any library.

Perestroika in the Baptist Union

What do the words 'official' and 'unofficial' mean in the world of Soviet publishing at present? The days of sharp division between official (heavily censored) and *samizdat* (uncensored) are gone, possibly for ever.

In November 1988 an unofficial publication, *Protestant*, appeared, produced by people affiliated to the official union (AUCECB). One of the declared aims of the editorial board is to encourage Baptist communities to be aware of and to exploit all the new opportunities which *glasnost* and *perestroika* offer. It is not enough, says Alexander Semchenko, an editorial board member from Moscow, to wait for the word from above. The AUCECB leadership has become conditioned over many years to be submissive to secular authority. Just as *zastoi* ('stagnation') atrophied many state institutions, so Christian thought had failed to develop.

For years Semchenko had been one of those who had tried to criticise the Moscow Baptist leadership from within, without going over to join one of the unregistered congregations. In 1978, when he was thirty and a youth leader in the church, the Soviet authorities had investigated him and two of his fellow-activists for having set up a secret studio where they recorded foreign Christian radio broadcasts, copying them on to cassettes for distribution among the young people of the church. Semchenko remained free that time, but in January 1984 he received a three-year sentence for distributing Christian literature. The leaders expelled him from the congregation (as their counterparts had done to Valeri Barinov in Leningrad). As a result, there are some tensions between *Protestant* and the AUCECB, with some of the old issues of the schism of nearly thirty years earlier surfacing again.

Protestant has increasingly become a forum where Baptists have felt able to call for changes in the official structure and for a more innovative response to the challenge of the new times. In January 1989 Anatoli Rudenko criticised the leadership for seeking to retain its authority and for holding on to the concept of 'bureaucratic central-ism', which gave it a style more reminiscent of the Communist Party than a church structure, particularly in a denomination which prided itself historically on the primacy it gave to the decisions of the local congregation. Leaders are too often appointed 'from above' for their conformism, rather than being elected by the church community for their spirituality and visionary qualities. This demonstrated, continued Rudenko, the effects of state restrictions and interference in church life, which have undermined the structures and reduced the ability to provide gifted and far-seeing leaders.[2]

At the Plenum of the AUCECB in May 1989, Vasili Logvinenko, President of the Baptist Union, reporting to delegates on its internal affairs, made some strong criticisms of the *Protestant* group: 'Zealots have appeared who are seeking to present our omissions and short-comings in such a way as to give the impression that nothing has remained sacred in the AUCECB.' This, said Logvinenko, curries favour with the West, while the real issue was not freedom of speech, but personal ambition:

> For example, take our own *Protestant*, which writes: 'How many people are straining under the regime created by our presbyters? . . . The truth is exchanged for a lie, those zealous for the Lord's work are deprived of their freedom and independence. This cannot go on. My friends and I have lost confidence in the AUCECB leadership; they are not encouraging revival in the church.' (*Protestant* No.6, article by A. Tsymbal). Some think that a new structure can be built only on the ruins of the AUCECB.[3]

Logvinenko put forward a proposal for reform of the structures which would increase the authority of the regions and allot a co-ordinating role to the central council, which would decide questions relevant to the whole church, such as missionary strategy, theological training and publishing.

Such suggestions were obviously in line with general feeling in the Baptist Union. A young leader, in a private conversation with a Keston College staff member in July 1989, emphasised that current thinking was to press for greater autonomy at local and regional level. This did not prevent the board of *Protestant* from publishing further appeals which added momentum to this debate, as the Baptist Congress scheduled for February 1990 approached.

Writing on the history of the Baptist Union, Alexander Semchenko developed the theme of greater independence by arguing that the most 'successful' churches had been those which were 'autonomously registered' and which were thus outside central control. They were the churches which had displayed most initiative in the Millennium year; they it was who invited outstanding foreign guests, such as Earl Poysti and Luis Palau, to lead evangelistic campaigns which were hugely successful.

Having suffered decades not only of control, but also formerly of Khrushchevite and Stalinist persecution, Semchenko continued, the church faced a major problem in needing to return to its original practices. Unfortunately, conservative attitudes were still very strong.

Writing in *Protestant* No.15, just a month before the congress, Nikolai Kornilov highlighted some of the problems the AUCECB needed to confront if it were to appeal to the wider population, particularly the intelligentsia. Many thought the Baptist Church consisted of uneducated sectarians, he wrote, whereas Russian Orthodoxy seemed to be the preserve of the cultured and well educated. He urged the unleashing of the creative potential of Protestant thinking and theology in the Soviet Union by publishing Karl Barth and Dietrich Bonhoeffer.

Another immediate difficulty facing the AUCECB is the nurturing of good pastors. In his lengthy article entitled 'Overcoming administrative hypnosis', Anatoli Rudenko pointed out that very few sermons appealed both to the mind and to the spirit; there was a 'vacuum of ideas' in the absence of any new creative thought, whereas *Protestant* does regularly publish articles on science and religion. As a result, many of the younger generation were not being challenged simultaneously on the spiritual and the intellectual plane. There was a catastrophic absence of truly gifted people able to step into leadership positions. This was partly as a result of over-centralisation: ordinary Christians have become passive and display little initiative.

A Baptist youth conference held in May 1989, unprecedented event though it was, did not appear to achieve very much. This is not such a surprise, given the complete lack of experience in preparing for such an occasion and the absence of materials to give it the substance one would expect in any comparable undertaking in the West. 'Opportunities are running ahead of our readiness and ability to grasp hold of them,' was one opinion. That said, the conference offers proof of the change in atmosphere in Soviet society, where for so long youth activities were kept under cover, for fear of reprisals by the authorities. It highlighted a number of key areas, such as the need for renewal and evangelism and the healing of the generation gap experienced in many churches, because older members dared not become too involved in youth-orientated activities. One way of overcoming this had been to establish youth choirs, which could hardly be clandestine, but which never really operated within the old law. Choir trainers would insert Christian teaching into the practices in churches where no one would dare establish a Sunday school. In Moscow, however, these choirs had achieved considerable prominence, apparently with the full cognisance of the Soviet authorities, doubtless because they deceived foreign visitors into thinking that such youth activities were widespread. Now the Moscow Baptist Church has two youth choirs and they enjoy such a reputation that even non-believing parents try to secure places in them for their children.

None of this, however, replaces the massive need to develop Christian teaching for young people everywhere. After years of petitioning, there is now provision for a residential seminary, but the AUCECB has had difficulty in finding suitable premises. To supplement this need, for several years there has been a scheme, 'Theological Education by Extension', to organise classes and correspondence courses from the outside by qualified teachers from the West, who have been able individually to visit the Soviet Union and meet students as and where possible. In February 1989 the autonomous groups established a new missionary enterprise called *Svet evangelia* ('Light of the Gospel'), which aims to have its own training courses and to reach areas such as Siberia and Central Asia, where there are either very few churches or where the local population belongs to Islam or other traditions.

By February 1990 voices calling for reform found a response from within the Baptist leadership. In tune, perhaps, with the 'new thinking', the council of the Baptist Union met on 21 December 1989 and elected a new president, Yakov Dukhonchenko. Speaking later to *Protestant*, he hinted at far-reaching changes in the AUCECB, with new statutes and a new structure.

Since 1963 the Baptists have been able to hold regular congresses, but the latest one, held from 21 to 24 February 1990, was the first where discussions and elections were entirely free and unfettered. The atmosphere was one of joy and hope, according to the several foreign delegates present. For the first time the AUCECB was able to hire spacious accommodation in the Izmailovo conference centre, instead of having to meet in the cramped conditions of the offices and church in Maly Vuzovsky Street.

Pastor Dukhonchenko, elected by the council only two months

earlier, stood down as President, because new regulations stipulated that the President be resident in Moscow, and he preferred to remain in Kiev. In his place the congress directly elected 44-year-old Grigori Komendant, also of Kiev. Immediately he took control of proceedings with authority, observers reported, and is bound to make his mark in the affairs of the church. He is to play the executive role which formerly belonged to the general secretary, Alexei Bychkov, whose post was abolished. Bychkov had spent many years travelling the world and tirelessly promoting his church, but without ever being caught in the trap of excessively defending state policies in the way that several leaders of the Russian Orthodox Church had done. Although this could be seen as a partial demotion – or perhaps a well-earned respite from the rigours of his office – Bychkov became one of the three new elected vice-presidents, allocated an executive role with differing areas of responsibility. The much-resented international department, which so clearly operated under the control of the KGB, would be abolished and there was to be no place for its former head, Alexei Stoyan. The new statute emphasised the autonomy of the local churches. The central body is now stated to consist of associations and unions of churches in the republics which come together voluntarily for fellowship and co-operation. This conforms much more closely to the original tradition of local independence.

Delegates were able to lead the discussion into areas which needed greatest attention, such as evangelism, youth work, publishing, social and charitable ministries and thinking out new programmes to suit local conditions. In practice, speakers said, *perestroika* had seen a much greater scope for independent initiatives, with new newspapers appearing both officially and unofficially and several regions starting their own training courses for preachers. Up to the time of the previous congress in 1985 there were at best only oblique references to such pressing issues.

The Reform Baptists

Quite separate are the Baptists who renounced allegiance to the AUCECB in the early 1960s and from then on were always *de facto* outside the law. An outstanding feature of their life was their organisation. So determined were the Soviet authorities to eliminate them that they could have no office premises, no publicly identified administrator, no access to normal post or telephone services (because of KGB interference). Yet they were able to co-ordinate activities across fifteen republics, document repressions nationwide and send that information systematically out of the Soviet Union over a period of nearly thirty years without ever making a serious factual error.

The single most astonishing aspect of this secret organisation concerned its top leadership. The two leaders, Pastors Georgi Vins and Gennadi Kryuchkov, each served three years in prison from 1966, following a notorious show-trial, a transcript of which was one of the earliest documents to illustrate the depraved lengths to which the authorities were prepared to go to repress those who sought fundamental reforms in church–state relations. On their release they tried to resume their work as Christian leaders, but the authorities refused to license them as pastors, so their lives continued under conditions of perpetual harassment. Georgi Vins was rearrested and sentenced to ten years in 1974, but when he had served half his term he was expelled to the United States in April 1979, following a deal between governments involving Soviet spies in American detention in which Vins was a pawn not even informed of his destination. Seeing that there was no possible legal way for him to continue his role as a leader, Pastor Kryuchkov decided he would go underground in order to continue his work. That he was able to do this for nearly twenty years without the police ever laying a finger on him was a quite astonishing feat of organisation, one of the most remarkable Christian stories of the Brezhnev period and beyond. There was no trace of him in public except the 'wanted' notices which the KGB posted at various strategic points. Over these long years he managed both to control the affairs of his church and to remain undetected within his underground network.

At the beginning of July 1989 *perestroika* changed all that. The annual conference of the Reform Baptists, now for the first time held openly, under surveillance, but with no attempt made to disrupt the proceedings, brought together no fewer than a thousand delegates in July 1989. Dramatically, Gennadi Kryuchkov appeared on the platform to address the congress. This produced a wave of uncontrolled emotion. It was a *coup de théâtre* which had the delegates hanging on every syllable. He said that the Reform Baptists would continue not to apply for registration since there was still no guarantee of freedom from state control, but they would review developments after promulgation of the new law on religion.

An official of the Council for Religious Affairs was present to hear these statements but made no attempt to interfere. Presumably realising the scandal it would have caused if they had arrested Kryuchkov in front of the whole assembly, the KGB began an intensive search for him immediately afterwards. However, he had made a contingency plan and he disappeared at once.

This incident clearly illustrates just how much the persecuted Baptists had been able to gain from *perestroika*. They had already been able to confirm at the end of the previous year that not one of their members was now under detention, except for one or two conscientious objectors, the first time that such a statement could have been made since the schism almost thirty years earlier and possibly the first time since Lenin's day that no Baptists at all were in prison directly for their religious activity. The congregation in Kirovograd (Ukraine) celebrated the homecoming of the last five on 3 December 1988. Nikolai Boiko, leader of the unregistered congregation in Odessa, thanked Christians worldwide for their love, prayers and support during his many years in prison. His last sentence had been five years' strict regime camp and five years' internal exile. When he was nearing completion of the first part of this sentence he had been charged again and sentenced to a further two and a half years. His early release from exile in November 1988 was the cause of much rejoicing.

However, these developments are far from the whole picture. Petty disruptions of legitimate activities continue, in some places almost unabated. This is particularly true of some areas in Ukraine, despite countless appeals sent to Gorbachev and Shcherbitsky, until the autumn of 1989 the hated Party Secretary there. Disruption of services and confiscation of literature continued. For example, on 14 November 1988 in the Kharkiv region, an unregistered Baptist, I. S. Pabylin, was stopped by the authorities when transporting Christian literature and 80,000 printed sections of the Gospel of John, published by the Khristianin press, were confiscated. Obviously, as always in the past, a great deal still depends on the goodwill or otherwise of the local authorities. This account, published in the unofficial *Ukrainian Herald*, assessing conditions over the last three years for unregistered Baptists in Ukraine, maintained that officials of the Council for Religious Affairs, despite liberal pronouncements from Moscow, actively participated in the repressions.

Thus a 'Communiqué' of the Reform Baptists of December 1988, immediately after announcing the release of prisoners noted above, goes on to list numerous instances of continuing harassment. Here is just one example, verbatim, from that document:

ROSTOV-ON-DON. Several times in the past twenty years the tents in which our congregations held their meetings have been destroyed. Services of worship now take place at 36 Shcherbakova Street. The regional executive committee's Injunction No.32, dated 13 September, required that the owner, L. A. Zaitseva, tear down the structure. Despite numerous petitions, P. I. Gaidenko, acting on orders of the local executive committee, informed her on 15 November 1988 that 'the injunction of the regional executive committee is lawful and does not need to be revoked.'[4]

On 4 April 1989 the bulldozers arrived before 9 a.m. and by midday had completely destroyed the building. Reports continue to come in detailing the destruction of churches in other places, too: Odessa, Kharkiv, Tashkent. Regular interruptions of services have occurred in and around Gorky, which is a matter for concern, seeing that this is the city where Yuri Khristoradnov, the new chairman of the Council for Religious Affairs, held sway for so long.

The local authorities still often levy fines on the organisers of unregistered meetings and on the owners of the premises where these take place. The usual sum is fifty roubles, about one week's average wage, though many people are threatened with worse punishment. However, there are individual examples of much harsher measures. The Mashnitsky family of Vinnitsa (Ukraine) is well known for its hospitality. They have been subject to recent fines of almost 2,000 roubles, 400 of which they have not been able to pay. Several of them have served prison terms in the past, but now personal intimidation has reached the point where packets of explosives have shattered their windows and caused structural damage. After seven such instances, there was an anonymous telephone call on 18 September 1988, threatening murder if the services that were being held in their house did not stop.

At the same time as the regime was considering making Sunday school classes for children legal, bands of atheist thugs were breaking up Christian camps for children. On 22 July 1988 the authorities discovered such a camp near Rostov-on-Don. They tried to record the names of all the children, but Grigori Bublik, the organiser, resisted this successfully. They drew up an indictment against him and tried to take all the children back to their homes. After a lengthy discussion, however, they took them only as far as the homes of some believers in the immediate area.

It goes without saying that, if the persecution of the Brezhnev years did not dim the ardour of these believers, then none of the more petty intimidation of more recent times could possibly have any effect.

In Ukraine the organisers of an unregistered congregation gathered together their most active young people and distributed among them cards containing the names of villages where there were no religious services, possibly not even any believers. After long preparation of prayer and careful delineation of tasks, groups of young people set out for these places. In one village, for example, a preacher began systematic house-to-house visiting. Almost everyone was keen to listen to what he had to say. Eventually he reached a house where an old lady said she was a Christian. She had long since given up active expression of her faith, but now she was overjoyed and insisted that her house should be made available for a gathering of anyone local who wished to come there to worship. There were conversions and this became the focal point of a new church.

In some places former persecutors have witnessed to their conversion. On 30 August 1987 Yevgeni Turchik came forward at a meeting in Tambov and declared that his membership of the congregation had been a fraud and he had been passing names and other information systematically to the KGB. He wrote reports on commission, answering such questions as how believers dressed, who was friendly with whom, who had fallen out, whether anyone went to the cinema, what were the subjects of the preaching and the young people's discussions. One day, so troubled by his conscience that he could no longer continue, he unburdened himself to the wife of one of the believers. He received such a sympathetic hearing that he knew he must make a complete break. Asked what the KGB fears most, he replied:

> *Glasnost, glasnost* and again *glasnost* – publicity is what they fear. And I believe that if the Christian public learns about my conversation, then the KGB, these enemies of Christ, will have to limit their reprisals against me. I ask every Christian who hears of my confession to pray for me: that will be the best support.[5]

The KGB put him under house arrest without sentence and tried to intimidate him into working for them once again.

Meanwhile, stories of evangelistic initiatives pour in from all corners of the Soviet Union. One pastor, Ivan Plett, had been imprisoned for his role in printing Christian literature on a clandestine press. Towards the end of his sentence he received a summons from the camp administrator. 'A Bible has arrived for you in the post and I'm obliged to pass it on,' he said. This little irony, so typical of recent times, not only provided the most immense fillip to the morale of the prisoner, but also provided him with a tool of evangelism right there inside the prison.

While this is happening in one area of the Soviet Union, in another the media attack the Reform Baptists for continuing to run their clandestine printing press. The daily newspaper in Moldavia carried no fewer than four connected articles attacking the Borinsky family, one of whom was accused of being the leader of the team carrying out the operation. This was, however, in 1986 and subsequently such articles mostly vanished from the Soviet press.

An exception was an attack against Gennadi Kryuchkov in the conservative newspaper *Sovetskaya Rossia* in December 1989, for still allegedly pretending to the world that he needed to live clandestinely in order to avoid persecution. In general, however, from the end of 1989 there was less news about the disruption of the activities of the Reform Baptists.

Unity

The advent of *perestroika* has naturally aroused hopes for the reunification of the Baptist factions. In 1986 new and important information came to light on the nature of relations between the AUCECB and the Reform Baptists in the early days and it is worth summarising it here. The Reform Baptists published an account of their conversation with the senior officials of the AUCECB on 26 November 1961. This meeting took place before the formal secession of the Reform Baptists from the official organisation. The conversation illustrates just how impossible it then was to conduct any serious internal church negotiations at a time of direct threats from the KGB. The issue at stake was the imposition by the state of new rules limiting evangelism and baptisms and keeping children away from the influence of the faith. A group, headed by Gennadi Kryuchkov and Georgi Vins, objected and tried to call a congress to elect a more worthy leadership.

The meeting took place in the AUCECB offices in Moscow. Gennadi Kryuchkov and Alexander Karev, general secretary of the AUCECB before Alexei Bychkov, were the main spokesmen. Karev announced that the Reform Baptists' request for a congress to repeal the 'Letter of Instructions' and the 'New Statute' had been categorically refused by the state authorities. He admonished Kryuchkov with these words:

> I don't believe in this congress, since our country is now bent on a course of highly destructive measures against the church. They have decided to wipe out organized religion in the shortest possible time. They do not want us to accompany them on the road to communism![6]

This betrays the measure of fear that had been sown in the church as the Khrushchev anti-religious campaign began to gather momentum.

State interference in the internal affairs of the church could also cause deep division, which the authorities also encouraged as a way of limiting the influence of the church over its members. Kryuchkov and the reformers were concerned that the church retain its integrity rather than give way to state pressure and the fear that it generates. Karev's replies vividly demonstrate the degree to which liberty had been curtailed. True freedom, argued the Reform Baptists, is a spiritual rather than a physical phenomenon: only repentance and a return to the truth would bring restoration. The intransigence of the AUCECB on the issues raised by the New Statute was a serious compromise born out of a time of crisis in the existence of the church. Kryuchkov asked: 'Why cannot the church have a united leadership of both registered and unregistered congregations? Why do we not have a common cause, why do we not unite ourselves in prayer for God's work at such a crucial time?'

This appeal for unity had no success: Karev instead blamed the reformers for inviting persecution and church closures by their action which was upsetting the state-imposed *status quo*. He even insisted on defending the legitimacy of the Statute: 'It does not contradict the Word of God. You talk about children being allowed into church. If you bring them to the Lord you'll get five years and your children will be taken from you.'

Clearly, there could be little progress towards re-establishing unity while there continued to be no free discussion of the events of 1960-61. Least of all could this happen while, as was the fact until relatively recently, many of the leaders of one side were still in prison, or, in the case of Georgi Vins, were in enforced exile in the USA. Now, at last, the atmosphere for progress exists. If the AUCECB and the Reform Baptists can find common ground, the 'independently-registered' congregations should be able to do so, though they would insist on not losing the precious autonomy for which they had successfully fought.

Both sides have insisted on the other's need for repentance for sins of the past as a precondition for sitting down together. Here is an extract from an interview given by Vasili Logvinenko, until December 1989 President of the AUCECB, to Valeri Smirnov and printed in *Moscow News*:

> The Statute of the Union of ECB in the USSR and the Letter of Instruction to Senior Presbyters of the All-Union Council of ECB, adopted by our church officials in 1960 and 1961, played a negative role. These documents curtailed the church's canonical and spiritual activities. When believers came to know about them, thousands of people left our brotherhood, preferring clandestine activities, and avoided registering

their communities. In a number of cases this resulted in conflicts between believers and the law, which in turn led to the emergence of the Council of Churches of ECB which split from us. True, the 1963 All-Union Congress of ECB repealed both the documents, and at the 1966 Congress the former leaders of ECB publicly repented for having signed them. Not all laymen were informed about this and the enlarged plenary meeting of the AUCECB in May 1987 decided it was important to make special mention of the incident in the Message to the Churches of Evangelical Faiths in the Soviet Union, published in our journal, *Bratsky vestnik*.

It was openly admitted that the decisions leading to the split were mistaken, which is very important. These sad events are now behind us, but great efforts are still needed if we are to achieve complete unity. We are doing our level best to help the separated brothers and sisters reunite. Unfortunately, leaders of the Council of Churches, those who split, are reluctant to have contacts with us. Some of the separated communities have recently been registered by the Council for Religious Affairs, their legal status has been normalized, but they are still autonomous.[7]

Since then there has been a strong response and a new initiative on the part of the autonomous Baptists, who are in a strong position to intervene as possible mediators, since they bear no affiliation either to the AUCECB or to the Council of the Reform Baptists. Three of their leaders, again emphasising the need for repentance on all sides, proposed the establishment of a new union in which the accent would be on promoting fellowship and evangelisation, rather than directing activities nationally and internationally. A working group representing the three tendencies should review relations with the state; membership of foreign religious bodies, especially the World Council of Churches; and internal structure, especially re-establishment of the traditional Baptist principle of independence of the individual local congregation. Papers and proposals would circulate for eventual consideration by a full free congress, which would establish a new Baptist Union. Some of these proposals were adopted at the congress of February 1990, which should clear the way for further talks.

Statistics

One result of the freer flow of information and the opportunity which the Soviet churches now have of operating without fearing reprisals every time they take an initiative is that it is more possible than in the past to establish reliable statistics. The number of believers belonging to any denomination was always treated as a state secret in the past. Registration meant that the Council for Religious Affairs had certain hard information in its files, but these were never opened to reveal the full picture and the snippets published from them were always selected for their propaganda or minatory value.

In 1989 the official Baptists were able to publish their membership and one can also compute the figures for the Reform Baptists. The figures overall are lower than expected. This is due to the emigration of so many to West Germany in recent years and to the defection of the Pentecostals after forty years of uncomfortable union. Mennonites, too, are likely to be seeking to return to their own traditions, which discourage active military service.

The latest figures for AUCECB membership are 204,156 in 2,260 congregations, whereas at one time there were claims of over half a million. What are the reasons for the earlier inflation of the statistics by the official Baptist Union? On the face of it, one would expect them to have been under pressure over the years to deflate the figures, rather than the opposite. The special factor here is that, with encouragement from the state, they had to appear to be the predominant body, having absorbed not only the majority of the 'dissidents' (Reform Baptists), but the Pentecostals and Mennonites as well.

In the 1960s official Baptist spokesmen represented the Reform Baptists as power-seekers, trouble-makers, people who brought suffering upon themselves by deliberately flouting Soviet law. As the Reform Baptists became better known, not least through the possibility that some of them had to emigrate to West Germany from the mid-1970s, it became demonstrable to the world that these accusations were untrue. However, one line never changed: the unregistered communities were a tiny minority who were losing influence and who would, they hoped, soon be absorbed into the 'mainstream'.

From the 1989 congress of the Reform Baptists at which Gennadi Kryuchkov spoke, it is possible for the first time to estimate their numbers also. The formality was that every forty full (that is, baptised) members of the church could elect one delegate to the congress, a very simple way of ensuring fair representation among both large and small communities (it is not known whether groups of under forty members, of which there must be quite a number, could be represented at all, so the following figures might need some marking up). There were something over a thousand delegates, which indicates a total of over 40,000 for the whole Soviet Union. As the qualification for membership (adult baptism after full preparation) is clear and restrictive, this leaves room for a large number of men and women touched by Baptist influence, and in many instances even regularly worshipping. The figure would also not include any children or those at various stages short of full commitment. The total of those who come under the influence of the Reform Baptists cannot be far short of 100,000. From all the accounts of vigorous evangelistic campaigns and of numerous converts at rallies, one might still have expected higher overall figures and it would be wise, for the moment, to treat them as provisional.

In comparison with the Orthodox Church, their numbers seem insignificant. If one put together all baptised members from all three groups and added on a considerable number representing non-baptised attenders at worship, the total would still be well short of half a million. The Orthodox Church, perhaps numbering as many as fifty million, has more than a hundred times as many members. Yet the influence of the Baptists, both in the Soviet Union and internationally, far outweighs their numerical importance. Given the new opportunities they are so ready to take under *perestroika*, their role is surely destined to grow.

Pentecostals

The challenging fact of Pentecostal history is that they are a 'Soviet' denomination, an adjective from which they would recoil in horror. They had very small beginnings in Tsarist Russia at the start of the century, but were particularly adapted to growth in the harsh conditions of the Soviet period. Their origin can in no sense be designated as a 'relic of the past', to use the Soviet phrase. It is an objective fact that their characteristics are a reaction to the society round them, often taking the form of a rejection of it. The 'union' with the Baptists of August 1945 agreed by some of their leaders was not reached after any democratic process, nor did it stand any realistic chance of success, as it reflected pressure from the atheist authorities, whose values the Pentecostals repudiated.

Almost nothing was known outside the Soviet Union about these Christians until the 1960s. Even then information became available only in the most fragmentary form – attacks against them in the Soviet press, or the occasional public incident such as occurred in Moscow in 1963, when a group of them attempted to gain asylum in the American Embassy by rushing into it past the guards. The American officials sent them back into the care of the Soviet authorities, an event fully reported at the time, but which never became an international incident. Fifteen years later, on 27 June 1978, a group, including some of the same people, repeated what they had done earlier, and this time the American Embassy had to be much more responsive to public opinion at home. The presence of the 'Siberian Seven' in the American Embassy over the next five years was a *cause célèbre* from the first day. The sole objective of this group was to emigrate, but the Soviet external guards would not allow them their freedom. Eventually they went to America after a negotiated agreement.

The overriding current concern among some Pentecostals remains emigration, while for the rest it is registration. It is estimated that approximately ten per cent of the total want to emigrate, even the benefits of *perestroika* having failed to persuade them that Soviet society has a place for them. Then, quite naturally, the majority who want to remain in the Soviet Union wish to establish a Pentecostal Union, which would help them to organise their affairs both nationally and internationally, but without losing the autonomy of the local congregation which is a characteristic of their tradition. Interestingly, this was an idea endorsed by one of the leading Soviet experts on Pentecostals in the Soviet Union, V. D. Grazhdan. In a pamphlet issued recently by the atheist publishers, Znaniye, he gave a detailed analysis of tensions between Baptists registered under the official union and Pentecostals, a conflict which absorbs a great deal of the energies of the Baptist leadership. With this in mind, Grazhdan proposes that the Council for Religious Affairs look carefully at the possibility of establishing separate denominational affiliations to suit the requirements of the various Protestant groupings both inside and outside the official union. Under the more favourable conditions, those Pentecostal churches in the AUCECB left in May 1989, with a view to establishing their own union.

The issue of registration remains a divisive one, however, especially as the Soviet regime allowed a very few Pentecostal communities to register independently after 1969. Having outlawed the Pentecostals as a denomination for so long, the authorities changed their tactics in the 1970s and 1980s, cajoling the leadership with promises of buildings for worship, the establishment of a headquarters with a department for foreign relations, a printing press and the release of Ivan Fedotov, the leader who had spent most of his adult life in prison. Such a momentous issue could not, however, be decided without Fedotov's participation and when eventually he was released without conditions, he came out against registration. Pentecostal leaders of unregistered churches in the USSR held a conference to discuss the issue of registration in Zagorsk on 17 September 1988, attended by over 150 representatives of churches opposed to registration under current conditions. Documents from the conference received at Keston College reveal that there is a serious split on this issue, with some church leaders fearing that those beginning to argue for registration are in fact being manipulated by the KGB. In the opinion of many, registration remains a sign of capitulation to the authorities.

The advent of *perestroika* has resolved some other issues, however. As with the Baptists, this is the first time for decades that there have been no Pentecostal leaders in prison. It seems that the handful of Pentecostals in prison in mid-1989 are there because of their refusal to do military service and the hope is that the new law on freedom of conscience will provide for an alternative form of service for those whose convictions do not allow them to carry arms. The Soviet authorities are now anxious to engage believers of all denominations in the *perestroika* process, which in turn means that their previously hard-line approach appears to be softening.

Apart from the 'Siberian Seven', the event which brought Soviet Pentecostals most forcibly to the notice of the outside world was the treatment of the community in Chuguyevka, eastern Siberia. After a series of threats to their children at school, the community renounced its Soviet citizenship in 1983, after which the campaign against them intensified. This did not deter them from their desire to continue in the faith and to share it with others, even when members of the community were arrested and sent to various camps in the Soviet Union to serve sentences ranging from three to five years. Names such as Victor Walter, Nikolai Vins and Victor Pavlovets became well known in the West. Victor Walter himself was able to give a moving account of the community's experiences as the guest speaker at Keston College's Open Day on 14 October 1989 – in itself a remarkable event. He spoke of the suffering the community had undergone, harassment from the authorities, arrest and imprisonment, where the youngest members of the community were put under severe pressure from the camp authorities to get just one of them to renounce their faith. They all stood firm, however, until their release and eventual emigration during 1988, having used their prison experiences as a further opportunity to spread the faith. To see Victor Walter addressing the crowd of British Christians who had prayed for his community and campaigned for the release of its prisoners was indeed a testimony to all present that God will build His church, and the gates of hell will not prevail against it.

7 The Baltic on Fire

Three Brave Nations

The young man's words stunned the public assembled in the court-room. The posse of armed guards tightened their circle around the five accused. The ranks of the KGB and the judicial authorities glared in disbelief, but no one made the first move. The few Catholic faithful allowed inside, relatives of the five men, held their breath, praying that the speaker would be able to finish. This is what they heard:

> Is this what you understand by freedom – the closure of Catholic churches and their conversion into warehouses and concert halls? The imprisonment of priests for teaching children the faith? . . . Even today there are many working for justice, freedom and the general good of the people. How many have perished in the snows of Soviet Russia, how many have suffered hunger, disease and torture? They died as martyrs, enslaved but unconquered. Today, no less, our best hearts and brightest minds are rotting in prison . . .
>
> Lithuania, land of our birth, our own dear country . . . How many times have the boots of foreigners trodden you down? How often have you been bathed in tears and blood? But you have always had many noble hearts fearless to suffer and die for you. There are such even today.[1]

This was December 1974. Virgilijus Jaugelis, the spokesman for the accused, was only twenty-seven. The prosecutor treated him and the four older men in the dock as though they were charged with treason, though the formal accusation was that they had produced and circulated in *samizdat* the *Chronicle of the Lithuanian Catholic Church* which 'denigrated the Soviet system'.

With hindsight, it is obvious that the prosecutor had more to be afraid of than was apparent at the time. Jaugelis already knew that he was not alone. Two years earlier a student, Romas Kalanta, had burned himself to death in Kaunas, the former capital of Lithuania, as a protest against the Soviet occupation of his country and the continuing persecution of the church.

Jaugelis's sentence was more lenient than one would have expected following his temerity: two years. Perhaps the authorities feared a more severe one would further incense the people; or maybe his ill health deterred them: they did not want to create a martyr and Jaugelis was already ill with cancer. This did not save him from a savage attack by criminal prisoners in the pay of the KGB who set on him and broke his jaw. Three years later he was secretly ordained as a Catholic priest, but he died in February 1980, the rough treatment he had received doubtless contributing to the further deterioration in his health.

When I published a book about Lithuania in 1979, from which the above extract has been quoted, people tended to ask where the country was and dismissed its aspirations as irrelevant to the politics of the late twentieth century. Now the world has discovered the three small Baltic nations of Estonia, Latvia and Lithuania; their names are almost daily on the television news. They huddle together at the east end of the Baltic Sea, rendered almost invisible and anonymous on the map by the massive dominance of the Soviet Union, into which they were incorporated fifty years ago. *Glasnost* has now prised out for the Soviet people the historical truth that the Germans and the Soviets abolished the independent existence of the three countries by the 'secret protocol' of the Molotov–Ribbentrop Pact of 1939, which carved up eastern and central Europe into two spheres of influence. Mr Gorbachev admits now that the protocol existed, but still maintains that the union with the USSR was voluntary.

On 15 June 1940 the Red Army marched in and there were elections under the threat of the gun, leading to their formal 'incorporation' as Soviet Republics. The Nazis invaded a year later and in 1944 the Red Army drove them out, leading to an even firmer subjugation of these nations.

The roots of the flame which seemed so decisively doused fifty years ago continued to smoulder beneath the blanket of oppression. Baltic bravery is now igniting the hearts of people in other Soviet republics who were impressed by the nationalist and religious ardour of these men and women, as well as by their self-discipline and the responsible way in which they marshalled themselves and honed their civic courage.

The bludgeon which the Soviets used to cow the three nations was that of deportation: the cream of two generations, politicians, scholars, clergy, leaders of industry, the armed forces, even 'internationalists', such as students of Esperanto and philatelists, was removed to the arid desert of Kazakhstan or the mortal cold of Siberia. The Soviet net caught 35,000 people in 1940–41 in Lithuania alone (out of a population of 3 million) and a further 200,000 in the post-war years, on top of the 40,000 the Nazis sent to do slave labour in Germany in the intervening years. So appalling were the conditions in the cattle trucks during both deportations that many died even before they reached their destination. The figures of approximately ten per cent of the total population for the smaller nations of Latvia and Estonia are proportionately comparable. The Nazis deported most of the Jews, who had formed a large community in Lithuania before the war.

These tribulations had the effect of more than ever uniting three nations very different from each other in culture, language and religion, but sharing a similar recent history of brief independence between the wars and then subjugation. The only gain from the Molotov–Ribbentrop Pact in the whole of the Baltic States was that Lithuania regained its ancient capital of Vilnius from Poland in 1944.

The death of Stalin and Khrushchev's 'thaw' led to the return of many of the survivors from the Gulag. They came back often broken in health, but almost always strengthened in faith, wearing a crown of martyrdom which would inspire the younger generation, people such as Virgilijus Jaugelis. The Soviets tried to temper these renewed nationalist stirrings by introducing a more subtle tactic: immigration. The Baltic States, with their tradition of hard work, their efficiency and 'Western' look (whether Scandinavian, Hanseatic or Polish) were always attractive to Russians. They needed no persuasion to move there in considerable numbers, to some extent compensating for the population depleted by deportation and kept small by a low birthrate. By 1989 nearly a fifth of the population of Lithuania consisted of Slav immigrants, while Estonia had about two-fifths and Latvia almost half.

Lithuania – Christian Revival

Lithuania is overtly the most 'Christian' of the three nations, with perhaps nearly eighty per cent of the non-immigrant population belonging to the Roman Catholic Church, which nurtured the spirit of the nation during times of great suffering. Where massive prison sentences awaited any suspected of independent political activity, attendance at church became a symbol of unspoken protest.

The renewed spirit following the returns from exile saw such enterprises as the building of a new Catholic church in Klaipeda, Lithuania, where on 30 June 1957 Bishop Petras Mazelis laid the foundation stone of a major church destined to replace the one blown up by the retreating Nazis. This extract from the *Chronicle of the Lithuanian Catholic Church* indicates the enthusiasm of the time:

> Offerings were collected throughout Lithuania for the construction of the church. The Catholics of Klaipeda joined in the enterprise with joy and enthusiasm. Even though the site was very boggy, within a few weeks the people had filled in the marsh, using small carts and even baskets of earth. After returning home from work, believers hurried to help in the construction and worked late into the night. Drivers brought the necessary materials in their own time and collected bricks among the ruins of the city. Even inspectors turned a blind eye as drivers helped in the work and some officials would come to help the believers. Among the helpers were some who had never previously been to church. The believers collected about three million roubles for the church building fund. Even poor Catholics gave joyfully of their savings. One worker who brought a considerable sum of money said, 'Put my heart among the bricks in the walls of this church.' It turned out that this man, who had a large family to support, had contributed one month's wages. When people sold anything, they allocated part of the money for the church. The church was completed during the summer of 1960 and the consecration ceremonies were to be held on the Feast of the Assumption.[2]

But the consecration ceremony of the 'Queen of Peace' church never took place. One of the inaugural and most grotesque acts of the new anti-religious campaign under Khrushchev in 1961 was to demolish the steeple, which the authorities themselves had asked should be visible from the sea, as a landmark and to impress foreign visitors to the port. The nave became a concert hall where orchestras played to empty houses and two priests who had done much to see the project through were imprisoned. In the 1970s and 1980s over twenty petitions (one with nearly 150,000 signatures) and delegations to Moscow presented the case for the return of the church.

In the Lithuanian Church several grievances overlapped. Nowhere were there sufficient churches open. Vilnius, the capital city, with a population of over half a million, had just six. St Stanislas Cathedral fell into the hands of the atheists after the war and became a warehouse, then a gallery exhibiting pictures which the local people made a point of calling third-rate. Even more provocative was the conversion of the nearby St Casimir Church into an atheist museum. Between the wars there were over 1,500 clergy, while in the 1980s the total had fallen to half that, with a high average age and therefore a disproportionate number who were sick or incapacitated. The original four seminaries had been cut to one, in Kaunas, which at its lowest ebb (because the state authorities strictly controlled the intake) produced only three ordinations in 1969, as against sixteen deaths of serving priests. In the fifteen years up to 1988, 308 priests died, while there were only 183 ordinations.

Particularly controversial and painful were the enormous gaps in the ranks of the episcopacy. For many years there were only two bishops administering six dioceses. The enforced exile of Bishop Julijonas Steponavicius (Vilnius) and Vincentas Sladkevicius (Kaisiadorys) to remote country areas of Lithuania, where they could have only sporadic contact with believers and none at all with their own dioceses, was a focal point of literally hundreds of protest documents.

Then there were the judicial proceedings against anyone who attempted publicly to defend the rights of believers, or who engaged in any type of allegedly 'nationalist' activities. This was the time when there was a ban on dressing dolls in national costume showing the red, green and yellow colours of the old flag. Despite vitriolic attacks in the press against such people as the five accused mentioned at the beginning of the chapter, Virgilijus Jaugelis and several priests who were put on trial became national heroes.

In 1971, following the post-Khrushchev lull, the anti-religious campaign resumed with full vigour and it was this which stimulated the attempt to document the attacks and present the life of the church to the world through the pages of the *Chronicle of the Lithuanian Catholic Church*.

One of the first cases to become known was that of Fr Juozas Zdebskis, arrested in August 1971 for teaching the catechism to children at their parents' request. Although this was his third arrest his sentence was only a year; his trial and the fearless testimonies in his defence became well known through a transcript which formed the substance of the first-ever issue of the *Chronicle*. Released a day early to prevent a demonstrative welcome for him outside the prison gates, he walked on a carpet of flowers which children strewed in front of him. This path, however, led to more suffering and eventually to death. In 1978 he followed the example of Gleb Yakunin, who had just established a similar group in Moscow, and became a founder member of the Catholic Committee for the Defence of Believers' Rights, furthering its work from the semi-exile of one of the most remote parishes in Lithuania. Far from limiting his activity, the intrusion of the authorities stimulated him to become virtually an itinerant priest, specialising, for example, in contacting Soviet soldiers and taking them the sacrament secretly. He ministered to unregistered Catholic congregations as far afield as Tajikistan and Armenia.

Several times the KGB attacked him physically. He never lived to see the better days which would so shortly come. Following the identical fate of others who had incurred the wrath of the system in various parts of the Soviet Union (and, incidentally, Poland) he became the victim of a 'road accident' on 5 February 1986. A fellow priest, executor of his will, searched his room just after and, apart from a few books, almost his only possessions – and they filled the drawers of his desk – were little stones of attractive shape, colour and texture gathered from the fields of Lithuania. At his grave, this priest said that every ordained minister of the Gospel should see this room to learn from it how to dismiss the value of worldly possessions and how to love his native land. Fr Zdebskis was only fifty-five when he was killed.[3]

During these years the person who achieved most international recognition and prayer-support for her campaign for religious liberty was not a priest but a nurse, Nijole Sadunaite, who was thirty-six at the time of her trial in 1975. It was she who had been responsible for continuing the *Chronicle* after the trial of the five and reporting their trial in the very next issue of a publication the authorities thought they had suppressed by jailing those who produced it. Her letters, sent clandestinely to Lithuania from the Siberian Gulag and then out of the country, inspired tens of thousands of people. Her devotion to God in these appalling physical circumstances was the keynote of every letter she wrote:

> How good it is that the hand of the good Father is steering the small craft of my life. When He is at the helm I have nothing to fear . . . We have many old and sick women here, so I rejoice that my journey enables me to fulfil my calling – to nurse and to love.[4]

The only response of the state authorities during this time was constant interruption of every local Christian activity outside the church buildings, the continuation of a crude campaign in the press and the summoning of priests to the offices of the Council for

Religious Affairs to harangues on how 'progressive' priests were keeping within the law.

Lithuania's Popular Front

In an era of unprecedented events in the Soviet bloc, the emergence of the popular fronts in the Baltic States forms one of the most astonishing developments: three tiny nations (though each, admittedly, with a population larger than that of Northern Ireland) prepared to take on the might of the Soviet system, with its double threat of military intervention and KGB terrorism.

The rise of the Popular Front in each of the three Baltic nations follows a parallel path, but for brevity's sake, we continue with an account of events in Lithuania.

The date of 16 February, marking the anniversary of Lithuania's independence gained in 1918, has always been the focal point of nationalist aspirations. The KGB would adopt a high profile on that day as a visible warning to any prospective demonstrator. In recent years the church found a way round the ban on political meetings by inaugurating 'masses for the fatherland' and over 600 of these (that is one in almost every church) took place in 1988. One of the largest was in Kaunas Cathedral, where lines of militia outside failed to deter 4,000 people from entering. Some known activists, such as Nijole Sadunaite, quite undeterred by her earlier prison experiences, were not only kept under house arrest during this period, but were also physically maltreated.

However, the deep-seated impulse for change was already meeting less resistance from the central authority in Moscow and people were less afraid, feeling that the threat of violence had receded. Hungary and Poland were beginning to show that the right of Moscow to dominate smaller nations could be successfully challenged.

The 'Popular Front' movement in the Baltic States represents a universal desire for national independence, but the presence of large Slav minorities, some second- or even third-generation immigrants, some of much more recent origin, complicates the ethnic and therefore the political map. With fewer Russians in Lithuania than in the other Baltic States, the task of Sajudis has been slightly less complicated than elsewhere.

Sajudis means simply 'movement' – short for 'Movement for *Perestroika*', originally a safe enough title to encourage Mr Gorbachev's support. Established on 3 June 1988, it immediately became a powerful presence on the Lithuanian scene, with its head office overlooking the demonstration ground of Gediminas Square, in front of the Cathedral of St Stanislas. Vytautas Landsbergis, its gentle and artistic president, a pianist and musicologist by profession, described its aims to me in February 1989. He was the focus of calm amidst the febrile activity of the cramped Sajudis offices. It is hard to imagine that he is now the first president of a Lithuania claiming independence, but Poland appointed another pianist, Paderewski, to a similar office after the First World War and the world has been acclaiming Vaclav Havel, the new playwright president of Czechoslovakia.

'Sajudis is not a political party, but a movement,' Professor Landsbergis stressed. 'It does not seek to seize power, but rather to exert influence over those in power and thereby have a say in the running of the country's affairs.' He said it acted as a kind of protective umbrella under which fledgling political parties could take root and evolve. Within it were not only Christians, Greens and anyone who sought to preserve the nation's heritage, but even a number of more progressive Communist Party members. Full religious freedom was a fundamental point in its founding document and the Party newspaper, *Sovetskaya Litva*, published the whole text of this on 12 October 1988. Almost all the leaders of Sajudis showed their Christian allegiance by attending an open-air mass in Gediminas Square marking the end of the inaugural congress of Sajudis.

The Latvian Popular Front similarly included significant points to guarantee religious freedom in its manifesto, recognising the role of the church in the moral regeneration of society and in the affirmation of universal human values. At the Constituent Congress of the Estonian Popular Front a whole section entitled 'Church and Society' was part of the debate promoting legislative changes and greater equality of believers and atheists.

In order to inform the world objectively of the aims of Sajudis, an understanding which Mr Landsbergis stated to be essential for the future of the movement, it publishes a *Congress Bulletin* in English and other languages.

The Sajudis umbrella also shielded the Lithuanian Freedom League, which demanded secession from the Soviet Union as the main plank of its platform. This was originally an underground movement which now surfaced ten years after its foundation, but soon Sajudis as a whole was working openly for independence. One of its leading lights is Antanas Terleckas, formerly imprisoned on political grounds and released in 1987.

When the unofficial 'Baltic Interest Group' of the European Parliament visited Vilnius on 6 February 1989, the 'Young Lithuania' movement associated with the Freedom League put a declaration into their hands asking the Parliament's help in re-establishing a 'free and independent Lithuania'. It continued: 'We hold Lithuania to be a full and free member of the European family of nations, and we therefore state that we do not want to be a Russian colony or a vassal state, nor do we care to have any ties with Moscow.'5

On 7 May 1989 the League unveiled a monument honouring the Lithuanian guerillas who fell in the struggle against the occupying Soviet forces forty years ago. Three thousand people attended the ceremony at Varniai, where the memorial is next to the former NKVD building which claimed a toll of 200 victims secretly buried within its precincts. Warnings from the KGB failed to prevent a priest from consecrating it in the presence of a large crowd. Only a year or two ago all those associated with the event would have had a prison sentence of at least ten years.

The more formal expression of this urge to give vent to the nation's feelings came with the elections to the new Congress of USSR People's Deputies on 26 March 1989. No fewer than thirty-one of the thirty-nine Sajudis candidates were successful and their formal role in Moscow briefly became important as the focus of the nation's aspirations. After the declaration of independence, however, the Baltic delegates withdrew from the debating and legislative process in Moscow.

The people went from strength to strength, on no occasion more impressively than in the three nation protest against the annexation resulting from the Molotov–Ribbentrop Pact, when hundreds of thousands joined hands across the three territories in a demonstration of their desire to shed the communist yoke. Sajudis went further than ever before towards embracing the cause of independence in stating that Lithuania 'must be reborn as a democratic and independent republic . . . It must be free from the jurisdiction and administrative system of the USSR.'6

With the preparation for free local elections in February 1990, the issue of independence dominated all else. First the Communist Party, under Antanas Brazauskas, declared itself independent of Moscow, but even this brave act did not secure for it any major support, while Sajudis became more and more openly wedded to the goal of independence, thus uniting the various tendencies within it. Sajudis won an overwhelming majority, which led directly to the formal declaration of independence on 11 March. Following Moscow's threats to rescind this, Mr Landsbergis has now become a familiar face on the television screens of the world.

Lithuanian Catholics and *Perestroika*

Looking back at the documents of 1986–87, one is amazed to see, even two years into Mr Gorbachev's rule, how the state persisted in its time-hardened attitudes. For example, on 23 April 1986 no fewer than 127 of the 130 priests in the diocese of Panevezys signed a protest to Gorbachev complaining about the continuing interference of the state in church affairs. Worst of all was the control, amounting to the right of veto, which the authorities exercised over the appointment of bishops, the assignment of priests to individual parishes and the admission of students to the single theological seminary in Kaunas.

There were still several prisoners, lay and clerical, who would have been exercising leadership in their communities if they had been free and they were still in the forefront of believers' minds as news continued to filter back about them from distant places.

Jadvyga Bieliauskiene, known to the world not least through the friendship she formed in prison with Irina Ratushinskaya described in the latter's prison memoirs, *Grey is the Colour of Hope*, continued the imprisonment begun in 1982 for teaching the Christian faith to children. She was seriously ill and there were fears for her survival. However, her release came soon and her exile was cancelled. Before that she had written:

> I became very ill, with three relapses, but my soul was flooded with a clear light never seen before, which still accompanies me when I suffer. If I die, rejoice and praise the Lord that the humble sacrifice of this most unworthy and wayward being has been accepted for the purpose of saving our children. I have come to understand that suffering is fruitful only when we accept it humbly – only then does it open the eyes of the soul.[7]

In February 1989 I had the joy of meeting her by chance on Gediminas Square in the company of Nijole Sadunaite. It was the spirit of these two more than anyone else who convinced me that no human force could quell the indomitable spirit of these people.

The imprisoned priests, Frs Alfonsas Svarinskas and Sigitas Tamkevicius, were never far out of mind, especially when the Lithuanian Commissioner for Religious Affairs, Petras Anilionis, singled them out for calumny. On 27 June 1986 he summoned all the bishops and diocesan administrators for one of his regular but futile intimidation sessions. Expressing satisfaction at the silencing of the priests, he nevertheless complained that others were making 'impossible demands' to mark the forthcoming 600th anniversary of Christianity in Lithuania, such as the return of the Cathedral and the Church of St Casimir (then still an atheist museum) in Vilnius and of the Church of the Queen of Peace in Klaipeda.

At the end of the year, however, there was a sign that not all was going the authorities' way when the Vatican appointed Mgr Vladas Michelevicius as an auxiliary bishop of Kaunas (under Archbishop Povilonis) and his consecration took place in the cathedral on 7 December.

The beginning of the jubilee year (1987) was obviously a time for taking stock, a time when there was the first breath of a warmer wind from the Kremlin, even if it did not at first appear to be blowing in the direction of the Baltic.

The Soviet authorities had said they would block any attempts by the Lithuanian hierarchy to travel to Rome that year; indeed Bishops Steponavicius and Sladkevicius were still banned from office. Archbishop Povilonis received permission to go to Rome in February 1987. The warm public welcome which the Pope gave him, news of which travelled back via Vatican Radio, must have encouraged every believer back at home. This led to a renewal of the hope, which Lithuanians had long entertained, that the Pope would be able to visit their country in the jubilee year. A message to him in the *Chronicle* read:

> Despite all the difficulties and the current conditions, we hope and trust that we shall see you visiting our motherland in celebration of the 600th anniversary of our conversion. The whole of believing Lithuania, determined to remain loyal to Christ and his representative on earth, the Pope, awaits this blessing.[8]

The Pope revisited Poland in June 1987 and while he was there he pointedly referred to his inability to travel to Lithuania next door. A Soviet spokesman hastened to state that there were no plans to invite him that year or next. Instead, the Pope marked the jubilee by sending a message of eighteen pages in which he praised the nation for 'not losing its own identity and self-awareness', despite many impediments and obstacles.

The celebrations of the jubilee year were muted. The banned bishops and the prisoners remained where they were and as late as October, the *Independent* correspondent, Rupert Cornwell, who

would soon be writing movingly of the resurgence of Lithuanian
Christian life, was still referring to the 'uneasy balance between a
population resigned to the *status quo* and the grudging acceptance by
the Soviet authorities that some leeway must be given the church in
the interests of stability'.[9]

   In 1988 the wind of change finally began to blow in the direction of
the Lithuanian Church. First, there was the reinstatement of Bishop
Vincentas Sladkevicius to the diocese of Kaisiadorys. He received
permission to travel to the Vatican in April with all the other bishops
(except one who was retired and Bishop Steponavicius, still barred
from office). Archbishop Povilonis formally requested retirement
on grounds of age and the Pope appointed Bishop Sladkevicius in
his place, raising him to the rank of cardinal a month later and
consecrating him in the Vatican at the end of June. In the spring of
1989 the Vatican took the initiative of appointing three new bishops.
By this time Fr Svarinskas had served five and a half years of his
ten-year sentence. He had constantly been in trouble during his
ministry. Now aged sixty-three, he had spent eight years in prison
after the war and a further six years under Khrushchev, half his adult
life behind bars in all. Undaunted, his most recent 'crime' had been,
with Frs Zdebskis and Tamkevicius, to found the Lithuanian Catholic
Committee for the Defence of Believers' Rights. Now finally he saw
freedom again on 15 July, but his release was conditional on his
emigration, to which he agreed only under duress. Before he left
for West Germany, however, he was able to say a farewell mass in
Vilnius and to visit two of the country's most sacred shrines, Siluva
and the Hill of Crosses. A great crowd gathered at the airport to see
him off and sang the Lithuanian national anthem.

   The release of Fr Tamkevicius followed on 4 November, without
the precondition of his leaving the country, though the authorities
had unsuccessfully tried to force him to sign an admission of guilt.
A crowd of about 400, waving the forbidden national flag and the
white and gold papal colours, gave him a joyful welcome on the
railway station in Vilnius and among them he saw other faces of
prisoners recently released, perhaps most notably the lay activist
Viktoras Petkus, amnestied two days earlier in the middle of a
fifteen-year sentence. Fr Tamkevicius wanted to do nothing more
than return to his former parish of Kybartai, where he celebrated
mass for his ecstatic parishioners.

   The return of the Queen of Peace Church in Klaipeda, a subject
of bitter dispute now for more than a quarter of a century, was
the cause of very special rejoicing for the Lithuanian faithful and

must have been humiliating for Mr Anilionis who, until recently, had been proclaiming that this was not even on the agenda for discussion. Fr Bronislovas Burneikis, the original priest of the parish, was still alive and active, having served a four-year sentence in the meantime for allegedly indulging in 'financial speculation' over the building materials. He was able to repossess his rectory at once and to begin restoration work to make the building again suitable for use as a church.

Just as symbolic was the return of the mother church of the whole land, Vilnius Cathedral. At the end of the jubilee year over 31,000 people from all over the country signed a petition and sent it to Mr Gorbachev, in which they drew his attention to the forthcoming Millennium of the Orthodox Church, when believers would be able to celebrate in the Danilov Monastery, which had recently been returned to them, while Lithuanian Catholics had been given no comparable privileges.

Finally, the authorities gave way at the end of October, their decision coinciding with the inaugural congress of Sajudis, founded three months earlier. Rupert Cornwell was again in Lithuania to witness this historic event. He wrote:

> What has bewildered and exhilarated here has been the sheer speed of events. A year ago, a visitor found Lithuania apparently cowed, sullen and hopeless . . . The crowd gathered from every direction, slow streams of people carrying candles, torches and the long-banned red, green and yellow flags of 'bourgeois' Lithuania. As they approached the square, the streams became rivers of their own, of old and young, children on their fathers' shoulders, walking to the soft rhythmic chanting of patriotic songs which everyone knew by heart.[10]

The authorities were not going to give up their hold on the cathedral without a struggle. Spokesmen demanded its return during the congress itself and finally an official came to the podium to announce the concession. To a man, the 3,000 in the hall stood and chanted *Lie – tu – va, Lie – tu – va* (Lithuania). As it was a Saturday, the church administration made hasty plans to celebrate an open-air mass in the square outside the cathedral at the crack of dawn next day. Rupert Cornwell continues:

> Thus it was in Sunday's icy pre-dawn that perhaps 20,000 people gathered before the great white columns of the cathedral's entrance. Again, the darkness was filled by rhythmic chanting. Picked out by television arc lights, Lithuanian and Vatican flags fluttered in the breeze.

From the building, Cardinal Vincentas Sladkevicius emerged like the Pope himself from St Peter's to celebrate mass. As the faithful stood transfixed, the sky over Vilnius gradually lightened. The symbolism was overpowering.

Before the end of the year there was a succession of events which underlined how decisively the tide had turned for the faithful in Lithuania. Following an announcement that this had been the best year in four decades for the ordination of new priests (twenty-seven all told), All Saints' Day once again became a national holiday for the first time since the Soviet annexation. Lithuanian television transmitted its second Christian broadcast, this time from Kaunas Cathedral (the first having been the open air mass just over a week earlier). The official Vilnius-based Russian-language newspaper, *Sovetskaya Litva*, proclaimed in a headline on 11 November that the 'legal requests' of believers were now being satisfied, following this a month later by an article in praise of the notable Lithuanian patriot, now beatified, Bishop Jurgis Matulaitis.

At last it became known that Bishop Julijonas Steponavicius of Vilnius would be released from his banning order. For the first time Lithuanian schools closed for their midwinter break on 24 December, so that Christmas Day, celebrated according to the Western calendar and not in January, as the Orthodox do, could become a family holy day once again. For the third time in two months mass was broadcast, this time at midnight from the Vilnius Church of Ausros Vartai ('Gates of Dawn'). The Lithuanian press carried the Cardinal's Christmas greetings. At the end of the year the church announced that it had received 209,000 Bibles and New Testaments in its own language from overseas during 1988.

On 7 February 1989 the local press, both in Lithuanian and in Russian, reported the presence in Vilnius two days earlier of the 'representative of Keston College, the Reverend Maiklas Bordo' (as the Lithuanian version spelled it).[11] A few local dignitaries from other denominations were on the list, but no one else from abroad. Behind these few words lay a private drama for me. I had been invited by Bishop Steponavicius to attend the reconsecration of Vilnius Cathedral. My own visa application, accompanied by presentation of the bishop's telegram, received a firm refusal, but strong pressure from the Foreign Office led to a last-minute reversal of the decision. With permission to visit all three Baltic States in my Soviet visa, I set off on the very last plane which would deliver me to Vilnius, via Moscow, in time for the ceremony on Sunday.

That morning, 5 February, Bishop Steponavicius was engulfed by the bustle of bishops and priests all greeting him at once when I arrived. Yet it was my privilege to share his car and be alone with him for a few precious minutes as we drove to the cathedral. He spoke of his long isolation as a period of unceasing prayer on behalf of his people, but he did not complain of the loss of nearly half a lifetime, twenty-eight years under house arrest in a remote Lithuanian village. Now he was returning to reclaim his diocese and to reconsecrate his cathedral. His illegal punishment, he said, had been for refusing to forbid the teaching of catechism to children: now he was greeted by the children of those children in national dress, bearing gifts of flowers as he approached the cathedral. The vast crowd on Gediminas Square welcomed him, not with soaring cheers, but with prayer and the near-silent waving of a thousand flags. The colours of pre-Soviet Lithuania, gold, green and red, were everywhere. Television cameras transmitted the scene throughout Lithuania and continued to roll through the next three and a half hours. The impact of this event, seen by the whole nation on TV, must have convinced them all that basic change was indeed well on the way.

Parting the crowds as Moses did the Red Sea, the bishop strode across the square at the head of his procession, then paused at the west door for a moment of prayer before walking majestically up the nave to prostrate himself at the altar steps. Filling every square inch of the cathedral, the 3,000-strong congregation prayed with him in silence. The years spent by the bishop in quiet study and prayer in his remote place of exile now brought their reward in this most solemn act of reconsecration: a natural leader under God among his people, no doubt using this occasion as an act of personal rededication in order to face the challenges of the new era.

After the reconsecration and the mass, the third hour was filled with special tributes. The first was from Nijole Sadunaite, speaking in the name of all prisoners, especially those who had not returned from exile.

Coinciding with this great event was the publication of No.1 of *Kataliku pasaulis* ('Catholic World'), the first official church journal to appear in Lithuania since the Second World War. I received a copy at the banquet after the service in the cathedral. Fellow-Catholics in Latvia also received permission in 1989 to produce their own journal.

To walk around Vilnius during those days was to share the joy of a people who were aware that freedom was already within their grasp. Perhaps the most amazing sight was a notice on the wall of the Church of St Casimir proclaiming, 'Museum closed. Property of the Vilnius Curia from 1 March 1989.'

The rest of 1989 saw nothing quite as dramatic as the events of October to February, but the Vatican raised Bishop Steponavicius to the rank of archbishop, which was more than symbolic, because this underlining of his authority gave him, at least nominally, sway over part of Belorussia and his archdiocese also extended into Poland. This was highly unusual, as at seventy-eight he was already well beyond retirement age, but as he had been banned from office for nearly three decades it was also a singularly gracious gesture and a public affirmation by the Vatican of the greatness of the man. Two further bishops were consecrated, one of whom, Juozas Zemaitis, had created a favourable impression in England as a member of a delegation to the British Council of Churches in 1983.

April saw a surge of determination to re-establish Catholic youth work nationwide. There was a revival of the organisation which had once been so influential among young people, *Ateitininkai*, with its motto, 'Everything must be renewed in Christ'. Vilnius University announced the founding of a chaplaincy and the radio put out the information that the Scout Movement would resume after a gap of fifty years. In the same month a group of women, with the blessing of the hierarchy, established a Lithuanian branch of the international Catholic relief agency Caritas, and Viktoras Petkus set up a new Christian Democratic Party, with a fifteen-point programme.

As the Soviet laws then stood, none of these activities could even remotely come within the framework of legality, but they all went ahead unimpeded, illustrating that the Lithuanian branch of the Council for Religious Affairs had now abandoned its authority. It is believed that Anilionis was dismissed some time in June or July 1989 and there can be no place for such a Council in a Lithuania which manages its own affairs.

What is certain is that the hierarchy, now more boldly than ever, and with Bishop Zemaitis taking the lead, called categorically for an end to the compulsory atheist programme in schools; all parents should also have the right to choose religious education for their children. The church is now fully recognised in Lithuanian law and the government is working out the legal side of how to return confiscated property in full.

Lithuanian émigrés were now, even though they had been barred from many of the preceding festivities, able to play a much more active role in events in their own country of origin. For example, Bishop Paulius Baltakis from the United States paid his first return visit since leaving as a refugee in 1944, receiving positive coverage in the Estonian as well as the Lithuanian press. His visit to the now functioning church in Klaipeda was an immense encouragement to the faithful.

In July Lithuanian TV inaugurated a regular weekly series of programmes on Sundays, having already televised mass on several special occasions. In August there came an announcement that a second theological seminary, at Telsiai, would open in time for the academic year beginning in September 1989. It had formerly served the western part of the country, where there was now a shortage of priests, and there were thirty applicants for places on the initial course.

For Lithuanian believers, who had lived through two invasions and fifty years of religious oppression, these events were indeed the dawning of a new age.

Estonia

One of the smallest nations in Europe, with only one and a half million population, Estonia is also one of the most remarkable. A close neighbour of Finland, just sixty miles across the gulf at the east end of the Baltic Sea, it has always looked and felt much more akin to Scandinavia than to its dominant neighbour, Russia. Its language, being close to no other except Finnish, has kept its people apart, though it feels a great loyalty to the other two Soviet Baltic States through the common history and suffering it has shared with them.

Estonia, like Latvia, has had to contend with growing numbers of immigrants from the Slav republics. This small country was perhaps more radical in its initial demands than either Latvia or Lithuania, receiving stern warnings from Moscow as early as 1988 for its pretensions to independence. Estonia has also been the centre for meetings of popular front leaders across the Baltic States to discuss policy and establish principles for future co-operation.

At the age of forty-two, in 1970, Harri Mötsnik abandoned his work as a lawyer to become a Lutheran pastor, thereby incurring the severe displeasure of the Soviet authorities. They pressurised him constantly, which only served to sharpen his determination to preach the Gospel in a form pointedly relevant to the oppressed people he was addressing.[12] In the early 1980s, some of his sermons (he sent copies out of the Soviet Union) seemed provocative to the point of foolhardiness. He spoke on freedom and peace in these terms:

Freedom is not understood or sufficiently valued until it is lost and the realisation of its absence becomes a personal experience. Freedom is not an illusion, but an experience of reality. It is a vital need. It is not out of place to remember the valiant men and women who have chosen the noble path of self-sacrifice rather than self-interest and furthering their own careers; they have chosen the struggle for freedom as the only way of hope for the Estonian people, setting on one side the fear which they surely experience within and in face of the totalitarian regime which confronts them . . . Peace is very precious, because it is necessary for life. To a Christian peace means a good and secure life, clean air and water, health and long life. This includes a democratic, independent homeland, freedom of conscience and religion.[13]

Vilification and imprisonment, followed by an enforced public renunciation of his activities and exile to Scandinavia, were Harri Mötsnik's immediate destiny. Yet within four or five years not only had thousands of others, including many believers, similarly responded to the urge for national independence, but they had even gained such a measure of success as must have seemed impossible when he first preached his message.

In the summer of 1987 an ecumenical group of Estonians formed a group to defend all believers in the USSR which they called 'Rock of Support'. They aimed especially to collect information about persecution in Estonia which they wanted to send abroad, naming Keston College as one of the intended recipients. Pressure continued on activists at this time to the extent that the authorities prevailed on the leaders of the official Baptist Church to expel from membership a large group of young people, on account of their Christian nationalism and the influence they were having on their contemporaries. They established an independent group called 'Word of Life', rejecting the official Baptist viewpoint that the church should be divorced from politics and claiming the right to involve themselves in social activities. About forty members wish to emigrate for the purpose of theological study, but with the aim of later returning to help evangelise Estonia.

It would not be long before the ecological concerns already being expressed by Harri Mötsnik would be taken up by no less a figure than Metropolitan Alexi of Leningrad, whose Orthodox archdiocese includes his native Estonia. The ecological movement is strong in Estonia and Latvia. Long known as a man of 'safe' views, he is now a member of the Congress of People's Deputies and the change in his outlook is indicative of the new mood in the Soviet Union. On the feast of the Assumption at the Puhtitsa Orthodox convent in August 1989, the Metropolitan severely criticised plans to dig a mine nearby in north-eastern Estonia which would have catastrophic ecological effects.

When the Estonians established their Popular Front in October 1988, the founders proclaimed in the press that the fight with religion was a relic of the past, that the obsolete Stalinist legislation must be changed, that Christians should actively promote holiness, patience, care for the old and the sick and inculcate moral values in the young. Going well beyond any concessions suggested earlier in the year by Mr Gorbachev, one speaker said that there should be an alternative form of service for those whose conscience did not allow them to bear arms.[14] On 6 February 1989 church leaders of various denominations had the opportunity of putting their needs and aspirations to the first secretary of the Estonian Communist Party, V. Väljas. On 21 April church leaders even more strongly requested return of their property in a meeting with Indrek Toome, Chairman of the Estonian Council of Ministers, who publicly stated his satisfaction with the contribution the churches were already making to the *perestroika* process.

In September the churches gained a significant concession with the abolition of special punitive taxation for the clergy, which had been a feature of Stalinist policy still operating in the rest of the USSR. At the same time the Estonian Government set up a commission to draft new legislation on religion, irrespective of what was happening elsewhere, which holds the promise of resolving the problem of confiscated church property. Unlike its Latvian neighbour, the majority Estonian Lutheran Church as an institution has not, as yet, made any public statements of support for the Popular Front or other political groupings which have flourished in the country.

The director of the Estonian Lutheran Theological Institute, Kalle Kasemaa, made it clear that the church did not feel it appropriate to be involved in politics in any official way:

> Officially the churches have not taken up any standpoint towards the Popular Front movement. We feel that these political movements are not primarily a matter for the church. As a body, we cannot afford to participate in the Popular Front, the Greens or in the struggle of the Party for the National Independence of Estonia.

This did not preclude involvement on a personal level, however:

> Of course, pastors can be involved as individuals; that is their own private affair. So far we have been able to establish that the only party in which no pastor is active is the Communist Party. But it is also true that membership of any of the others tends to be the exception, as far as our pastors are concerned.[15]

Estonia seems set to make a significant new contribution to the worldwide ecumenical movement. It is well known that many Soviet Christians are dissatisfied with the relations of their leaders with the World Council of Churches, particularly with its failure to support suffering Christians unambiguously through the time of their recent persecution. The Lutheran Archbishop, Kuno Pajula, made the first move towards rectifying this by inviting young WCC representatives to come to Tallinn for a meeting in January 1989 and the next month church leaders took the significant step of establishing an Estonian Council of Churches. This was the first such body anywhere in the Soviet Union, the absence of which had always been a great weakness. The choice of ecumenical representation in international forums had always been very largely in the hands of the Council for Religious Affairs.

Later in the year, in mid-August, Estonia played host to the largest Christian youth festival ever to be held in the USSR, organised by the local churches. The opening rally took place in Tallinn's vast Oleviste Church, belonging to the Baptists. There were services also in the Lenin sports stadium, which seats 6,000.

Baptists in Estonia have recently set up their own small seminary, initially with five students, as part of a new administrative and publishing centre for the denomination.

There is a strong feeling among active Estonian Christians that the existing church leadership is, by long exposure to the attrition of the communist system, unable to take advantage of the age of *perestroika*. As one young man put it to me, speaking in the Lutheran Cathedral in February 1989, 'It's one thing to have new opportunities; it's something quite different to have the nerve to grasp them. Those people who lived through the terror of the 1940s and 1950s – and we sympathise with them – cannot respond to the new conditions. Our senior people have not trained themselves to take the initiative; rather, they keep out of the limelight, away from the gaze of the authorities. Even under present conditions it will take decades for the church, as well as society as a whole, to adapt.'

There are, however, growing grounds for optimism in Estonia. Kalle Kasemaa stated in September 1989 that for the first time since the war there had been a rise in membership – by several thousand – of his church. The number of baptisms had tripled and there were now seventy theological students, as compared with forty in 1980. Several church newspapers had begun, including one for children (still illegal, according to the letter of the Soviet law). Some 40,000 copies of the Bible were in the process of being imported and a new translation of the New Testament was in the later stages of preparation. So good were relations with other churches that the institute had admitted both a Methodist and an Orthodox student.

Whatever the difficulties which the Estonian churches continue to face, it is clear that they are set to be the focus of lively new ideas and rapid action.

Latvia

In 1988–89 the church in Latvia also experienced unprecedented revival and a determination to use every new opportunity which the improved political situation offers. Although less reported than similar demonstrations in East Germany and Poland at the same time, an indication of the ferment was the turn-out of over half a million people on the streets of Riga, almost one-fifth of the total population of the country, to celebrate 'Independence Day' on 19 November 1989.

Latvia is the middle one of the three Baltic republics, being closer to Lithuania in its language, but to Estonia in its predominantly Lutheran tradition. There is, however, a large Roman Catholic enclave in the east (Latgalia) and the Orthodox and Baptists also have an important presence.

Religious ardour seems to have been absent from Latvia during this century. Before the war some 56 per cent (one million) of the population officially belonged to the Lutheran Church, a figure which dwindled to 350,000 by 1980, according to the church's own statistics, but some pastors there reckoned that the number of the truly committed was less than ten per cent of this. Worse, the church had acquired a poor image with Latvian patriots, due to its unfailing support of Soviet foreign policy.

The 'Rebirth and Renewal' movement started with a conflict – just the sort which the atheist authorities always used to win.[16] A bright young theological student was in trouble with the authorities for his energetic youth work and the local Council for Religious Affairs refused to sanction his ordination. This time the outcome was different. The year was 1985; there was a Lutheran bishop in Lithuania who was prepared to be bolder than his Latvian counterparts. The new young pastor, Maris Ludviks, could scarcely have imagined that his ordination would set in train a series of events leading to the deposition of an archbishop, the reopening of Riga Cathedral and a national revival of the church.

Under Stalin, Ludviks would have been shot, under Khrushchev or

Brezhnev imprisoned. Gorbachev came to power just in time. It was also a period of uncertainty in the Lutheran leadership, for Archbishop Matulis had just died and his successor, Eriks Mesters, though equally compliant to the Soviet authorities, had not yet been consecrated. It was this hiatus which had prompted Ludviks to approach Bishop Kalvanas in Lithuania. Archbishop Mesters sought to help him by agreeing to his appointment to a parish, but quickly caved in under pressure from the Council for Religious Affairs.

On 7 January 1987 the Latvian newspaper *Padomju jaunatne* ('Soviet Youth') mounted a scurrilous attack against him, calling him a black-marketeer and a work-shy parasite. Enter one of the two key figures in the events of the next three years, Modris Plate, pastor of Kuldiga and lecturer in the Riga theological seminary. He himself was still only in his early thirties. He led a group of five clergy in a visit to the editorial offices of the newspaper to protest and demand withdrawal of the calumny.

Inevitably, the only response was a switch in the focus of the attack to Plate himself. He was already on the unofficial blacklist of the Council for Religious Affairs, as under his leadership the number of church members had increased by fifty per cent above the original 300, and there had been a threefold increase in the number of communicants. He had instituted Bible courses for the laity, even teaching some New Testament Greek, and had introduced some liturgical reforms in holding 223 services in a year, more than any other parish in Latvia. His support for Ludviks provided just the pretext the authorities needed to dismiss him.

They could have done this directly, of course, by simply removing his registration, but Eduards Kokars-Trops, head of the Latvian Council for Religious Affairs, preferred the more damaging method of leaning on the Archbishop to carry this out, which the Consistory (governing body) did on 18 March 1987. A group of nineteen clergy signed a petition in Plate's defence, which stated:

> Try to imagine how we feel when, before our very eyes, we see one of the best clergymen in Latvia being punished and transferred elsewhere, so that all the activities which he initiated in the parish of Kuldiga are disrupted. His only fault is consistent and uncompromising service rendered to God and dedicated to the future of the Evangelical Lutheran Church in Latvia . . . Which of us will be the next victim?

Additionally, 350 of Pastor Plate's parishioners supported him and he continued to serve them, but on 5 May the Consistory confirmed the dismissal, without having discussed the petitions. Even then Pastor

Plate stayed on, and it was by this time a little more difficult for the Council for Religious Affairs to intervene by force, because the age of *perestroika* was beginning to dawn. Plate said he had received assurances of personal support from the Archbishop, who was nevertheless afraid to repeat them in public. At this point the more secular Latvian human rights group, Helsinki '86, publicly expressed its support, which clearly increased the nervousness of the Archbishop and the Consistory, who now felt they were becoming isolated from everyone. Under great pressure from active pastors, from the Council for Religious Affairs and increasingly from opinion abroad, the Consistory offered a compromise on 3 June: Plate could stay on in Kuldiga if he would 'calm down' his congregation and stop defending Ludviks. It was probably this unprincipled behaviour which discredited the Consistory and the Archbishop in the minds of many believers.

Pastor Plate's response was now not one of words but of deeds. He and fourteen other pastors, prominent among them being theological lecturers, announced the formation of a new group called 'Rebirth and Renewal', the aim of which would be to 'defend openly the right of Latvians to lead a Christian life'. In a declaration to the Consistory, they said that they wanted to engage with its members in discussion of a 'few points', including an alternative to military service, religious instruction for children, legal rights for the church, more religious literature, the establishment of radio and TV programmes and the right of believers to work in hospitals and old people's homes.[17]

Archbishop Mesters was so terrified at what he read, not least because of the clear links the group had with nationalist dissent, that he decided to act quickly, possibly not even waiting for instructions from the Council for Religious Affairs. To add to his dismissal from the parish, Modris Plate received an order banning him from the seminary, too, and Dr Roberts Akmentins was removed from the post of rector because he had signed a letter supporting Plate. Forty-five students and lecturers protested at this, which led to the suspension of all teaching. Yet still Plate continued to officiate at Kuldiga and when an appointee of the Consistory arrived to replace him the parish council gave him the unambiguous message that he was unacceptable. Even the denunciation of Plate in the press as a CIA agent rang hollow in the improved climate for believers of 1987. Maris Ludviks emigrated at the end of the year, but the focus had long since passed from a specific to a much more general protest.

Lutheran opinion outside the Soviet Union began to play an influential role. Dr Gunnar Staalsett, General Secretary of the

Lutheran World Federation (Geneva), visited Archbishop Mesters for a discussion, and the Archbishop had a rough ride from questioners when he visited West Germany and the USA, after which the Consistory yielded and reinstated Plate on 26 January 1988. Roberts Akmentins would be allowed to lecture once again, though without regaining his post of rector. This did not satisfy the students, who proclaimed a boycott. The Consistory, in an unprecedented challenge to the state's authority, appointed the Rev. Uldis Saveljevs as 'youth pastor' to the Latvian Lutheran Church. Not only was he a sympathiser with the Rebirth and Renewal movement, but this move took him well beyond the limitations of the law, which still categorically banned youth activities in the church.

During the course of 1989 there was a significant revival of the Latvian Sunday school movement, with an unprecedented call for their legalisation in what is still officially the atheist press. By mid-1989 a semi-official children's Christian magazine, *Zvaigznite* ('Little Star'), had begun to appear.

A young man still in his twenties and who had completed his theological education as recently as 1983, Juris Rubenis, now stepped on to the centre of the stage. He had signed the original petition in support of Modris Plate. When I met him in Riga in February 1989 I found him outgoing, but with a gentleness which gave little hint of the steel will beneath the mild exterior of a devoted family man. I asked him about a great event of four months earlier, the first service in the great Lutheran Cathedral of Riga for thirty years. He replied:

> I was sitting at my desk one day when the idea came to me that we should ask permission to hold a service there. We could scarcely hope for success, because its conversion in 1959 into a concert hall stood as a symbol of the triumph of communism over religion. However, the Popular Front took up my proposal and, miraculously, we held a service at which Modris Plate and I officiated, but we were told it was just a one-off event. People packed out the church and spilled out across the square outside, but there were loudspeakers and those who did not come were able to watch on TV or listen in on the radio, the first such transmission since the war. Of course our people now demanded regular services; after protracted arguments the authorities agreed last month and now from Easter Sunday (26 March) there will be regular services, with a reconsecration of the altar.[18]

The large Orthodox community in Riga has also been promised the return of its cathedral, but this huge building is in need of massive restoration before it will again be suitable for worship.

Later Pastor Rubenis said that the TV transmission 'led to a kind of seismic disturbance in people . . . On that day a great many people reconsidered all that they had built up against faith in God.'[19]

The church authorities were quite amenable to sharing the building with the concert promoters. With the gift of a fine set of reversible pews from the Dutch churches, both uses were possible. Concerts take place in front of the organ at the back. When the focus is in that direction, the pressure of one hand is enough to lever the back of the seat forward, with the wooden seat itself remaining fixed to the floor. Transformation of the whole building to face the altar again for worship takes only a few moments.

Pastor Rubenis lives with his wife and three children in a suburb of Riga. He used to travel to a parish at Liepaja, 200 kilometres away, to take regular services. He has received insistent requests to take charge of the cathedral, not to mention to stand as a candidate in the new democratic elections. In addition, he has co-founded a new theological journal, *Cels* ('The Way'). There is now also a Christian weekly newspaper. Rubenis is actively involved in television, where he has many friends – which I experienced myself when he took me along to record an interview and the reception was one of warmth and enthusiasm. He became vice-rector of the seminary after the reinstatement of Pastor Akmentins and travels regularly to the USA to encourage financial support from the Latvian émigré community.

One point emerged in our conversation which could turn out to have more long-term significance even than the return of the cathedral. The Latvian Lutheran Church, under the influence of the outstanding young men whom we have mentioned, became the first in Soviet history to demonstrate that it could vote out compromised leaders and vote in those whom the faithful trusted. This will certainly have been noted by all other Soviet church leaders, aware now that they are accountable for their actions more to their fellow-believers than to the state. Pastor Rubenis primed me what to look out for in April, when there would be an election of a new Consistory, but I do not have the feeling that even he expected events to be as dramatic or decisive as they turned out to be.

Formerly only thirty per cent of the clergy, a hand-picked minority, were allowed to participate in the election of pastors to senior office. In his Christmas message of 1988 Archbishop Mesters promised that all would be able to vote in the election of a new Consistory. This was not enough to save him from being voted out on 11 April, together with the whole Consistory. Into their place came the key figures of Rubenis

and Plate, together with six others who had been active in the Rebirth
and Renewal movement. The effective work between meetings would
be done by an inner council of three people, of whom Rubenis is one.
Roberts Akmentins would resume his role as rector of the seminary,
with Rubenis as his deputy.

In the sight of the world at large, the deposing of Archbishop
Mesters was the most dramatic event. For the ninety-five members
of the synod his change of heart had clearly been too little and too
late. His replacement was to be Archbishop Karlis Gailitis, a man
of only fifty-three at his election, who is a member of the Latvian
National Independence Movement, which, as the name suggests, is
much more openly engaged in a political struggle for independence
than the Popular Front, to which Rubenis and Plate belong.

After a heated debate, the synod itself endorsed the readoption of
the old 1928 church constitution, which naturally reflected all the
conditions of a free society. It went further. It passed a resolution
on 'Justice and Freedom' which supported the political movements in
their aim of 'annulling the Molotov–Ribbentrop Pact and [supporting]
the self-determination and independence of Latvia'.

At its first meeting after the election (mid-July), the Consistory
made a statement which, remarkably, an official secular newspaper
published:

> [We denounce] the arrogant and heartless policies on the ecological,
> economic and spiritual state of Latvia . . . Only in an independent
> Latvian state, free from the dictates of any imperial centre, will our
> people be able to realise fully either its national values or the universal
> values given to us by the Christian faith.[20]

Up to the time of writing, there has been no Kremlin reaction
to this astonishing departure, through which a church which had
seemed moribund as recently as five years ago is now leading its
nation and bids fair to play a role in international Christian relations.
Archbishop Gailitis has spoken out in a statesmanlike way and pointed
out to the World Council of Churches, for example, that its own policy
had been to align the struggle for peace and justice in the world: it
needed now to turn special attention towards the second concept.[21]
He also noted the progress away from atheism at home, with many
head teachers having called in clergy to inaugurate the new school
year with prayer. I myself received a telephone call in October relaying
an invitation from a Latvian collective farm to come and give lectures
to the pupils in its school – a school where I had met the teachers in
February 1989.

On 3 September the consecration of Archbishop Gailitis took place in the resplendent setting of Riga Cathedral in front of a crowd of foreign guests. Archbishop Wekstrom of Sweden officiated and the Bishop of Gibraltar, John Satterthwaite, represented the Archbishop of Canterbury. A Latvian nationalist has now taken his place among world Protestant leaders and he seems destined to play an international role far different from other clergy from the Soviet Union who have followed a conventional political line.

In each Baltic state, in a very different way, the church is now playing a vital role. As these countries seek to implement their expressed intention to achieve independence, the responsible leadership they are exercising promises well for the future of these societies. Excessive allegiance to a nationalist cause is a danger for Christianity, but the leadership seems aware of such a pitfall. As the Soviet Union becomes destabilised, the church will be more often called upon to mediate rather than to incite, but never again can it play the subservient role it did under Stalin.

8 Ukrainian Catholics: Tragedy to Triumph

Background

Violence breeds violence. Everywhere he turns, Mr Gorbachev sees the legacy of Stalin's brutal policies. In many republics on the periphery of the Soviet Union his problem is not only that nationalities too large to call minorities are sick of decades of Russian-Soviet imperial domination; there are also many true minorities within them who feel doubly threatened, both by communism and the larger ethnic group surrounding them. The relaxing of central and local police control has had the effect of rapidly bringing these tensions to the surface. Stalin, both in the Soviet Union and in many other parts of Eastern Europe, deliberately drew borders in the wrong places, so as to be able to play off an enclave of one minority against its neighbours. Probably only the great and idealistic goal of a truly united Europe (from Portugal to Vladivostok, not the Urals!) could fully undo the mischief of Tsarist expansionism, made a hundred times worse by Lenin's reconquest of the empire and then Stalin's malice at Yalta.

Of all the disadvantaged groups, the Ukrainians rank among the worst off. They are a nation with a complex history, now one of the largest in Europe (52 million people), yet one which has never managed to establish independence for long enough to secure its identity within the world community of nations. This incenses those millions who have come, through a combination of factors, to feel increasingly distinct from the Russian people. They have their own language, written in the Cyrillic alphabet, close to Russian, but quite separate from it.

In this chapter we shall, in the main, use the Ukrainian form of proper names, except where English usage more or less demands that the Russian should be used (thus we write 'Kiev', the Russian form, but 'Lviv', the Russian for which is 'Lvov').

Fearing that the Ukrainians were the biggest threat to his sovietisation policy, Stalin set out on a path of systematic genocide in the 1930s, the aim of which was to break every institution, political, cultural or religious, which could in any way be identified with Ukraine as a separate entity. The devastation of the richest agricultural areas on Soviet soil ensured that those who could not be beaten into submission were starved into it. The death toll ran into millions.[1]

Having achieved this goal, Stalin found himself in 1945 the possessor of a 'second' and unsubjugated Ukraine. This area itself subdivides into what for convenience we will call 'Western Ukraine', with Lviv as its capital, bordering on Poland, and 'Transcarpathia', east of Hungary. Both of these areas first came under Soviet domination in 1939 as a direct result of the Molotov–Ribbentrop Pact. Although they had been under Polish rule since the sixteenth century, they had been the setting for a nationalism of growing intensity, for which the Catholic Church had provided a special focus. Here are pages of European history virtually unknown, except to the specialist, and it is impossible now to do more than indicate some of the boldest outlines.

It is incorrect to call this a 'Roman' Catholic Church. It belongs to that branch of Catholicism which is designated 'Eastern Rite'. Formerly its adherents were known as 'Uniates', and the name 'Greek Catholic' is also in use.

'Uniate' refers to the Union of Brest of 1595–96, an early ecumenical initiative which has perpetuated the very rivalries which it was designed to avoid. For two centuries the Eastern Church, with its centre in Constantinople, had become progressively weaker and unable to withstand the advance of Catholicism. The defenders of the Orthodox Church on its western extremity concluded an agreement with Rome to set up what one might in another context call a 'buffer state' – the local church would keep its essential traditions of liturgy in Church Slavonic and ecclesiastical practices, such as married parish clergy (though bishops, as in the Orthodox Church today, were celibate), whilst accepting the supremacy of Rome. The Metropolitan of Kiev concluded this agreement, but Transcarpathia followed in 1646.

No settled state evolved out of this policy. The next three centuries saw these lands divided and redivided, with political and ecclesiastical rivalries dying down only for a year or two at a time. While it is true to say that some of these believers remained Orthodox in their hearts, with no more than a notional allegiance to Rome, it is also of utmost importance for understanding the events of the Soviet period to know that in the nineteenth century the 'Greek-Catholic Church' in the Austro-Hungarian Empire became the focus of emergent Ukrainian nationalism. In the twentieth century the great Andrei Sheptytsky, Metropolitan of Galicia 1900–44, carried this forward, with most of his flock finding themselves on Slovak (Eastern Czechoslovakian) and Polish territory.

This sets the scene for one of Stalin's most grotesque acts. Not without reason, he feared that the Eastern-Rite Catholics in the new territories would provide the focus for that very Ukrainian nationalism which he had expended so much blood to eliminate in the previous decade. Kiev and lands further east, it must be said, had to some extent become Russianised in the tsarist period, whereas Ukrainians in the west now nurtured a much more intensive nationalism.

Stalin acted swiftly and dramatically to carry out in a year the political subjugation which it had taken him a decade to accomplish in the east. There was no other area within the new borders of the Soviet Union, except possibly Lithuania, with such an intense adherence to the Christian faith. The plan was to destroy Ukrainian nationalism not by removing one of the main foci, the church, but by terrorising it into allegiance to Moscow. The idea was Stalin's alone, but he with utmost cunning persuaded – by what means we do not know – the Patriarch of Moscow and his senior hierarchs to become accomplices. There always was a strong tendency towards Russian nationalism within the Orthodox Church and so there were some, at least, who saw this as an opportunity of expanding its influence.

Even before the end of the war in Europe the arrests of senior Eastern-Rite clergy began, starting with Metropolitan Iosyf Slipyi, who had just succeeded Metropolitan Sheptytsky. It was easier to bring married clergy than celibate into submission through threats against wives and children; the bishops remained firm under torture and refused to renounce their allegiance to Rome.

However, the state organs managed to find two priests ready to be converted and they were hastily ordained as *Orthodox* bishops in Kiev. On 8 March 1946 a 'Reunion *sobor*' convened virtually at gunpoint in St George's Cathedral in Lviv, under the chairmanship of another renegade, Fr Gavriil Kostelnyk. There were 216 intimidated delegates present, but they received no agenda, rules or draft resolutions in advance. The first the general public knew about the move was the announcement of the key decision, which to this day remains one of the most irregular in ecclesiastical history. A *sobor* supposedly of the Greek-Catholic Church claimed canonicity under *Orthodox* canon law through the alleged prior conversion of all its members to that faith.

Those clergy and parishes in the area which subsequently refused to transfer their allegiance to Moscow joined Metropolitan Slipyi to face decades of imprisonment.

The Revival of Nationalism

The suppression of the Eastern-Rite Catholic Church was accompanied by a violent campaign against all other manifestations of Ukrainian nationalism. Any open expression of it would lead to direct confrontation with the security organs and a punishment of up to twenty-five years in prison. Therefore the Ukrainian ideal went to ground and remained out of sight of the world for twenty years.

Ukrainians outside the Soviet Union were strong in Canada, the USA and Australia and there was a sizeable community in Britain. They became a vocal force proclaiming the rights of their people, but public opinion, quite out of touch with the hidden realities of the Soviet Union, regarded them as hopeless reactionaries, people whom history had left behind. Now, as is evident for all to see, it is they who nurtured the secret of the future.

They would not, of course, have been able to do so, were it not for the almost superhuman bravery and determination of their fellows in Ukraine itself and scattered in exile around various parts of the Soviet Union. Indeed, perhaps it was primarily in the prisons where these ideals survived.

Gerald Brooke, a close friend, with whom I shared the first-ever exchange year for British students in the Soviet Union, told me long ago that something was going on in Soviet prisons, about which the world outside knew nothing. He himself is a heroic, though modest, figure, a man who suffered five years in a labour camp in the second half of the 1960s for having done nothing other than actively support the democratic rights of the people he loved. While undergoing those years of deprivation he was at one point greatly encouraged spiritually and emotionally by sharing his cell with a wonderful old man, Dr Volodymir Horbovyi, a Ukrainian nationalist incarcerated in Vorkuta prison for many years for opposing Soviet policy openly.

Bishop Pavlo Vasylyk, too, kept his faith and ideals alive in prison at the same time, becoming secretly ordained there and eventually, in 1974, being consecrated bishop at a time when the world at large, even the Vatican, failed even to acknowledge the existence of the Ukrainian Catholic Church (the name which has become most common in recent years and which we shall use from now on).

Yet while these men were still in prison, others outside were brave enough to signal their allegiance openly. In 1968, along with the first tentative emergence elsewhere in the Soviet Union of what was to become a human rights movement, 139 Ukrainian intellectuals protested in a letter to the Kremlin against the violation of their rights. Such documents immediately set the alarm bells ringing again. Moscow removed the moderate Ukrainian leader, Petro Shelest, in 1972, replacing him by the formidable Volodymir Shcherbitsky, whose sole task, it seemed, was to use strong-arm tactics to suppress dissent. He retained power until September 1989, one of the last representatives in high places of the pre-*perestroika* mould of thought.

Under his aegis a new round of savage sentences began and the Ukrainian movement had to go underground once again. Such pressure was exerted on some that they were forced, following another common KGB tactic, to make a public recantation of their activities. Such a man was Boris Kharchuk, a 'new Soviet man' who had been only ten years old when the Germans invaded his country. He had signed the *Letter of the 139* and then renounced his patriotic allegiance. Yet when he died in 1988 he left among his unpublished papers an indictment of Soviet nationalities policies: 'Ukraine has been proclaimed a sovereign republic, but in practice everything is done to make this a fiction, to make the very nation a fiction.' At the end of 1988 the Ukrainian literary journal *Prapor* published this essay posthumously.[2]

Iosyp Terelya is one of those heroic figures who was prepared to sacrifice his life for his beliefs and his loyalty to his nation. He is a layman who openly proclaimed allegiance to the Ukrainian Catholic Church at a time when it was highly dangerous to do so and when the propaganda was that it did not even exist. Born in Transcarpathia in 1943 of communist parents, Terelya became a Ukrainian Catholic believer under the influence of his grandmother. His first arrest, on a falsified criminal charge, was in 1962. Later persecuted for his religious activities, he was sentenced to seven years in labour camp, charged in 1969 with anti-Soviet agitation and propaganda. In 1972 he was sent to the Serbsky Institute of Forensic Psychiatry for investigation and committed to the Sechkova special psychiatric hospital. In 1976 he was released but suffered continued harassment from the authorities. Unable to get a job, he was subjected to a further term in labour camp for 'parasitism'. In September 1982 he was the co-founder (with Fr Hryhori Budzinsky and three others) of the Action Group for the Defence of the Rights of Believers and the

Church, set up to campaign for legalisation of the Ukrainian Catholic Church and for equality with all other groups in the Soviet Union. After renouncing his citizenship in May 1984, Terelya was forced to go underground to escape the growing campaign against him by the authorities. He was arrested again in February 1985, tried for anti-Soviet agitation and propaganda and sentenced to seven years' strict regime labour camp and five years' exile. Terelya was one of those sentenced under Article 70 who benefited from one of the two prisoner amnesties in 1987: he was released in February and finally emigrated from the Soviet Union on 18 September 1987, after spending more than twenty years in Soviet prisons, labour camps and psychiatric hospitals because of his beliefs. Now resident in Canada, he has continued his vigorous defence of the Ukrainian Catholic Church.

A man of equal toughness who is still in the Soviet Union is another layman, Stepan Khmara, a dentist by profession, who sacrificed not only his career but also his liberty to join Terelya in the struggle. He was arrested in 1980 and charged with anti-Soviet agitation and propaganda for editing the Ukrainian *samizdat* journal *Ukrainsky visnik*. He was released under amnesty in 1987 after serving seven years in the notorious Perm 36 labour camp and immediately launched himself into the growing campaign for the legalisation of the Ukrainian Catholic Church.

When I met him in Kiev in June 1988 I was impressed by his utter determination and single-mindedness. Short of physical elimination, the KGB, one imagines, could never silence him or break his will. This was the time of the Millennium celebrations and he naturally felt that Moscow had usurped what should have been Kiev's glory. More important to him, however, was to impress upon me the unconditional inadmissibility of the Russian Orthodox Church's having any say in the future of the Ukrainian Catholic Church. He and his committee would not acknowledge the legitimacy of any discussion in which the Russian leadership played a role, either with or without the participation of the Vatican.

The Ukrainian Catholic Action Group

After the departure of Terelya for the USA in 1987 Ivan Hel, another man who had spent many years of his life – seventeen in all – in Soviet prisons, came to the forefront as the principal spokesman inside the country for the Ukrainian Catholic Church. His emergence more or less coincided with the beginning of *glasnost* for the church, so his name achieved considerable prominence. He has given numerous interviews to the press and TV crews have filmed him on a number of occasions. I met him, other members of his committee and several 'underground' priests and bishops in Moscow in June 1988, just before I met Stepan Khmara in Kiev.

Alongside what now became the highly-organised and vocal work of the Action Group, parallel and more secular movements emerged. 'Memorial' was dedicated to the elimination of the Stalinist heritage in Ukraine (it had branches in other republics also) as was 'Rukh', in full, 'Popular Ukrainian Restructuring Movement'. Rukh meant simply 'movement' and was therefore identical in name and in its ideal of unifying various nationalist trends to Sajudis in Lithuania. This infuriated Volodymir Shcherbytsky, who launched a final unsuccessful attack on Rukh before Mr Gorbachev relieved him of office on 28 September 1989. His fall was one of the key factors in the acceleration towards the legalisation of the Ukrainian Catholic Church.

At the beginning of the *perestroika* period, the Ukrainian Catholic Church faced the combined might of the central anti-religious policy of the Soviet authorities, exercised through the Council for Religious Affairs, local Ukrainian anti-nationalist policy and the Russian Orthodox Church, both national and local. As *perestroika* progressed, it became increasingly obvious that ranged against this policy was something far more substantial than a group of dare-devil leaders backed by vocal Ukrainian émigrés. For many years informed commentators on Ukraine had been saying that in the region of Lviv and Transcarpathia was a church which still, after decades of suppression, numbered four or five million adherents, not only by far the largest illegal religious body in the Soviet Union, but also in the world. It was obvious that the general emergence of freedom of expression under *glasnost* would affect Western Ukraine in a major way. And so it has proved, with the church once again in the forefront, as so often in those places where communism was until recently in power. In addition, the public support now coming from Pope John Paul II, which had been so muted as to be almost absent while Pope Paul VI's *Ostpolitik* was dominant, played a decisive role, not least when Ukrainians observed the effect he had had on Poland, with his first visit back there as Pope leading directly to the founding of Solidarity.

The mass of Ukrainian Catholic faithful needed leadership and example. For forty years the only choice had been between abandoning their faith and accepting the ministry of the Russian Orthodox

Church. In a sense they were more privileged than Christians in other areas of the Soviet Union, because one legacy of Polish rule in the inter-war years was a far greater number of churches open proportional to population than anywhere else. No less than two-thirds of all Russian Orthodox Church buildings open in the whole country were in Ukraine, with an accompanying preponderance of vocations, which some believe to be as high as seventy per cent of all theological students. The system clearly intended to use the Orthodox Church as a 'russianising' influence, as no theological seminary was permitted in Western Ukraine to take account of these vocations.

How far the average church-goer in Lviv or Ternopil retained loyalty in his heart to Rome while continuing to attend Russian Orthodox services is questionable. What is certain is that as soon as a defined Ukrainian Catholic leadership came out into the open, huge numbers of people were ready to follow it. Clandestine publications such as Terelya's *Ukrainian Catholic Herald* undoubtedly played their role. Without them the movement for legalisation would have had no focus, but it was always difficult for the average believer to acquire such literature. More influential was personal example, and in particular the bravery, of the first priests who were willing publicly to leave the Orthodox Church and join the Ukrainian Catholic Church. Another unofficial publication, *The Chronicle of the Ukrainian Catholic Church*, devoted nearly the whole of its eighty-three pages in the spring of 1987 to a biography of Fr Mykhailo Havryliv, a priest of only thirty-eight, born after the liquidation of the church which he had now decided to join.

From this time on, information about the growing activity of the Ukrainian Catholic Church began to come in abundance. In August 1987 Bishops Ivan Semedi of Transcarpathia and Pavlo Vasylyk of Ivano-Frankivsk announced their emergence from the underground and stated that they would from now on act openly as bishops of the Ukrainian Catholic Church. A key moment occurred a month later, when the Synod of Ukrainian Catholic Bishops (in exile) in Rome announced that the head of the Church was now Bishop (later Metropolitan) Volodymyr Sterniuk, then eighty years old and living in a small room in Lviv. He had never yielded to the Soviet authorities and had been secretly consecrated bishop eleven years earlier. The Synod made it known that there were now seven other bishops, besides the three whose names were now public.

This stimulated the growing feeling of self-confidence in Ukraine and encouraged people to come out on to the streets in their thousands. If it was impossible to celebrate the liturgy in church buildings, then this would happen in the open air. Public processions became a weekly event in many places and their visibility in town centres, as they gathered in the open spaces outside the great churches not available to them, persuaded yet more people to join the movement. The leadership began to reinforce its case by frequent appeals to world public opinion and by sending delegations to the Council for Religious Affairs in Moscow and to other Soviet officials.

At a time when the open and physical repression of religion seemed to have ceased in other areas of the Soviet Union, there were many reports of continuing harassment of believers in Ukraine. There were interrogations of the organisers of processions, leading to fines of usually a week's salary (50 roubles) for each offence, sometimes accompanied by detention without trial for two weeks (a common practice permissible under the Soviet legal system). This might be explained by the pervasive influence of Shcherbytsky and the provocation – as it seemed to the authorities – of the public and illegal events, though one must stress their essentially peaceful nature and point out that Ukrainians in general have shown much restraint during decades of oppression.

Having said all this, one notes that the attacks of the KGB against Ukrainian believers from 1986 were far less violent than they had been earlier and there were no major trials of those who the authorities considered were breaking the law.

Reaction of the Russian Orthodox Church

The invective which the Moscow Patriarchate has systematically directed against the residue of the Ukrainian Catholic Church since 1946, which intensified every decade to mark the anniversary of the Synod of Lviv, would fill many sorry pages of the church history of our century. By the twentieth anniversary in 1966 a softer approach should have emerged, given that the Russian Orthodox Church itself was now undergoing yet another period of persecution under Khrushchev. However, it was not to be and these old attitudes were to persist for another two decades. Even in 1986 the tone was not only anti-ecumenical but unpleasantly self-justificatory and falsehoods appear as truths in the mouths of the hierarchy. The prime spokesman against the Ukrainian Catholic Church has in recent years been Metropolitan Filaret (Denisenko) of Kiev, who has taken on the role of proclaiming the Russianness of all things Orthodox in his Ukrainian homeland.

In May 1986 he stated in *Izvestia* that 'Greek Catholics live in unity of faith and spirit with the Russian Orthodox Church . . . benefiting from the freedom of religion which is characteristic of our whole country.'[3]

Referring back to the original events of the sixteenth century, Makari, the Russian Orthodox Archbishop of Ivano-Frankivsk (one of the key episcopal seats in the Western Ukrainian heartland), said at the same time: 'Our believers recall the Church Union as dark days in history, as an insult which can be neither pardoned nor forgotten. The return of the Union is out of the question.'[4]

The Journal of the Moscow Patriarchate celebrated the anniversary in many 'academic' pages, the scholarship of which we may judge from this extract from a speech by Metropolitan Nikodim of Lviv and Ternopil, another church leader in a difficult diocese:

> By uniting with the Russian Orthodox Church in 1946, the believers of the western regions of Ukraine proved the depth of their faith, their true maturity and showed they had moved from slavery to become masters in their own house and in their homeland and had set out on the path of their fathers and forefathers, from which they would never deviate.[5]

This tone persisted through the Millennium celebrations of 1988, where there were several sharp and unpleasant attacks on the Ukrainian Catholic Church during the closed sessions of the *sobor*, and right into 1989, when there was even a hardening of attitudes. It perhaps does not become us to speculate whether such words derive from ignorance, malice, fear or uncontrite shame at the deeds of the past, but we cannot gloss over the kind of statement that was being made at the very time when legalisation of the Ukrainian Catholic Church began to look inevitable. Metropolitan Filaret of Kiev said in June 1989 (the English text is original, as printed in a Soviet publication):

> In the 20th century the Uniate Church disgraced itself by collaboration with Nazis and whipping up ethnic strife. It was doomed by history . . . As to the Lvov Council, it fully conformed with the Orthodox canon law . . . both in form and the content of its resolutions . . . There are many Catholic churches in the Ukraine, no less than in other Soviet republics, and the parishioners are free to profess their faith . . . The self-styled Uniate zealots are out to set the church and the state against each other and make a rift between Orthodoxy and Catholicism . . . With its multiethnic clergy and flock, the Russian Orthodox Church is vitally interested in stronger unity within the Soviet nation . . . If – God forbid! – the Ukrainian Catholic Church acquires a legal status,

its zealots will brew a terrible strife and hinder the effort for beneficial change in Soviet life – to live in peace and concord.[6]

The 'collaboration' jibe is an old one, a standard confection of the KGB. Anyone wishing to counter it would probably begin by asking a question about Russian Orthodox collaboration with Stalin immediately afterwards. The Metropolitan's statement about the availability of Catholic churches in other republics is simply untrue. The tone of these remarks speaks for itself: nevertheless their content reflects a certain shift of ground from earlier pronouncements. Previously the Ukrainian Catholic Church did not exist (though why then expend so much energy celebrating its demise?). Now, by implication, it is strong enough to cause a major upset in Soviet policy.

When one looks at the unofficial reactions of Orthodox believers at the grass roots – those very people who had suffered imprisonment and vilification for their stand on religious liberty over the past twenty years – one finds precisely the opposite attitude to that prevailing among the hierarchy. The view, expressed with increasing frequency and conviction during the 1980s, is that the continued outlawing of the Ukrainian Catholic Church is not only a major blot on the Soviet human rights record, but that support of this aspect of Soviet policy and the church's implication in it is a cancer within the body of the Orthodox Church.

Fr Georgi Edelstein, already known in Moscow for his support of human rights, wrote an impassioned defence of the rights of the Ukrainian Catholic Church at the beginning of the year of the Millennium in the new independent journal *Referendum*.[7] The Leningrad layman Vladimir Poresh, veteran of the prison camps for his work with Alexander Ogorodnikov's 'Christian Seminar', addressed a letter to Patriarch Pimen on 29 April 1988 (as it happened, the very day on which Gorbachev received Pimen, but there is no record that the subject received any mention on that occasion). Poresh wrote:

Will the Russian Orthodox Church deny these thousands of Ukrainians their freedom of conscience, their right to decide their faith for themselves, when according to the law twenty people are enough to form a congregation? Or do you consider that there are not twenty Greek Catholics in Ukraine? The Greek-Catholic Church has existed now for decades in the catacombs. Many of its children have perished in the camps and prisons. They are defending their faith just as Russian clergy and laity were doing until not so long ago . . . Stalin wanted to settle this question by just this method of liquidating people, and it was not his fault that he failed. It is a terrible and insupportable thought for me that the Russian Church might come out on the side of the persecutors.[8]

Alexander Ogorodnikov himself took up this argument at the seminar which he organised to coincide with the Millennium celebrations in Moscow. The whole group took up the call for legalisation and offered hospitality to the delegation from the Ukrainian Catholic Church which was trying, with eventual success, to meet Cardinal Willebrands and other Vatican representatives in Moscow for the main event. It was here that I met Bishops Kurchaba and Vasylyk, Fr Havryliv and Ivan Hel.

When Frs Georgi Edelstein and Gleb Yakunin were able to leave the Soviet Union in June 1989 for their first visit to the West, they began in Rome. It was an impressive moment when these men of such spiritual authority in their own church spoke there in defence of the rights of Ukrainian Catholics. When Academician Andrei Sakharov visited Italy on the one occasion he was able to travel there before his death, he added his respected voice in support of the same cause. On 6 February 1989 Sakharov called on Cardinal Lubachivsky immediately after his audience with the Pope. One of his most solemn public pronouncements in the last six months of his life, from an open air platform in Moscow, was to call the continual repression of the Ukrainian Catholic Church 'absolutely inadmissible'.[9]

The Millennium

The celebrations of June 1988 came at a transitional period in Soviet church policy. The key decisions, however, such as making Moscow the prime focus and therefore emphasising the role of the Russian Orthodox Church in unifying the Slav nationalities of the Soviet Union, were obviously taken some time beforehand, though by the time of the event itself, Kiev received some concessions which would have been unexpected earlier. It would have been entirely correct and logical to have organised all the main events in Kiev, the city where the baptism of St Vladimir took place, with Moscow one of the subsidiary places to be visited by foreign church leaders immediately afterwards. Instead, the reverse was true and Kiev became one of three main centres which these visitors could choose after Moscow.

While the main events in St Vladimir's Cathedral were closed to all except invited guests, to the disappointment of local believers, there were more accessible open air events. An atmosphere of joy prevailed in the Pecherskaya Lavra, the Monastery of the Caves, a foundation going back to the very earliest days of Kievan Christianity. Its monks had been banished in 1961 and in a dramatic gesture prior to the celebrations the Soviet authorities had announced the return of part of the monastery complex to the Russian Orthodox Church. I had been one of the last visitors to the monastery before the expulsion of its monks nearly three decades earlier, so it was an especially moving experience to be one of the first to see at least a small part of it again in the hands of the monks.

One incident will remain deeply etched in my memory. St Vladimir's Cathedral is a building of the nineteenth century, whereas the holy shrine of St Sophia's Cathedral, with its apsidal mosaic of the Praying Virgin, is the city's most direct link with Constantinople. It has been in a 'museum of architecture' since the early days of Soviet power. During my visit to it, crowds of pilgrims were visiting it in an attitude of quiet reverence. Then softly, almost imperceptibly, an Orthodox chant broke out – a foreign choir from Canada, as it transpired, but filling the whole space with a timeless awe.

Few foreign visitors reached Western Ukraine during this time, but many towns and villages witnessed 'clandestine' celebrations of the mass according to the Eastern Rite in their central squares to offset the Orthodox ones which took place inside the churches.

From this time a new policy began to emerge. The Russian Orthodox Church leadership started to proclaim the reopening of churches, something long overdue in the wake of the massive closures of the Khrushchev period. On examination of the evidence, however, it became apparent that the majority of these were in Ukraine, where already there was a higher proportion of Orthodox churches open compared with population than anywhere else in the USSR. In view of subsequent events, this can only have been a signal that the church (after an indication from the state?) was preparing itself for the loss of other churches, which would follow the legalisation of the Ukrainian Catholic Church. For example, Radio Kiev announced in English on 3 February 1989:

> Nearly 130 Orthodox churches were consecrated and almost fifty organi-
> sations of believers were registered in Ukraine last year. Upon the
> requests of believers, most of the new Orthodox churches were opened
> in western regions of Ukraine, where some time ago the Uniate Church
> was very influential.[10]

There seems to have been especial urgency in those areas where the Ukrainian Catholic Church was clearly gaining the upper hand in the local struggle to reclaim its rights. Suddenly it became easier for any group of twenty Orthodox parishioners to find ready collaboration from the local representatives of the Council for Religious Affairs in reopening a church.

The most curious aspect of this development is that in the areas where churches are sometimes hundreds of miles apart, such as Siberia, towns and villages with no provision for worship whatsoever are still deprived several years into the *perestroika* process. It is sad that local believers have been drawn into an ecclesiastical dispute not of their making. If political and nationalistic considerations had not been so dominant in their thinking, church leaders would have guided believers in a more positive way. However, the fact that they did not stimulated the spiritual renewal of the Ukrainian Catholic Church during these difficult days.

The Soviet Press

The change of heart, or perhaps one should say failure of nerve, on the part of the Soviet authorities towards the question of legalising the Ukrainian Catholic Church is reflected only dimly in what we can gather from the policy pronouncements of officialdom.

It is not true to say – as some do – that the Ukrainian Catholic Church was the only major denomination banned by law in the USSR. Even a cursory reading of Stalin's legislation of 1929 or of subsequent single decrees indicates that all laws apply to all religions and it is expressly stated that they are all equal before the law. There never has been a roster of banned denominations, though the official list of banned activities is lengthy and comprehensive. Therefore officials such as Fyodor Burlatsky, the Soviet Government's main spokesman on human rights issues, were putting forward a spurious argument when they began to say in 1989, 'Let us wait for the new legislation and include the Ukrainian Catholics in it.' As subsequent developments would soon show, one cannot lift a ban which has never been officially imposed. Instead, the argument should have been over the certain fact that unpublished and therefore illegal administrative orders have always existed and religion suffers heavily from these, the Ukrainian Catholic Church most of all. Therefore what was needed from the first was the correcting of an illegality, not the promulgation of a new law. Again, for Soviet officials to claim, as they often did for propaganda purposes abroad, that this was an 'internal matter for the churches' was disingenuous, to say the least.

We have already raised the question of how far a change of heart on the Ukrainian Catholic issue, leading to collusion between the hierarchy of the Russian Orthodox Church and the Central Committee, was the cause of the downfall of Konstantin Kharchev. There is some evidence of a policy shift in official pronouncements; it is from the Soviet media that one can glean important information on the general change in attitude with a clarity appropriate to the period of *glasnost*.

In 1986 the media attitude was still universally negative. For example, a television programme was screened on 11 November 1986, repeating the claim that the pre-war Ukrainian Catholic Church had been an ally of German fascism; now its representatives abroad were 'shipping in ideological poison and contraband'.[11] A year later Kiev radio was still characterising Iosyp Terelya as a common criminal.[12]

However, already the new unofficial journals which were beginning to proliferate were providing space for atheists to call for the restitution of the rights of the Ukrainian Catholic Church. Vitali Shevchenko, an apprentice from Kiev, wrote in this vein to *Izvestia*, but when they refused to publish his letter he sent it to *Glasnost*, by then a leading alternative voice, which printed it in November 1987.

By the end of the year there were already the first signs in the Soviet press of a change in attitude. *Moscow News* printed a commentary on the dialogue which had just taken place in Rome between the Vatican and a delegation from the Russian Orthodox Church, still repeating old accusations, but at least showing that there were two sides to the question and that the Vatican, at least, supported the Ukrainian Catholic Church.[13]

The next month, December, *Nauka i religia* ('Science and Religion', the atheist monthly) admitted that there was now massive support for the Christian faith in the Western Ukraine, though it did not directly raise the Ukrainian Catholic issue: 'In our region about 35–40% of the population are believers and some villages have a solid adherence . . . with overall about 70% of workers being believers.'[14]

This amazing admission, unique in the Soviet press at the time, sets the scene for the Christian demonstrations on the street which were to erupt the next year. These seem to have shocked the press into silence, for there were very few reports on the Ukrainian Catholic Church in 1988.

Mykola Kolesnik, head of the Ukrainian section of the Council for Religious Affairs, claimed early in 1989 that the Ukrainian Catholic Church was losing support. Referring to the mail pouring into his office, he claimed: 'In hundreds of statements, signed by tens of thousands of citizens living in the regions indicated, there is a request to register specifically an Orthodox society, and not that of some other religion.'[15]

The following June, however, the first crack appeared in the Soviet press, insignificantly tucked away in a corner of the central trade-union newspaper, *Trud*. In reply to a reader's enquiry about a Ukrainian Catholic demonstration on the Arbat in Moscow, the editorial response significantly referred to the 'self-liquidation' of the Ukrainian Catholic Church in inverted commas – a subtle but powerful signal – and went on to say that the question of its official status was under consideration.[16]

On 21 July *Pravda* indicated that the question of the Ukrainian Catholic Church had been raised at a conference of the Central Committee of the Communist Party, with negative results. But by this time *Moscow News* was keeping readers abreast of the developments in what was now a hunger strike on the Arbat. The newspaper gave space to Metropolitan Filaret of Kiev to adduce the old arguments, but underneath Sergei Filatov, a research associate at the Institute of the USA and Canada in Moscow, made an astonishing statement (in the wording of the English-language version of the publication):

> Western experts in religion believe that today Uniates have five bishops, hundreds of priests, two monastic orders, and put the number of Uniates at 2.5 to 4 million (3.5 million in 1943) . . . For many years it has been hoped that Uniates will return to Orthodoxy. It was widely believed that the Uniate Church owes its existence solely to the support of foreign governments. Life has shown that this was a delusion . . . I believe that if the Cathedral of St Yura [that is St George] in Lviv remains in the hands of the Russian Orthodox Church, it will serve as a reminder of a humiliating, insulting 'gift'. I think that the St Yura Cathedral must be given to its real owners, and that the Russian Orthodox Church should claim the return of its ancient shrines in the Ukraine – the St Sofia Cathedral and other old churches of Kiev, the Chernigov Region, etc. If the St Yura Cathedral is returned to the Uniates, this will restore justice and will stand as evidence of the triumph of courage and spiritual strength over arbitrary rule.[17]

In August the same newspaper published a sympathetic interview with Archbishop Sterniuk and then in September *Ogonyok* brought the whole issue to the court of Soviet public opinion, as it were, the lead-in being the hunger strike on the Arbat. The organisers must have been overwhelmed at the success of their efforts and the Soviet public at large could now see what a determined effort by an unofficial group could achieve. Filaret and Kolesnik receive the space to put forward their 'unreconstructed' views, but this leads the author, Georgi Rozhnov, into a lengthy re-examination of the Lviv *sobor*. He points the finger at the NKVD as the guilty party in an act of terrorism against innocent people. Now that the church has emerged from the catacombs, there is only one way in which justice can be done – reinstatement – and as the state instigated the persecution, so it must play the leading role in the restitution of those rights lost forty-three years ago.[18]

Legalisation Becomes Inevitable

Probably from the moment that *Ogonyok* printed its article, bearing in mind its large circulation and enormous influence, the Soviet authorities had accepted that there was no viable alternative to legalisation of the Ukrainian Catholic Church. As it was by now known that the Pope would receive Mr Gorbachev in the late autumn, there was a general feeling that this event would provide the occasion for the formal lifting of the ban.

Transcarpathia, with Uzhhorod as its main city, now began to play an important role also. It is ethnically one of the most mixed areas of the Soviet Union, and the predominant language is Hungarian. The Eastern-Rite church has here strongly re-emerged in recent years, though they call themselves 'Greek Catholics' because they are not, in the main, ethnic Ukrainians. Their leader, who survived from before the liquidation of his church, is Bishop Ivan Semedi. When Western visitors called on him in the summer of 1989, they discovered that he did not even possess a cassock, but he was in good spirits and determined to play a role in what he believed would soon be the turning point for his church. In a curious way, because of the peculiarities of Soviet legislation, the church there had already achieved a kind of legalisation. Every Friday a group of the faithful would go to the town hall and register the open air service to be held on the coming Sunday. Obviously by this time local political tensions were less than they were in Western Ukraine. Religious tensions could not be avoided, however. When Cardinal Paskai of Hungary paid a notable first visit across the border in May 1989, he visited only the local Roman Catholic flock, though he did have a meeting with the auxiliary Greek-Catholic bishop, Iosyf Holovach. The one convent in the region contains both Orthodox and Greek-Catholic nuns, which typifies the problems that lie ahead. Perhaps they can set an example of how the two communities can learn to live together in peace.

The story of 1989 is one of gathering determination by different groups of people in various parts of Ukraine to regain their rights, though in a territory as vast as this one cannot talk of unity of purpose in the same way as the Lithuanians are demonstrating it. However, the gains have been considerable.

The elections to the Congress in Moscow at the end of March and beginning of April showed people, quite unexpectedly, that *perestroika* had gone so far that, while the system of choice of candidates was still gravely flawed, the vote count itself was not rigged and in certain instances a candidate 'of the people' was able to beat an official representative of the communist system.

The miners' strike in the summer began in Siberia, but Ukrainians in the key industrial area of the Donbass took it up in a specially organised way and won key concessions, though time has yet to tell whether they will be fully implemented.

The Ukrainian Catholics, being one of the most highly organised large groups in the Soviet Union, began to feel the tide was running in their direction as soon as individual priests began to cast off their Orthodox mantles and declare their allegiance to the Pope, whose election eleven years earlier had given them the first feeling that one day something might change.

Outside the Soviet Union observers at last began to see and understand an issue which had long been shrouded in mystery. When Mr Gorbachev visited London in April, it was one of the issues which the Foreign Office raised with him, following a very constructive meeting which William Waldegrave, the minister responsible for Eastern Europe, had had with Cardinal Lubachivsky. When the new human rights conference under the renewed Helsinki Agreement convened in Paris in June, the Ukrainian Catholic Church was one of the main issues regularly raised with the Soviets and some sections of the press picked this up with good reporting.

On several occasions the Ukrainian Catholic bishops visited Moscow in order to petition Mr Gorbachev and the Council for Religious Affairs. These efforts did not achieve any immediate and measurable results, but they were part of the process of attrition which would eventually show that a group bereft of temporal power could nevertheless breach the Kremlin's defences. Perhaps it was the Ukrainian Catholic demonstration on the Arbat with its successive hunger strikes which did more than anything else to impress Moscow. Certainly, this peaceable group of people which assembled on the city's most popular street on 19 May became one of the local sights for nearly five and a half months until they were eventually removed and escorted back to Ukraine by militia in mid-September. It began with about a dozen people, but gained numbers significantly as the faithful from various parts of the Western Ukraine heard about it and came to the capital to join in. There were always banners on display and sometimes the priests in the group would lead an open air liturgy. On 24 May Fr Petro Zeleniukh celebrated mass, while still being severely harassed by the KGB at home. About 200 Ukrainian Catholics were present, but local people attended, more than doubling this number. They formed a band which would move, as they did later that same day, to hold an act of worship outside the central Moskva Hotel, where delegates to the Congress of People's Deputies were staying. They also ensured that their presence was noticed by delegates to the first meeting of the Central Committee of the World Council of Churches to be held in Moscow, which took place in July.

At the same time, parishes in Western Ukraine were beginning to return to the Ukrainian Catholic Church in greater numbers. Metropolitan Sterniuk received Fr Mykhailo Nyzkohuz into the Ukrainian Catholic Church on 5 May and the congregation in his village of Stara Syl came over with him. A group of Party officials descended on the village, accompanied by no fewer than eighteen Russian Orthodox priests, in an effort to confiscate the church keys and expel Fr Nyzkohuz, but about 1,500 people formed a phalanx to keep out the intruders. The next day, 14 May, perhaps the biggest congregation ever seen assembled to participate in the liturgy which Fr Nyzkohuz celebrated.

In the larger cities people surprised even themselves by the vast numbers who turned out, encouraged by the fine summer weather. On 18 June, designated as an international day of prayer for the legalisation of the Ukrainian Catholic Church, about 100,000 people in Ivano-Frankivsk, more than a third of the total population of the town, came to an open air mass in support of the banned church. The police intervened, arresting Bishop Vasylyk and four priests who had planned to officiate, but a sixth clergyman appeared to take their place. The police charged him with disturbing public order, but the fifteen-day sentence he received without trial, the maximum punishment the authorities felt they could impose in the prevailing local conditions, seemed risible – and even so it misfired, because the faithful kept vigil outside the prison where he was serving his sentence, which doubtless attracted the attention of many more people.

By the end of August Ivan Hel, in an interview with Keston

College, was able to name fourteen towns and villages where the churches had reverted to the Catholic Church. On 17 September perhaps the greatest crowd ever seen in Lviv, estimated to be at least 150,000, came out on to the streets for a mass, followed by a protest march against the Molotov–Ribbentrop Pact, the fiftieth anniversary of which had fallen the previous month. There were rousing speeches (but not advocating violence) outside St George's Cathedral, the seat of Metropolitan Nikodim. The rally continued all day, and as darkness fell thousands of people kept their lights off, placing candles in their windows to commemorate the victims of Stalin. All of this is preserved on film and some highlights were shown on British television. David Alton, MP, and a BBC film crew were present, which probably ensured that this time the police did not intervene.

The Sunday before Mr Gorbachev met the Pope, 26 November, the people of Lviv and surrounding regions showed that they were not merely summer demonstrators, for on this occasion the numbers were up to 200,000, according to some observers. Here is a brief eye-witness account from a Western observer of what it was like in Lviv on any day during that period:

> Every evening there is an open-air Greek-Catholic service in Lviv, usually outside the closed Carmelite church (the location is convenient and the courtyard in front of the building can easily accommodate up to 20,000 standing worshippers). The esplanade down Lenin Prospect [from the Opera House to the Intourist – or St George – Hotel] has become a permanent centre of unofficial political gatherings and discussions, where the (theoretically illegal) Ukrainian national flags are always flying.[19]

Gorbachev and the Pope

As 1 December approached, the hierarchy of the Russian Orthodox Church clearly showed they were losing their self-confidence over the bitter issue of legalisation. In August Metropolitan Nikodim of Lviv addressed a letter to all the Orthodox bishops, with copies sent abroad, the tone of which one commentator has called 'hysterical'. In it he complained that the Ukrainian Catholics were persecuting the Orthodox, whereas comparatively recently he had been saying that they did not exist in Ukraine. This letter almost certainly contributed to his removal by the Holy Synod and assignment to Kharkiv. There must have been at least some at the top of the hierarchy who could see the damage that such men were doing and that the struggle was by now virtually lost. However, his successor, Archbishop Irinei, showed himself equally unable to cope with these fraught circumstances and would soon be embroiled in even deeper trouble, for it was he who was destined to preside over the dismemberment of the Russian Orthodox Church in Western Ukraine.

These events must have had some bearing on the resignation in November of the 'other' Filaret (Vakhromeyev), the Metropolitan of Minsk and Belorussia and head of the Foreign Department of the Russian Orthodox Church, known to have such a negative attitude to the Ukrainian question that he reportedly asked the Pope, when he met him in Rome in August, to recommend to all Ukrainian Catholics that they should join the Orthodox Church. His successor was Archbishop Kirill of Smolensk, already known to us as the possessor of perhaps the keenest mind among the Russian hierarchy. A man known for his advocacy of stronger links with Rome, he was therefore someone who believed that a realistic solution of the Ukrainian Catholic controversy must be found. Sadly even he, in statements made since his appointment to the Foreign Department, has displayed a negative attitude to the Uniate question.

Yet even now some very influential bishops were unable to accept the inevitable and even inflamed the atmosphere on the very eve of legalisation. Metropolitan Yuvenali was in Rome as a kind of advance ecclesiastical guard for Mr Gorbachev's visit. The transcript of a broadcast which he made for Vatican Radio on 28 November illustrates attitudes which must have tarnished the Metropolitan's considerable international reputation. In order to appreciate the full significance of what he says, it is necessary to note that the Transfiguration Church in Lviv, by now having declared itself back in the Ukrainian Catholic camp, is a place of deep symbolism, for its parish priest had been Fr Kostelnyk, one of the protagonists at the 1946 *sobor*. Yuvenali said:

> The Vatican delegation came to Moscow on 2 November. Unfortunately at that time certain events took place which threw a shadow over the resolution of the Uniate issue, when people took the Transfiguration Church by force and demonstrations began. That was the reason for the issuing of the joint declaration appealing for an end to violence and for the cancellation of the delegation due in Moscow on 18–24 November. These meetings were to address the Uniate issue, but how can you have a peaceful discussion when a pistol is being pressed to your neck? From the Ukrainian Catholic side there was no attempt to exhort its faithful to act as befits believing people. The Transfiguration

Church is a symbol of violence; only through dialogue can we reach a solution.[20]

It ill becomes the representative of a church which participated in the events of 1946 to refer to discussions under the threat of the gun. That aside, Keston College contacts in Western Ukraine commented that the Transfiguration Church was first taken from the Catholics by violence and there was no guarantee that it would not be taken by force again; therefore in the meantime a peaceful occupation of the premises, a permanent vigil, was a necessary safeguard against this.

No transcript is available of the conversation in Rome between Mr Gorbachev and the Pope, nor is there ever likely to be. The most momentous aspect of it took place far away and was low-key. Many people, including myself, had publicly forecast that this meeting was certain to prove decisive in the long struggle of the Ukrainian Catholic Church to achieve legal recognition, yet in the few days beforehand, quite a number seemed to go cold on the idea and suggested that it would be too cynical for Mr Gorbachev to offer the Pope this as a kind of present. In the end, he did not have to, because the decisive moment had arrived earlier. Back in Kiev, Mykola Kolesnik had already announced on television two days before that the way was now clear for Ukrainian Catholic parishes to register. This was not published anywhere, so news reached the West only on the morning of the meeting. Cardinal Lubachivsky in Rome greeted this news in a firm and statesmanlike way:

As head of the Ukrainian Catholic Church, I call upon our faithful in Ukraine to avail themselves of the right and begin to register our congregations with the authorities as soon as possible; to respect the request of the Council for Religious Affairs in Ukraine to proceed in a peaceful manner; to identify themselves as Ukrainian Catholics when they are questioned by the authorities; to respect churches which at this time are functioning as Orthodox and to work patiently and according to the law with the authorities.[21]

The meeting between Mr Gorbachev and the Pope produced the unexpected announcement that diplomatic relations would now be established between the Vatican and the USSR, while Mr Gorbachev's promise of new legislation for the churches was a reiteration of an as yet unfulfilled promise to the hierarchy of the Russian Orthodox Church. A visit by the Pope to the Soviet Union is now clearly on the agenda. Were he to go, it would have to be at the invitation of the local Catholic churches rather than of any government. Clearly, if he were to go and not visit Lviv, this would cause immense disappointment to some of the most faithful Catholics anywhere in the world, but the implications of this for the Russian Orthodox Church and its relations with the Vatican are immense and problematical.

A Charged Atmosphere

Since Mr Gorbachev's visit to the Pope, the situation in Western Ukraine has, if anything, become more complicated. There is still no legal process to ensure just decisions about the future of individual church buildings. Then some parishes have wanted to remain Orthodox, but switch allegiance to the Ukrainian Autocephalous Orthodox Church. This is yet another difficult and contentious issue which raised the temperature in 1989. Suffice it to say here that this branch of Orthodoxy, separate from the Russian, did in fact exist from 1919 to 1922, while Ukraine was free of Soviet domination. Those who established it clearly intended it to be a barrier to growing Russification; then, as now, the political aspect of doing so was obvious.

On 15 February 1989 a group of Ukrainian believers, under the leadership of a priest, Fr Bohdan Mykhailechko, who had broken with the Russian Church, issued a statement that they had inaugurated an 'Initiative Committee for the Restoration of the Ukrainian Autocephalous Church'. From the point of view of the hierarchy of the Russian Orthodox Church, this was already bad enough, but one can only imagine their shock when on 19 August more than one thousand parishioners of the Church of St Peter and St Paul in Lviv rejected the jurisdiction of Moscow and became the first Ukrainian Autocephalous church, declaring its allegiance to the Ecumenical Patriarch Demetrios of Constantinople. Even worse was the defection of the retired Archbishop Ioann (Bodnarchuk). The Holy Synod met on 14 November and defrocked him, decreeing that he should revert to his baptismal name: Vasili Nikolaevich Bodnarchuk.

Recent developments in the Russian Orthodox Church seem to be attempts to stave off the emergence of this church, since it has now declared that the Exarchates of both Belorussia and Ukraine are to be the Belorussian Orthodox Church and the Ukrainian Orthodox Church respectively. It looks as though these will remain under the jurisdiction of the Moscow Patriarchate, which is obviously trying to regain the loss of its influence in these areas.

By this time the hierarchs of the Russian Orthodox Church were in no frame of mind to countenance the loss of further parishes, and therefore clergy and income, in the Western Ukraine and Transcarpathia.

Instead of a timetable for transition, Soviet spokesmen made a vague promise on television that there would be some sort of local vote, which brought a sharp reaction from Ivan Hel:

> Taking into account that the communist leaders are very capable of fabricating the results of the elections and of the votes, Ukrainian Catholics are not in the least happy with such a 'plebiscite'. According to this declaration by the authorities, the lawful owners are being asked to plead with those who stole their property. This is totally devoid of any intelligent thought.[22]

As for a measured and serious guarantee to the Orthodox that there would be no coercion and that they would be able to open new parishes in other areas, such as Siberia, where the need was so desperate, there was not a word to be heard from the Council for Religious Affairs at the very time when, at last, the way seemed to be open to them to do something really useful.

The situation quickly and sharply deteriorated, though it should have come as a surprise to nobody that there was an immediate and massive response to the statement on legalisation. Marko Bojcun, an acknowledged expert in Britain on the Ukrainian Catholic Church, wrote:

> By 21 December over 600 Ukrainian Catholic parishes had applied to register with the Council for Religious Affairs, more than 300 parishes were functioning inside church buildings, and 200 priests of the Russian Orthodox Church had applied to and been accepted into the Ukrainian Catholic Church . . . The congregations simply stayed in the church buildings which their ancestors had built, which had passed into the hands of the Russian Orthodox Church in 1946, and which were now returning to their original owners by the congregation declaring a collective change of denominational affiliation.[23]

Clearly, however, at this very time there was considerable muddying of the waters. The KGB must have been frustrated by the final failure of their longstanding plans permanently to eliminate the Ukrainian Catholic Church. With considerable manpower still at their disposal, provocations would be easy. Was it Orthodox priests on their own who attempted to organise counter-demonstrations outside the Transfiguration Church in Lviv to demand its restitution to the Orthodox Church? Did the KGB go even further and plant false information on senior clerics of the Russian Orthodox Church, so that they could pass on 'disinformation' to the West? In a private communication to Keston College a respected commentator wrote immediately after receiving news of the legalisation that 'there is little doubt that the Ukrainian Catholic Church will be provoked in the coming weeks, if not days.'

Further accusations of violence began to pour forth from the Russian Orthodox hierarchy. Metropolitan Filaret of Kiev claimed that 'gangs of violent people' were engaged on a campaign to seize Orthodox churches. Making a dubious reference to the legislation still in force, he claimed that wherever twenty people remained faithful to Orthodoxy, they should have the right to retain the church. The Holy Synod passed a resolution, printed in *Izvestia* on 20 December, condemning the 'cruel and illegal actions' of Ukrainian Catholic representatives and four days later reported that Metropolitan Alexi of Leningrad had spoken to the Congress of People's Deputies, firstly saying that his church could help the government in its campaign against violence and crime, but then making an unexpected switch to accuse the Ukrainian Catholics of 'outrageous acts of illegality' which were forcing people to turn to the Ukrainian Catholic Church against their will. As a result, he continued, one priest was in hospital and another had died.

One of the most respected church leaders in Britain, Metropolitan Anthony Bloom, chose the occasion of his broadcast Christmas sermon (night of 6–7 January 1990) to repeat these allegations in a particularly sharp way. The tape reveals him to have said (in English), 'One church after the other is being taken away by violence, parish houses are being burned down, priests and their families murdered.'

Some positive developments then took place: in mid-January Ukrainian Catholic and Orthodox bishops met at the Moscow Patriarchate in the presence of the Vatican delegation which had arrived there on 12 January. At this meeting the Ukrainian bishops had an opportunity emphatically to deny the allegations of violence which Russian Orthodox spokesmen had made in the press and elsewhere and asked the Moscow Patriarchate to put forward their evidence. Such evidence was not forthcoming. The worst that has come to light is that one priest did indeed die after a disturbance in his church, but this was an old man whose third heart attack proved fatal. There is also the case of Archbishop Makari of Ivano-Frankivsk, who took the drastic action of going on hunger strike in his own cathedral, in order, he stated, to protect himself and the building against threats of violence, after six of the seven parishes in the city had already gone over to the Catholics. He abandoned his hunger strike in mid-January, apparently without suffering any ill effects.

It was clearly a time for dispassionate and well-organised negotiations. There was considerable excitement and a sense of optimism in Western Ukraine when church leaders there heard that a Vatican delegation was to visit them in March. In the event, the occasion was a very considerable disappointment. It was reported as a 'quadripartite' conference, the four groups being the Vatican, the Ukrainian Catholic Church, the Moscow Patriarchate and the Ukrainian Orthodox Church, each represented by two participants. The imbalance in this arrangement is there for all to see. The last two are the same body, the Russian Orthodox Church having simply renamed its Ukrainian dioceses to make it appear they enjoy some autonomy.

The basic account of what occurred comes from Cardinal Lubachivksy's secretary from Rome, Fr Iwan Dacko, who arrived on the spot in Lviv the day after the Vatican delegation had left. One can only speculate on why Fr Dacko himself, not only the best informed person outside the Soviet Union, but also the direct representative of the head of the Ukrainian Catholic Church, was not included in the delegation as an adviser to its leader, Archbishop Marusyn. The Pope apparently in person appointed the Archbishop, under the impression that he was fully informed and the right man to represent the Cardinal. However, he proved himself unable to find his way through several highly sensitive issues, although a great deal of information had been put at his disposal before he left Rome. We are here at the edge of impenetrable Vatican politics, on which it is impossible to comment further with too little evidence even for sensible speculation. Therefore all we can do is to report the facts as related by Fr Dacko, himself an impeccable source.

There was a public announcement in Rome on 28 February 1990 that a visit would take place from 5 March. Cardinal Lubachivsky asked Fr Dacko to dictate fifteen major agenda points by telephone to Metropolitan Sterniuk in Lviv, giving the Cardinal's firm views on the rights of his church. The second member of the Vatican delegation, Metropolitan Stephen Sulyk of Philadelphia, received these points in writing from the Cardinal the day before he left for Moscow.

On 6 March the first major mistake occurred – or rather two mistakes compounded into one. Archbishop Marusyn sent a telegram from Moscow to Archbishop Sterniuk asking him to come to Kiev from Lviv for talks the next day. He received it at 4 p.m., giving him only two and a half hours to catch the overnight train – hardly the way to treat any archbishop, let alone a man of 83, nor the way to prepare for a major conference. What gave gravest offence, however, was the fact that Archbishop Marusyn sent the telegram via the Russian Orthodox Archbishop Irinei. On innumerable previous occasions representatives of the Ukrainian Catholic Church had stated that they believed that the Russian Orthodox Church had no *locus standi* in the negotiations at all, yet here was its representative being treated by the Vatican as though he was senior to the Catholic leader on the spot. Metropolitan Sterniuk's fellow-delegate was 73-year-old Bishop Dmyterko. Fr Dacko later commented that here were men not only unpractised in the art of diplomacy, but who had spent their lives cleaning out toilets in prison or, after their release, working as dustmen. They were leaders of a simple flock who needed every consideration from other participants; least of all should they have been put at a disadvantage before they started. As it was, they appear to have been playing little more than walk-on roles in some drama of power politics enacted between Moscow and the Vatican, the subtleties of which they could not even begin to comprehend.

The two Ukrainian Catholic bishops arrived in Kiev from Lviv at 8 a.m. on 7 March. Metropolitan Filaret of Kiev – whose views on the Ukrainian Catholic Church had long since discredited him in the eyes of millions of Ukrainians – insisted on entertaining the visitors to breakfast, instead of allowing them to confer in private with the Vatican delegation.

Talks began – with no agenda – precisely two hours after they had stepped off the train. It had earlier been stated that the talks would be for bishops only (thus excluding Fr Dacko), yet with no prior warning Archimandrite Nestor, a man not known for any sympathy towards the Catholics, walked into the room to strengthen the Orthodox delegation. The door of the meeting room stayed open, so a variety of unseen people behind it could hear every word. They created a noise and constantly disrupted the proceedings by sending in notes of unexplained content to the Orthodox participants.

This should have been a historic meeting: the first ever where the Vatican, the Orthodox Church and the deprived Ukrainian Catholics could sit around a table in Ukraine and set out all the main issues. Yet the key questions of principle, such as the status of the 1946 Synod of Lviv, were left on the sidelines. All the Orthodox side was willing to discuss was the future designation of individual churches. Frequently the Catholics objected to phrases such as that a certain church had been 'seized by Catholics of the Eastern Rite'. The Orthodox agreed to withdraw such remarks, but a subsequent press release reinstated them.

The next day, 8 March, the commission flew to Lviv, still with no Vatican-Ukrainian consultation having taken place. From here on the work was exclusively practical, with progress through towns and villages attended by stops on the way to discuss the future of individual churches on the spot. Here any informed observer could have seen the enormity of what was occurring. The Orthodox team were able to telephone ahead to acquire intelligence on whether there were more of their own people or Catholics gathered in a particular place and they changed the route frequently to avoid meetings which would have been detrimental to their own cause.

The most distressing example of this occurred at Ivano-Frankivsk, where Ukrainian bishops, priests, nuns and the faithful in their tens of thousands were waiting, but the Orthodox delegation found out about it and cancelled the visit on the fictitious pretext that Archbishop Sterniuk was ill.

The result of such machinations was that the Orthodox regained six churches which had already passed into the hands of the Catholics. People complained to Fr Dacko that the commission had done more for Moscow than for the local people. This has itself caused unrest in Western Ukraine, even to the extent that the mayor of Lviv appeared on television to appeal for calm.

Finally, on Sunday 11 March, after a liturgy in the Transfiguration Church in Lviv, attended inside and out by about 30,000 people, the Vatican delegation received representatives of the laity and the newly elected deputies to the Ukrainian Supreme Soviet, but it was only the next day that they met all ten Ukrainian bishops. Even then the agenda of the meeting was to gather information for publication in the *Annuario Pontificio* and to discuss a few pastoral problems.

The next day the conference reconvened and at this point Archbishop Sterniuk decided to walk out as a protest against the continued refusal to discuss the fundamentals. He stated that no documents issuing from the discussions had any legal value. Any future discussion could take place only with the government, because it was Moscow which had been responsible for the liquidation of his church, while these discussions were valueless because they were taking place between two sides which did not enjoy equal rights. He presented a fourteen-point statement underlining this and then left. The only signatures on the final document were those of Archbishop Marusyn and Metropolitan Mefodi of the Moscow Patriarchate.

The next Saturday, 17 March, seven of the Ukrainian Catholic bishops were able to meet in Lviv. They agreed on the fourteen points. Amazingly, Archbishop Sterniuk was able to maintain his

high standing with the Ukrainian people by reading the declaration
on television on 21 March and a Lviv newspaper published the full
text – thus leaving the impression with some observers that the Soviet
media were now more open than the Vatican.[24]

Clearly, the restoration of justice to the Ukrainian Catholic Church
is still some distance away, let alone the establishment of some kind
of ecumenical relationship with the Russian Orthodox Church. The
new Vatican envoy in Moscow will have a great deal of real diplomacy
to undertake if he is to salve wounded feelings. Be this as it may, the
Ukrainian Catholic Church has now become fully and openly active,
already participating in the public life of Ukraine and organising
charitable work, just like its Orthodox and Protestant counterparts.

9 The Quality of Mercy

The Need for Compassion

Addressing the ranks of one of Moscow's most elevated ideological institutions, Konstantin Kharchev asked whether it was right, in this great socialist society, to allow a man's dying vision to be of a believer bringing him a bedpan. Should he go to his grave in the realisation that our socialist state is incapable of organising someone to bring him this relief? The debate, in March 1988, was on whether it was correct to allow believers to help out in these most elementary aspects of social care where the Soviet State had so abysmally failed. Kharchev went on:

> Another reason why we cannot allow the church to engage in charitable activities is that the Catholics would seize upon it: that well-known Mother Teresa has already offered, also Protestants, Baptists, Adventists. Only the Orthodox Church is too beleaguered to have financial resources available at present for anything like that.[1]

Kharchev's speech was virtually the last bastion of resistance to the calling in of Christian resources to supply relief in the huge and growing areas of need which were now being publicly admitted in the social services. A state which had proclaimed itself around the world as the most humanitarian yet devised – for three generations Soviet citizens had suspected this to be a sham – was now open for public scrutiny in the era of *glasnost*. What the newspapers were beginning to print caused shock-waves inside and beyond the Soviet Union, as the propaganda of the past began to be ruthlessly exposed.

The state of affairs was much more serious than Mr Kharchev's reference to bedpans might imply. A nation which had been able to send a rocket to the moon as long as thirty years ago could still not, in the late 1980s, supply the most elementary pre- and post-natal care for mothers. One of the unspoken reasons for the low birth rate in the Russian Republic is that young prospective mothers are terrified to expose themselves to the dangers and indignities of maternity units. Not that this is the only reason for the falling birth rate in a country where the abortion rate is abnormally high. So insanitary are the conditions that infant mortality figures in some areas are now considered comparable to some of the less favoured third-world countries.

Some commentators have seen Mr Gorbachev's reception of the leaders of the Russian Orthodox Church in the Kremlin in April 1988 as the turning point. The true emergence of a new attitude predates this by over a year, however. *Miloserdiye* has become one of the great and resonant words of the society the present leadership would like to build. Literally 'dear-heartedness', it is loaded with Christian associations. It is the biblical word for 'mercy', *kharis* in Greek, *caritas* in Latin, which lies at the basis of the English word 'charity'. But to say that the church in the Soviet Union can now engage in 'charitable activities' does not begin to convey the richness present in the Russian word – particularly striking when it has not only been banned in practice for seventy years, but when *miloserdiye* has almost been excised from the dictionary with the symbol 'obsolete' beside it.

Snatching *miloserdiye* from this limbo, the writer Daniil Granin brought it back with immense power in a prominent article in the Soviet press in March 1987.[2] The poem which sets the tone for the piece claims that man has an innate capacity, even a desire, to respond to another's pain or need, but if this lies long unused it will atrophy. When he slipped and badly hurt himself in the street recently, people passed him by, assuming he was a drunkard. A friend's wife became ill; he was told he should offer money to the surgeon, who said, 'I need ten times more,' when offered twenty-five roubles. The woman died, but the surgeon told her husband he would not return the money, as the fault was not in his surgery, but in the woman's heart, which gave out under the strain.

It is the church, Granin continued, with its last rites and the forgiveness of sins which can teach the medical profession how to treat people on the point of death. The systematic elimination during the purges of any feeling except fear and the need for self-preservation caused Soviet society to lose its compassion. People had to approve sentences of appalling injustice even though they were self-evidently wrong. James Herriot's Yorkshire vet, Granin told his readers, shows infinitely more compassion towards an injured dog than this society does to a person whom a loving gesture could save from an undignified death.

So far had the debate unfolded by the end of 1989 that a priest was able to write in the same newspaper and put forward the argument that the virtue of compassion was so much more developed in pre-revolutionary society that it was not uncommon for the aristocracy not only to found hospitals with the best available medical equipment but for titled women to give up the comforts which their inheritance guaranteed in order to devote their life to nursing the sick, exercising just those virtues so lacking today.[3]

National Tragedy and the Churches

The onset of a series of disasters, some natural, some man-made, from 1986, made it clear that Soviet propaganda concealed a system barely able to cope with routine emergencies, let alone national disaster on a grand scale.

First came Chernobyl. It is doubtful whether even pre-*glasnost*, the system could have concealed a tragedy as enormous as the Chernobyl explosion, though had the effects been confined within the Soviet borders there would undoubtedly have been an attempt to do so. That night much more than a concrete lid blew off a nuclear reactor: Soviet self-confidence suffered irreparable damage also.

It is the belief of many observers that the full scale of the disaster has still to be made public and it is certain that the Soviet authorities have systematically withheld from the affected population information about the consequences of nuclear radiation.

The state showed itself from the first to be virtually bereft of the means to offer help on the scale needed. During the period of initial reaction, one could see the church preparing for a defensive propaganda exercise, as, for example, when Metropolitan Filaret of Minsk stated on 21 May 1986 that some foreigners were trying to 'gain political advantage from someone else's grief' – a deeply unfair remark when one considers the readiness of Western people to respond to humanitarian need in a wide variety of contexts.[4] The Soviet press quoted a visiting pastor from West Germany as saying that the real danger to the world was not nuclear reactors, which will inevitably have accidents from time to time, but the deployment of American nuclear weapons.[5] Archbishop Makari of Ivano-Frankivsk, instead of thanking a major Western agency for its offer of help (Aid to the Church in Need), criticised it for championing the cause of the Ukrainian Catholic Church.[6]

However, at the same time there was a new note in the pronouncements of one or two of the most forward-looking of the Soviet church
leaders. The head of the Armenian Apostolic Church, Catholicos
Vazgen I, who two and a half years later would see his people
engulfed by a horrific tragedy in his own homeland, announced
the opening of a disaster fund to raise 150,000 roubles to help
refugees from Chernobyl. The strong Baptist churches in Kiev did
the same and provided temporary accommodation for them. Especially
welcome in Kiev were members of the two Baptist churches right in
the affected area. The Chairman of the Council for Religious Affairs,
Konstantin Kharchev, stated in an interview with the atheist monthly,
Nauka i religia ('Science and Religion') in November 1987 that the
churches had donated more than three million roubles for the relief
of Chernobyl victims.[7] Three years after the accident an estimated
20,000 people gathered outside the Cathedral of the Assumption
in Lviv, Western Ukraine, to pray for those who had died, for the
health of children and for those who had been held responsible.
Priests from the then still outlawed Ukrainian Catholic Church led
the service.[8]

This was a new departure for the churches. They had regularly
contributed to the Soviet Peace Fund, but this was purely a government agency over which ordinary people had no control and about
the workings of which they had little knowledge. Therefore in no real
sense could supporting it be considered an act of 'charity'. Over forty
years earlier the Orthodox Church had contributed financially to the
support of a tank division in the Second World War, while the Baptists
paid for medical supplies. Even at this stage Vazgen felt he had to
apologise for taking this initiative: the church had a moral duty to
contribute, even though 'our state has taken all measures to provide
flats, foodstuffs and medicines to the evacuated population'.[9]

Chernobyl was already a more major factor in forcing open the
average Soviet mind than commentators have realised. People who
had put up with indignity for decades in the belief that somewhere
a long way away there were men who did care for their ultimate
wellbeing began instead to experience apocalyptic visions of the
fallibility of the system. Some saw it as a time to turn their thoughts
to the existence of a superior power. Others even rationalised the
series of rail, air and ecological disasters which struck the Soviet
Union in 1987–89 as God's judgment on the sinful leadership
in the Kremlin. The very name 'Chernobyl' (wormwood) echoed
for some a biblical prophecy of the imminence of Armageddon:
'The third angel sounded his trumpet and a great star, blazing

like a torch, fell from the sky on a third of the rivers and on the springs of water – the name of the star is Wormwood' (Revelation 8:10–11). The insecurity caused by this and other disasters, coupled with the growing realisation that all was far from well with the Soviet system, has led to a very real apocalyptic feeling even among non-believers.

The shock of this disaster was undoubtedly a factor which made people ask questions. Why was the Party unprepared to cope with social and humanitarian need? Christians had shown by their deeds that they cared more than communists did. Within the Party, people cared primarily for their privileges, for the allocation of massive resources to special housing, private medical care, high-grade shops and elitist schooling. Indeed, in Kiev after the disaster Party officials sent their own children away on early summer holidays, while publicly proclaiming there was no danger.

Not only did the rulers show contempt for the less privileged in society: they treated the environment as badly. People started to become aware of 'green' issues. The Aral Sea was being poisoned by the wash of chemical fertilisers, the soil around it exhausted by cotton monoculture.

After Chernobyl there followed floods in Georgia, rail and air crashes and, most horrific of all in its immediate effects, the Armenian earthquake of December 1988. By the time the massive earthquake devastated Spitak and Leninakan in Armenia not only Vazgen but all other church leaders had struck a new note in their public statements. For Orthodox bishops, their memory of the collection for the train disaster during the *sobor* was very recent (see Chapter 3). There can have been scarcely a Christian in the Soviet Union whose heart was not moved to prayer or financial support for the victims, though we should mention that this same event seemed only to make Muslims in the neighbouring republic of Azerbaijan more hostile and more determined not to relinquish their power over the disputed Armenian enclave within their territory of Nagorny Karabakh, taking advantage of the temporary weakness of Armenia and Moscow's indecision on ethnic issues to enforce their will by physical means.

Already before the earthquake various groups, but with the church as the most prominent, had come together to form the 'Armenian Charitable Union', building on the old traditions of Christian involvement in setting up schools, hospitals, children's and old people's homes. Formal recognition came on 8 October, two months to the day before the earthquake struck. There was, therefore, an embryonic aid fund already in existence and the Catholicos was the natural figure of authority to step in front of the TV cameras to spearhead the worldwide relief operation.

The Orthodox Church showed itself in a new light, able to respond at once to the grief of those outside its fold. In Estonia it offered immediate public prayer for the victims, while its counterpart in Lithuania organised a concert of religious choral music in Vilnius Orthodox Cathedral, with a collection for the victims. Foreign support provided for a 'temporary Pentecostal village', while most notably of all there was a donation of 100,000 roubles from the persecuted and then officially non-existent Ukrainian Catholic Church. The transfer of the money, however, was not so simple. The Ukrainian authorities in Lviv, where the money was gathered, did not want to accept it for transfer from an illegal body, demanding that it should be sent in the name of the Russian Orthodox Church, but eventually good sense and compassion prevailed.

Baptist churches in the Russian Federation, giving detailed statistics on their membership and activities for the first time, revealed that in the course of a few days 180,000 roubles were collected for the Armenian Earthquake Relief Fund. In February 1989, a group of young people from the church visited a ward in the children's hospital in Moscow where children injured in the earthquake were being treated. They gave a concert of religious music, preached and prayed with the children, including those who were too sick to attend the concert. The beneficial effect of this was so great that the head doctor asked them to come again.[10]

Suddenly *miloserdiye* became a buzz-word in the Soviet press. Earlier the resurrection of old religious terminology would have been unthinkable. Now, in 1988, it became a reality. Soviet citizens had to begin to accustom themselves to headlines such as 'Charity for all' (*Sovetskaya Moldavia*, 7 March 1988) and 'Hurry to do good' (*Pravda*, 17 September). Groups of people began to form charity societies in response to this call.

Although there was entrenched opposition to this initiative, some headway was made. The Leningrad Miloserdiye Society was the first to register, headed by Granin, the writer who had done much to initiate the debate. It did so on 5 April 1988, just before Gorbachev was to meet the leaders of the Russian Orthodox Church and challenge them to help him in the social aspect of *perestroika*. Within two months the movement had spread to twenty cities and on 16 September the first All-Union conference of the 'Soviet Mercy and Health Fund', an organisation apparently running parallel to

the Miloserdiye Society, took place. In December the All-Union
Miloserdiye Society was established. On 14 June 1989 *Literaturnaya
gazeta* listed the cities in which the main opposition was to be found.
At the same time, some city councils were much more enthusiastic
and took the initiative, such as Rostov, which held a *miloserdiye* week
in May 1989 involving all local schools in holding fund-raising fairs.
Then the Russian Republic inaugurated an 'Action-Miloserdiye' six
months in August 1989, due to end the following February with a
series of charity gala concerts involving many leading performers
from at home and abroad. For the first anniversary of the Armenian
earthquake, and therefore in good time for Christmas and the New
Year, the state issued charity stamps to help continue raising funds
for the homeless and the families whose lives had been shattered.

A charitable activity of an especially sensitive nature was the
establishment in February 1989 of an Association of Afghan War
Veterans, who put relief for mutilated victims and for bereaved
families at the top of their agenda. The agency established a foreign
bank account, not only to collect donations from abroad, but also to
be able to order such essentials as artificial limbs, the manufacture
of which remains at a primitive level in the Soviet Union. Those
continuing to need injections would also be able to secure foreign
needles for the purpose and thus avoid the very real extra danger
of contracting AIDS – for recent revelations by the Soviet medical
profession itself show that here is another crucial gap in the supply
system, which puts the whole population in peril.

Sisters of Mercy

We have already mentioned the readiness of Christians from abroad
to help in disaster relief and the consequent formalising for the first
time of the wish several dozen societies have of involving themselves
in some form of direct aid within the Soviet Union. For decades any
such aspirations were rejected out of hand by the authorities, who
often arrested and confiscated goods from foreign Christians at entry
points and harassed the would-be recipients to an extent intended
to deter the donors. For a few years there was a legal system, later
abolished, of sending in parcels, but this was always accompanied by
punitive taxation.

It is too early to assess the overall impact of this foreign effort. However, one enterprise deserves special mention (and indeed received
it from Konstantin Kharchev): the persuasiveness of the redoubtable

Mother Teresa of Calcutta in obtaining permission to establish a bridgehead for her Missionaries of Charity.

Before the illness which disrupted her life in the second half of 1989, Mother Teresa visited the Soviet Union no fewer than three times in seven months and saw her work firmly established there over that period. It is understandable that some Soviet believers have expressed cynicism at the welcome, little short of ecstatic, which officialdom extended to her and which was reflected in the media. 'Why can't our own nuns receive premises to do similar work in central city locations? We have hundreds of nuns who can't even follow their vocation openly and the Catholic Church doesn't have a single convent' was one reaction from a dedicated priest. Nevertheless, taking the longer view, one must welcome this development, not only for the intrinsic goodness of the act itself, but because it opens an important channel for Western Christian aid. Furthermore, the authorities will find it much harder to ban the work of indigenous religious orders in the future. Mother Teresa had requested permission to establish her work long before 1988: in the autumn of 1987 she was refused permission to do so. However, in the words of Father Mark (Valeri) Smirnov, one of the foremost figures in the Miloserdiye movement, 'Sorrow has made us wiser.'[11]

Mother Teresa's first visit in December 1988 was an emergency one in the immediate aftermath of the Armenian earthquake. The second was the following February, by which time she was able to agree a co-ordinated programme for help in Moscow's Burdenko hospital, which has a section under Professor Arkadi Lifshits for treating spinal disorders and where several victims of the earthquake were undergoing treatment. All of this group were trained nurses and would be there initially for six months, but with the hope, the professor said, that the arrangement would then be ongoing. A further four nuns, Mother Teresa said, would go directly to Armenia to participate in the continuing relief work there. She went on to express the hope that some Soviet women would be able to join the order and continue this work. There were already thirty-five nationalities represented among the 3,000 sisters of the order and the group in the Soviet Union represented Italy, India, Poland and Yugoslavia.

For her third visit at the end of June 1989 Mother Teresa received a telegram of welcome from Raisa Gorbachev and she was able to announce that by now no fewer than thirteen of her sisters were at work in Moscow. Professor Lifshits reported: 'All the patients who have been lucky enough to meet sisters of the Order of Mercy speak of the unprecedented warmth of soul coming from these people.'[12] Mother Teresa visited the new centres recently opened in Tbilisi and Spitak and said that people had come to her 'literally day and night to receive a blessing and ask for help'. The Moscow civic authorities promised all the necessary help for her to develop her work, which was so urgently needed.

On 8 October 1989 *Moscow News* was able to give the addresses of two permanent premises in the capital, little two- or three-storey buildings with gardens, where the seriously ill, including people suffering from AIDS, or the homeless would be able to find shelter. Work would be done by Soviet volunteers supervised by a priest. The writer went on to complain that the municipal authorities were now putting bureaucratic objections in the way of the essential repair work, even though one of the buildings had been sitting empty for two years and foreign companies had volunteered to carry out the work free of charge. Doubtless these obstacles will disappear, though it is difficult to imagine how the warden will operate the physical controls necessary to stop the buildings coming under siege from the needy – and would the Moscow 'homeless' be the thousands who live illegally in the city, not being able to obtain precious residence permits?

Difficulties certainly lie ahead, but one can only marvel at God's economy: someone who might have grown up bereft of any religion among her own Albanian people was able, in her sunset years, to supervise personally the breaking-down of a bastion of Soviet atheism and establish the right of Christian sisters to nurse and to love.

Prison Visiting

For believers to establish a precedent, even with visible opposition, of visiting criminals in prison and bringing them a message of Christian salvation illustrates another breakthrough – one which must have seemed momentous for generations of Christian prisoners of conscience who had sought to preach the Gospel while themselves sharing the fate of their fellow-prisoners.

Such thoughts were present in the mind of a certain Mr Kiselyov, who reported the visit of Metropolitan Filaret of Kiev to a strict regime prison camp at Bucha, near Kiev, in *Literaturnaya gazeta* on 19 July 1989. This was the first time in seventy years, he reflected, that a priest had visited a labour camp without being one of its inmates. The director of the political section of the local *soviet* had come to the conclusion that the camp system, despite tireless propaganda to the contrary, had done very little to re-educate criminal offenders and it was time for a new and more 'human' approach. This was the motivation behind the recent decision to introduce parole as a reward for good behaviour; allowing Christians access to the camp was an experiment to help improve internal morale and conduct. The disintegration of standards in Soviet prisons was vividly illustrated by an article in *Moscow News* on 2 July, documenting a mutiny in a prison colony in the Peschanka District, Vinnitsa, Ukraine. Dramatically entitled 'Give us a Journalist and a Priest', the article explained that what lay behind the inmates' demand for a priest was that they wanted 'someone to talk to us as human beings'.

Metropolitan Filaret spoke to a gathering of 700 prisoners and the public address system relayed his message to anyone who was not there in person. The newspaper reported that the prisoners were receptive to the message. One said that, if the church could help bring about a reconciliation between criminals and the society from which they are outlawed, he at least would be prepared to try to put the Ten Commandments into practice. Prisoners were now permitted to wear crosses around their necks, reported Kiselyov, an offence until recently punishable by solitary confinement. The camp governor promised that any Christian literature which the Metropolitan had brought would be available to the prisoners without restriction and in future there would be a room where a priest could hear confessions and administer communion.

Kiselyov continues with a reflection on how hard all this must be for the ranks of professional atheists to stomach. There will be some who will try to reverse what is happening, but he ends with an affirmation from Metropolitan Filaret that it is the church's responsibility to care for all these people and to be a positive influence in society as a whole.

The same newspaper followed this article three weeks later with another which reported that Hieromonk Sergei had visited the Moscow prison of Butyrki, an occasion arranged jointly by the press office of the Ministry for Internal Affairs and the new Orthodox publication, *Moscow Church Herald*. A ministry spokesman said that this was a response to the call made by the Congress of People's Deputies to make every effort to combat crime. In recent months there has been a spate of articles in the Soviet press revealing disturbing trends in the frequency of organised and violent crime. Father Sergei had talked to the prisoners, trying to inspire hope and the courage in them to undertake to lead a new life. Photographs of the priest at the entrance to the prison and talking to the inmates accompanied the article.[13] Metropolitan Alexi of Leningrad who, incidentally, was nominated by the Soviet Fund of Mercy and Health and stands on this mandate, said in a recent speech to the Congress of People's Deputies that if men and women had been taught the biblical commandments, 'Do not steal', 'Do not kill', 'Do not bear false witness', it would have saved Soviet society from many of its present ills.[14]

In Riga the main Protestant denominations have come together to form a 'Latvian Christian Mission', the principal aims of which are social initiatives and evangelism. They list prison work as one of the objectives: 'Corrective labour colonies are an area for our special attention. Initial practical experience suggests the most positive results.'[15]

One of the new evangelical Christian publications printed a remarkable article three months later entitled 'Within the prison gates', continuing the story of the Latvian Christian Mission. The 'boldness' of the officials of the Ministry of the Interior in Latvia has given Christians the opportunity to preach the Gospel in prisons and to distribute Christian literature. The author notes the diversity of nationalities among the 250 or so people participating in this, while regretting that there are not more Latvians involved. The first visit to a women's prison had been very emotional, thanks especially to the singing of a Baptist choir and a remarkable gesture from a Roman Catholic gardener:

> He gave each of the female inmates a daffodil. Afterwards the women told me that this flower, even more than the words accompanying the gesture, had moved them. Many of them had never in their lives received such a gift. And, they went on, even though they did not yet understand many of the words which passed over them, yet the feeling of warmth and love remained. This light remaining in the soul could not be confused with anything else.[16]

The second visit in April 1989 concentrated on a service of worship, prayers and a question and answer session, where everyone observed a great openness to the Word of God. Not all were total strangers to the faith: some had been brought up in it, but had subsequently abandoned it. There were those who requested prayers for them in their own local churches. The prison officials later testified to such an improvement in the outlook and behaviour of the inmates that they wanted to establish these services as a regular event – but the writer points out with sadness that so very little Christian literature is available in Latvian as a follow-up that a unique opportunity is not being taken to the full.

Similar initiatives are being undertaken not just in the Baltic States, but also by Baptists in Ukraine, who published three reports in their Ukrainian language publication, *Khristianskiye zhitya* ('Christian Life') about prison visits in their area. Young Baptists visited the Berezansky corrective labour colony for the first time on 13 August 1989 and conducted a service of songs, readings, prayers and a sermon by a man who had himself sat behind bars more than once for his religious faith. Such was the impact of this visit on at least one of the inmates that he sent a letter of thanks to those who had taken part in the service. Another group went to the Bila Tserkva strict regime corrective labour colony and their visit was reported in the local newspaper, *Kievska pravda*, on 12 September 1989.

A decade which had begun with evangelists such as Valeri Barinov, the Leningrad rock musician, in desperate trouble for trying to reach lost souls at first on the street, later in prison himself, ended with the state encouraging the church to give priority precisely to this ministry. In the challenging world of *perestroika* there are few more dramatic examples of official *volte-face*.

Hospitals, Psychiatric Clinics and Old People's Homes

The development of Christian work in hospitals, psychiatric clinics and old people's homes is less dramatic than that in the prisons, but none the less real.

One effect of *glasnost* has been the general recognition and acknowledgment of the appalling conditions prevalent in every institution set up to care for people. With no possibility of travel the populace had until recently accepted what they were seeing as standard and inevitable, just as anyone would have reacted to visiting an operating theatre in the days before anaesthetics. The main problems fall into two categories: lack of personnel and physical conditions. Some sources, including Kharchev in the speech cited at the beginning of this chapter, claim that in the Moscow region alone there is a shortfall of 20,000 medical personnel, which in itself can only prejudice the relationship between the hospital staff and the individual. Add to this a prevalence of filth, overcrowding and sometimes the lack of even the most elementary needs of clinical medicine, and the picture which emerges is inferior to conditions in some parts of the third world.

An article in *Literaturnaya gazeta* charting the growth of the *miloserdiye* movement opened with a horrifying description of corruption and negligence in an old people's home in Voronezh, a city of approximately one million 500 kilometres south of Moscow. Nurses expected extra payment before they would give even the most elementary nursing care and sanitary conditions were such that there was only one shower room to two hundred people. Clearly, someone took a high-level decision early in 1988 that it might be possible to alleviate the effects of the enormous shortfall in personnel and to improve staff–patient relationships if it were permissible to summon help from the only available source which would cost the state nothing: the local churches. Mr Gorbachev implied such a request at his meeting with the leaders of the Russian Orthodox Church in April 1988.

The response was immediate, though uneven. Leaders of the Russian Orthodox Church correctly claimed that such 'charitable' activity had been an essential part of Christian concern since time immemorial, but they were clearly caught unprepared, as Soviet law had specifically banned any such work since 1929. As Fr Matvei Stadnyuk, Dean of the Moscow Patriarchal Cathedral, stated in an interview with *Ogonyok*, an article, incidentally accompanied by a heart-rending photo reportage of priests in cassocks and other believers going about their task of hospital visiting, people have become passive, have lost the prompting to take initiatives:

> Everywhere they are waiting for some directive . . . a decision, an order, a telephone call. You can compel someone to go out on a *subbotnik* [so-called voluntary Saturday labour, such as tree-planting] – we go, we're used to it. But can you force someone to go and exercise charity? Hardly.[17]

Far fewer people have volunteered for charitable work than needed or expected. For example, according to Metropolitan Alexi, there have been only eighty-four in a huge city like Leningrad.[18] Then there have been many who dropped it just as quickly as they had taken it up:

> Many parishioners who had taken up charitable work on the spur of the moment abandoned it within a month or two. Some of them, especially young people, proved to be unprepared psychologically for the sight of the suffering of the gravely sick and the dying. The dispersion of believers in the parishes and lack of contact with the

local clergy also have a negative effect. The inertia of the stagnation period is still there. The church's estrangement from public life, the blame for which was not hers, resulted in believers adopting a guarded attitude towards society. Today, when the conditions for public activity by Christians are favourable, many of us are not ready for it morally.[19]

This article – important because the *Journal of the Moscow Patriarchate* has always been among the most timid of publications and this exercise in self-examination is a new departure – goes on to state that in one place 'about half of the forty people who volunteered for hospital work have dropped out' and the only answer is to bridge the estrangement between the clergy and their flock. If there is no history or practical experience, then there must be parochial libraries, where activists can learn at second hand from the knowledge of others – but that resource is non-existent, too.

At the same time, the article makes it clear that even these modest beginnings are achieving positive results:

> For instance, there is a very active group of young men and women. Interestingly, after the hospital was visited by young believers many patients expressed the desire to receive Holy Communion, wear a pectoral cross, have small icons and memorise prayers. Some of the nurses too wished to receive Holy Communion . . . A woman of about sixty enters the ward. She holds a book. She tells me she is a parishioner of St Nicholas Church . . . She proceeds to read the Lives of Saints to the patients . . . Professor Anatoli Fedin, Chief Neuro-Pathologist of Moscow . . . says: 'Since volunteers first appeared in our wards, the nurses and other personnel have shown more consideration for the patients. It is no secret that we do have cases of rudeness and negligence in hospitals. When nurses see people come here in their free time to look after the patients, they begin working better themselves. The volunteers' work is having an especially strong educative effect on the young nurses.'[20]

It is clear that, even with optimum help from outside its own ranks, it will take the Orthodox Church years, probably decades, to be in a position to take advantage of all the new opportunities. The article above did not go far enough. Better communication between priests and their parishioners is only a very small part of the answer. The clergy themselves are not prepared for this extension of their activities. Their demanding duties would not allow them to be extensively involved in hospital visiting, but they are not experienced enough to train others to do it, either. Why? Because pastoral teaching at theological seminaries has deliberately excluded training for any activity which was not strictly in accordance with the letter of the law. Propagandist spokesmen for the church went further than this: they claimed that teaching was entirely according to needs and all social welfare was safely in the hands of the caring state. Therefore there could be no question of the Orthodox Church turning to foreign agencies for help. This attitude, expressed in public Christian forums in the West over decades, has produced its own sad consequences. Reiterating the message that 'everything is all right for us' has led to an atrophy in the West in those very areas where aid agencies might have become active. No tradition has arisen; only in scattered places is there the will to establish training or exchange programmes, and even when the desire exists, the linguistic skills to back this up are virtually non-existent.

The Protestant Churches in the Soviet Union are bound to some extent to suffer from the above strictures, but have they shown a more co-ordinated response to the new possibilities? While some of the early evidence is impressive, it is too scattered to make even an interim judgment on this question.

Pastor Mikhail Zhidkov is the co-ordinator of the Baptist *miloserdiye* programme. In a meeting I had with him in his Moscow office in February 1989, he underlined the immensity of the needs in local hospitals, and therefore of the task confronting a very much smaller cadre of people than the Orthodox community. Although Baptist leaders were not present at Mr Gorbachev's Kremlin reception, within a week (3 May 1988) the leaders of the Moscow Baptist Church had had a meeting with the head doctor of the Kashchenko Psychiatric Hospital and practical work was able to start immediately. That this was the first venue for such work was itself remarkable, for this was one of the hospitals where until recently there was systematic abuse of psychiatry as a punitive measure under the aegis of the KGB. However, the visiting immediately became a highly organised activity. Every month after the morning service those involved would meet to review the technical side of the work, to ensure that all the arrangements were in order. They would go on to talk about any problems they may have encountered and to pray for the special needs of any individuals.

Five days a week two separate teams of believers enter the hospital, morning and evening. At least a hundred Baptists are now regularly helping in four different sections of the hospital, each with sixty to seventy patients. In November 1988 the hospital administration asked for increased help with old people, feeding them, changing their bedlinen and generally improving their morale simply by spending time with them. There is no restriction whatsoever on the subject of conversation, so there is free discussion about any aspect of the faith, Bible reading has become standard practice and there is regular prayer.

On 24 September 1988 an unprecedented event took place at the Moscow Baptist Church. All the volunteers assembled for a special service, at which they received not only the expected blessing of the elders of the church, but, quite without precedent inside the walls of a Christian building, of the hospital authorities, too. There are remarkable photographs of the event, which concluded with a 'fellowship meal' – not, of course, a communion service, which would have excluded the non-believers from the hospital administration, but a very warm occasion for both groups to come to know each other. During the service a further thirty volunteers came forward to offer their help. All the non-Christian participants received a Bible and a recording of the church choir. Perhaps most remarkable and moving of all was what Valentin Kozyrev said, the first 'sermon' ever given by an atheist in the Moscow Baptist Church, but spoken by someone who was visibly moved by the unexpected surroundings in which he found himself:

> Had I been told several years ago that I, the chief physician of a major hospital, a communist, would stand here before you in a Baptist church, I would never have believed it . . . Pierre Dusson, a famous psychotherapist, in his book *Fighting Insanity* drew a formula for curing these unfortunate persons – 'chemistry plus love'. And although we as doctors and scientists are able to fulfil the first part of this formula to some extent, we are virtually incapable of fulfilling the second part, which is love. When you brothers came to my hospital and offered this co-operation I immediately agreed to it, though I usually need some time for making decisions. As a psychiatrist, I knew what kind of people would come to us, what kind of hearts they would have, and I knew as a specialist that it would be an example of lofty charity. Some of our personnel workers doubted the success of this project, but after two or three days of our joint work every doubt disappeared . . . I want to thank the whole church and ask you to see to it that this small detachment of nurses should be just the first of many.[21]

Subsequently, Western visitors have reported that now relatives of those waiting for admission to the Kashchenko hospital are trying to insist that patients should be assigned to those wards where they can expect the ministrations of the Baptist helpers.

Children

It is in the sphere of child care that the church has made the most significant breakthrough. Children, as representatives of the 'glorious future', were untouchable, their ideological purity guaranteed by the strictest laws. Even a group of two or three children from outside the household assembling there in strictest privacy to receive encouragement in upholding Christian moral standards was treated as an infraction of Soviet law and over the last twenty years hundreds, possibly thousands, of men and women have received prison sentences for organising such meetings. To reinforce the imposition of communist morality, it was common to remove children from parents as a result of a judicial decision and place them in state boarding schools. To what conditions? There are dozens of heartbreaking stories from the 1960s continuing right into the 1980s which recount the horror and the shock of the child victims and their attempts, sometimes successful, to run away.

Now the appalling conditions in those homes are open for the inspection of *glasnost* and it is not a pretty sight. One of the extreme ironies in the turn-about of *perestroika* is the open invitation to Christians in many places to come in and clear up the mess.

The Russian word for boarding school, *internat*, itself sends a shudder down the spine of many Soviet people, being synonymous with just about everything which has gone wrong with the system of care for the deprived. The one in Zhelybino, near Tula, two hours' drive from Moscow, is unusual only in that it has been recently well documented because someone special decided to do something about it. In Moscow in February 1989 I met a remarkable priest, Fr Mark Smirnov, whom we have already quoted, a man himself long since 'barred from office' by his own church for his sympathy with dissidents. Now he has re-emerged in the role of religious affairs correspondent for *Moscow News*. He published this article just before I met him – an Orthodox priest exposing Soviet incompetence in the official press and extolling the initiative of a group of Seventh Day Adventists who did something about it. Fr Mark described the conditions thus: '"Sanitary norms" were violated to the limit and the sick rate among the pupils skyrocketed . . . Regional television showed a sad spectacle: premises resembling barracks, beds standing edge-to-edge without even ordinary bedside tables . . .' The local authorities took the decision to build a new classroom wing, but the whole project became bogged down because the essential construction materials were not available – or so officialdom said. However, someone appeared on the scene who disproved this contention:

> One cannot say what would have happened to the boarding school were it not for Yevgeni Zaitsev, a paediatrician at the Yasnogorsk district hospital. The young doctor repeatedly visited Zhelybino and was shocked by what he saw. Zaitsev couldn't relax knowing that the children were sleeping in the orphanage's former church in overcrowded conditions, and knowing that the boarding school had no money even to buy a refrigerator for its medical room.[22]

Now comes the amazing revelation: it turned out that Dr Zaitsev was a Christian, a Seventh Day Adventist, for whom helping his neighbour was to put his faith into practice. He recounted to his church in Tula what he had seen. They took up a collection in the name of the 'Lenin Children's Fund', with the specific request that the money be used for the boarding school. Not only did they manage to purchase the building materials which the state had declared unavailable, but volunteers went themselves to undertake the work. No one turned up drunk, Fr Mark tells us, no one smoked on the job and the work was finished in five months. The local authorities were delighted, but the author reflects on the continuing anomaly that Soviet law still expressly forbids such enterprise. Why should believers be presented with such a crisis of conscience when they are acting only for the good of humanity?

It is, however, encouraging that the Adventists, for the first time in Soviet history, have been able to establish an administrative centre, a church, publishing house and seminary near Tula. It seems certain that they will be able to develop such activity more readily in the future, while in the past the whole movement has been only on the fringes of legality.

The Orthodox Church has readily responded to the new opportunities in a number of places, though it is still too early to assemble any overall picture of what has been taking place. Alcoholism in the family is one of the social evils which *glasnost* has exposed and the Orthodox Church has begun to rise to the challenge of doing something about it. 'Unusual Grandfather Frosts' (Father Christmases) is how the Soviet press describes a group of monks from a monastery in Lithuania who visited child victims of alcoholism with presents at New Year 1989.[23] The Orthodox Church there is engaged, the article tells us, in the collection of funds to combat alcoholism in the family and most of the children in the home are there because of their parents' conduct.

Metropolitan Mefodi of Voronezh was elected to the board of the Lenin Soviet Children's Fund at its inaugural congress in October 1987, an indication of the developments which were to occur the next year. It seems that, despite its name, this organisation is entirely open to Christian influence. In an interview with the *Journal of the Moscow Patriarchate*, the Metropolitan referred to the Patriarchate's workshops at Sofrino, which manufacture ecclesiastical goods for the whole church, and therefore make a tidy profit (the text is original, from the English-language version of the journal):

> The workshops have taken patronage over one of Moscow's children's homes and not merely transfer money to a certain bank account, as was done before, but give the home specific practical help. We visited the institution, met with its director, found out what they need most, and are now buying equipment for them, clothes for the kids, television sets, bicycles – in short, everything they really require.[24]

The Metropolitan goes on to criticise the abysmal standards in Soviet children's homes, saying that those who come out of them are simply not equipped to deal with life. They do not know how to use money, or even in one instance how to make a cup of tea. The only really practical solution is to begin the practice of adoption, unknown in the Soviet Union, where 'Czechoslovakia is setting a good example'.

The context of the article would suggest that, if this plan goes ahead, the authorities could well be looking for Christian homes for these deprived children – an astonishing reversal of earlier practice. The daily, *Sovetskaya Rossia*, has focused recently on just such a question and published an article about the plight of Soviet orphans on 16 December 1989. It opens with a heart-rending statistic, revealing that 1,100,000 children currently live in Soviet orphanages. When one takes into account the stories related above it gives a sorry picture of the sheer scale of the problem. The article goes on to focus on several families who have adopted children. This is still in the earliest stages, as a government decision was taken on this only a year and a half ago. Some 180 families in the Soviet Union have now adopted a total of 800 orphans who would otherwise have had a bleak and loveless existence. Metropolitan Mefodi has made a house belonging to his diocese available to a family who have adopted six orphans and hopes that others will follow his example.

Following up their earlier contact with the young delinquents who were still in the Danilov Monastery when the monks returned to repossess it after so many years (see p.46), clergy from the centre of

Orthodoxy in Moscow are now involved in one of the most difficult forms of work with children: they are helping at the Children's Psychiatric Hospital No.6. They have repaired and made furniture, returned the piano and bought a television set, a refrigerator and games for the children. They have enlisted parishioners to sew bedlinen and clothes. But the main mission of these men is to aid the spiritual and moral education of these children who have been disturbed psychologically as a result of unfavourable social conditions. They are able to teach them and give them moral examples from the past (presumably, direct Christian teaching, although the article does not say so), which should lead to understanding the concept of love for one's neighbour. Then there are practical activities, with choral singing taking pride of place.[25]

Physical or severe mental handicaps sometimes lead to the abandonment of a child by its parents and institutions which provide a roof over the head of such 'hopeless cases', some of whom have only a few weeks to live. It was into such a place in Moscow that one of the parishioners of the Church of the Tikhvin Virgin first penetrated early in 1989. She could not rid her mind of the terrible desolation. She soon returned with a friend, then with another, and soon they established a pattern of visiting. It was the staff of the home who, when they realised that all the visitors were Orthodox believers, asked that the children should be baptised. The administration first took the question to higher authority, but it was referred back as a local matter. Fr Vladimir Chuvikin and various other clergy became involved:

> We decided that each child should have a baptismal outfit. We bought forty-eight white shirts, candles, small crosses and presents and with a group of parishioners we went to the children's home. Everyone was in a holiday mood and looked forward to that Saturday in anticipation as a great celebration. Two weeks later, 15 April, the children received communion [there is no confirmation in the Orthodox tradition]. In the future we shall support them spiritually and give help to these sick children who so much need human contact and warmth.[26]

While physical conditions in the home are good, the article continued, and there is more than enough individual care, with seventy-six nurses to fifty children, there is still a lack of love. Such activity was central to the Christian tradition of the past and should become so again, concludes the writer. Clearly, the spirit of Mother Teresa is not confined to the Catholic Church or excluded from the native tradition of the Russian people.

The Baptist Church is in no way lagging behind the Orthodox in this sphere of activity, either. In Kishinyov, Moldavia, its members have helped with repairs in a children's home and bought clothes and crockery for them. Clothing, again, was on the supply list in the village of Antonovka, Brichansk District, and here they alleviated the primitive conditions by building a new bath house.

Such examples of Christian conduct can influence others – and in the new Soviet conditions this is already beginning to take effect. Baptists work in the Karl Marx hospital in Leningrad and twenty-six of them now have a permanent entry pass. It is remarkable that boys from a local school came to hear of what they were doing and managed to follow their example and perhaps even more amazing that this was held up as a public instance of exemplary conduct by one of the leading government organs – *Izvestia*, no less.[27]

The way is still not universally smoothed for these developments, however. Questions are still being raised in the Soviet press as to whether it is correct for believers to be allowed to look after sick children. Priests are still sometimes barred from hospitals and one may expect a continuing rearguard action from local organs of the KGB. However, the spate of articles in the Soviet press extolling *miloserdiye*, Christian charity, even at the highest level has already significantly reduced that opposition and believers in many places are launching with great determination into activities which are still technically against the law, as well as flying in the face of generations of Soviet dogma.

Organised encouragement and help is now needed from the outside to render good the inevitable deficiencies resulting from atrophy. Much of the goodwill is there already, but where it is not it should be possible to cultivate it in the present climate. From Brest on the Polish frontier to Vladivostok on the Pacific, training programmes for local organisers are needed on a massive scale. Visual aids, especially videotapes, to illustrate what is being done elsewhere, could encourage believers nationwide. The prospects are limitless, but the lack of preparation for them in the West is frightening. This book, we trust, will encourage and stimulate a far greater effort by the rich churches of the world than ever before – and Mother Teresa of Calcutta has already demonstrated that Christians from the third world can be practically involved as well, and perhaps provide the most convincing example of all.

Postscript

Professor David Marquand wrote recently:

> For the first time in seventy years there is a chance that a free
> and democratic Russia may take its place alongside the other free
> democracies of Europe. It is only a chance: as the brave men and
> women who are now trying to turn Russia into a free democracy know
> only too well, the obstacles are immense.
> A free and democratic Russia would, however, be a prize of incalculable
> value, not just to the Russians themselves, but to the whole of Europe and
> indeed to the whole world. Meanwhile, it is becoming more and more
> clear that the alternative to it is a return, not to restrained Brezhnev-style
> stagnation, but to a nationalist and probably adventurist authoritarianism
> – armed, of course, with nuclear weapons.
> It must be in the interests of the West to encourage those Russians
> who are struggling to use the window of opportunity which President
> Gorbachev has opened up to their country into the mainstream of
> European history . . .
> The best way to make sure that they fail – the best way to ensure that
> darkness once again descends on their long-suffering country, to whose
> blood and tears we owe so much, and whose artists and thinkers have
> made such a glittering contribution to our common civilisation – is to
> restrict our European sympathies to what we misleadingly think of as
> Eastern Europe and to forget that the real Eastern Europe includes
> Moscow and Leningrad as surely as Warsaw, Prague and Budapest.[1]

Has anyone put the challenge of the new Europe more succinctly
than this? (It was in a letter to the *Independent*.) It is now a continent
of hope and opportunity, of excitement and change. Every politician
has to discard the old assumptions of a lifetime and join in drawing
a new map of Europe. Mr Gorbachev's 'common European home'
has come into existence in a few weeks, but hardly in the way he
envisaged. The house contains a Christian altar, but not all leaders

have come to pray at it. Democracy has run way ahead of the creation of new institutions to contain it.

The dangers are as apparent as the opportunities. Ancient rivalries have resurfaced, but the settling of each old score creates a new problem. The church in the new Europe faces the urgent challenge of playing a mediatory role.

Nowhere is this more evident than in countering the rise of anti-semitism in the Soviet Union. This is an area where there is cause for trepidation, though it is far from clear as yet whether the disturbing reports highlight individual and isolated instances, making untenable generalisations from them, or whether there is a major menace threatening disaster. One letter I saw recently from a Jew in the Soviet Union talks of a situation not unlike that in Germany immediately before the holocaust began. This surely must be an exaggeration, though in saying so one must be careful not to minimise the very real dangers which exist. After all, there never has been a time when anti-semitism was absent from Russia. Since the creation of the state of Israel it has often taken a semi-official form, with attacks against Zionism acting as a code for strictures against the Soviet Jewish community itself. In the age of *glasnost*, some degree of popular anti-semitism has once again surfaced. It is here that church leaders in the Soviet Union should unite in their categorical condemnation of such attitudes and it is more than a little worrying that, so far, there have been only a few isolated voices doing so. There are, for example, some priests who are active in *Pamyat*, an organisation which is more or less openly anti-semitic, even if its founders did not originally intend it to be. They should be disciplined. The Moscow Patriarchate is perfectly ready to condemn Fr Gleb Yakunin for standing for election to the Moscow City Council, yet this very priest stands against anti-semitism and, following his election, is in a position to do something about it.

The Soviet Union is unquestionably in the early process of dis-integration. Soviet action against Lithuania proves, not surprisingly, that Mr Gorbachev is prepared to use whatever measure of force is necessary to prevent this from happening. He knows that the West is likely to back him, rather than introduce any measure which will seriously harm his prospects, in the belief that this will benefit Western commercial and security interests. It is hard to find words to describe such a short-sighted and self-seeking attitude. Politicians agree that the Baltic States have the right to independence, but they reluctantly concede that it is a right which cannot be exercised, in view of the greater concerns of the interests of the great powers. This is an argument we have heard often enough before. Until recently the same was being said about Poland – yet its unilateral stance against communism eventually became the trigger which fired the charge that freed Eastern and Central Europe from foreign domination. What moral right has the world to criticise President Landsbergis for speaking in the same way?

The stance of the West over this issue is not only morally wrong. It is also shortsighted. Western leaders are formulating no contingency plans for dealing with what might replace the Soviet monolith. Do the politicians of Europe and the USA really believe that Georgians, Armenians, Azeris, Tajiks, Uzbeks and dozens of other nationalities, about whom we have been able to say virtually nothing in this book, are not themselves at various stages along the same route? Whatever the Kremlin inherited from the Russian Empire, the Molotov-Ribbentrop Pact or the spoils of the Second World War, the system which is the end product of all this has no more legitimacy than did the old Eastern Europe. Perhaps it would be utopian at the moment to expect world politicians to admit as much, but it is absolutely realistic to expect church leaders, East and West, to say so publicly, loudly and insistently. Their silence on such issues continues a long and sorry tradition where condemnation of communism is concerned.

Growing ethnic tension, combined with the insoluble economic problems which Mr Gorbachev has not even begun to solve, will speed the disintegration of the system. Inter-ethnic tensions will inevitably increase. Here the churches of the Soviet Union have a major role to play. It is they, perhaps alone, who can mediate, just as they are already positively encouraging the development of charitable work in their own communities. But they must go much beyond this in proclaiming new values in a society which is already well into the process of rejecting communism. With the election of Patriarch Alexi, with his known conservative views, in June 1990, the Church has not made the task easier for itself. Whatever the inner tensions within the Orthodox Church which will undoubtedly develop, Christians nevertheless have the opportunity of playing a role in the various electoral bodies.

Never has it been more important for the West – and not only Christians – to understand the nature of this challenge and to involve themselves morally in the processes which are unfolding. There are, of course, huge dangers ahead which no one would wish to minimise. But there are also unprecedented opportunities. We must not be engaged in paternalistically imposing our own solutions, but rather setting out together in a spirit of common adventure together with those people now liberating themselves on Soviet soil. The spiritual answers belong to the world, not to those living under one particular political system. Materialism affects the whole world. Many believers in the Soviet Union have long since shown the ability to retain spiritual values in seemingly hopeless conditions. We have as much to learn from them as they from us.

Notes

Chapter One: The Crisis of History

1. *Independent*, London, 1 March 1990.
2. Quoted in Michael Bourdeaux, *Patriarch and Prophets*, London, 1970, pp. 154–5.
3. Quoted in Michael Bourdeaux, *Religious Ferment in Russia*, London, 1968, pp. 105–13.
4. Quoted in Bourdeaux, *Patriarch and Prophets*, p. 191.
5. *Moscow News*, Moscow, 16 Aug. 1987.
6. Quoted in Bourdeaux, *Patriarch and Prophets*, pp. 126, 127, 142.
7. Daniil Granin, *Kartina*, published in the journal *Novy Mir*, Moscow, Nos 1–2, 1980. I am indebted to Mary Seton-Watson, 'Religious Themes in Recent Soviet Literature', in *Religion in Communist Lands (RCL)*, Keston, Kent, Vol. 16, No.2 for these quotations.
8. *Neva*, Leningrad, No.8, 1987.
9. *RCL*, Vol. 16, No. 3, pp. 211, 212. I have drawn upon the article 'Religious Themes in Recent Soviet Cinema', by John Dunlop, for this section. He makes a detailed study of Andrei Tarkovsky and Andrei Konchalovsky, while noting that there are several other directors who could have been brought into the study.
10. *Komsomolskaya pravda*, Moscow, 10 Dec. 1986.
11. Irena Korba, 'Atheism in the Eighties: A New Look', in *RCL*, Vol.15, No.3, pp. 325–8.
12. *Sovetskaya kultura*, Moscow, 25 March 1989.
13. *Izvestia*, Moscow, 8 March 1989.
14. *Semya*, Moscow, No.24, 1988.
15. *RCL*, Vol.17, No.1, pp. 4–18.

Chapter Two: Gorbachev and His Times

1. I am indebted to David Remnick, 'The Making of Misha', *Sunday Times*, London, 7 Jan. 1990, for the basic facts of Gorbachev's early biography.

2. See Christian Schmidt-Hauer, *Gorbachev: The Path to Power*, London, 1986, pp. 53–7, for a detailed analysis of the significance of Raisa Gorbachev's thesis.
3. I am indebted to Gail Sheehy, 'The Making of Gorbachev', *Sunday Correspondent Magazine*, London, 25 Feb.–14 March 1990, for these additional details.
4. Interview on French television, 30 Sept. 1985, *Summary of World Broadcasts*, BBC, Caversham.
5. *L'Humanité*, Paris, 8 Feb. 1986.
6. *Izvestia*, Moscow, 11 April 1989.
7. *News Network International*, Santa Clara, California, 12 Dec. 1988. (Curiously, the interview itself had taken place three months earlier, in Washington D.C. I met the journalist, Ted Okada, on the day it occurred.)
8. *Pravda*, Moscow, 26 Oct. 1985.
9. *Pravda*, 26 Feb. 1986.
10. *Pravda*, 7 March 1986.
11. *Pravda*, 2 Oct. 1986.
12. *Izvestia*, 30 Nov. 1986.

Chapter Three: Orthodox Millennium

1. *Frontier*, Keston, Kent, No.2, May–June 1987.
2. *Celebration of the Millennium of the Baptism of Rus*, Press Release No.1, Moscow Patriarchate, 1988, p. 4.
3. *Ibid*, p. 5.
4. Statistics based on 'Orthodox Church Life since the 1971 Sobor', Moscow Patriarchate, 1988; Trevor Beeson, *Discretion and Valour*, London, 1982 (revised). Supplementary (1989) statistics come from *Keston News Service* 339, 30 Nov. 1989, Keston, Kent.
5. 'Orthodox Church Life since the 1971 Sobor', typed report in English as circulated by the Moscow Patriarchate (500 copies), p. 5.
6. *Ibid*, p. 7.
7. Kharchev's speech to the Higher Party School, March 1988. Later published in *Russkaya Mysl*, Paris, 20 May 1988.
8. 'The Economic Activity of the Russian Orthodox Church', typed report in English as circulated by the Moscow Patriarchate, p. 5.
9. From the typescript of the speech as circulated by the Moscow Patriarchate.

Chapter Four: New Laws and Old Institutions

1. Michael Bourdeaux, *Patriarch and Prophets*, London, 1970, p. 17.
2. *Moscow News*, Moscow, 20 Sept. 1987. Original English text.

3. *Religion in USSR*, Novosti, Moscow (designated for foreign readership), Dec. 1987.
4. *Keston News Service (KNS)* 300, 12 May 1988, Keston, Kent.
5. *KNS* 316, 5 Jan. 1989.
6. *KNS* 340, 14 Dec. 1989. (Wording is taken from the draft published on 18 Nov. 1989.)
7. Quoted by John Anderson, 'Drafting a Soviet Law on Freedom of Conscience', *Soviet Jewish Affairs*, Vol.19, No.1, 1989, to whom I am indebted for this section.
8. *Independent*, London, 14 Feb. 1990.
9. *Church Times*, London, 6 June 1986.
10. *Nauka i religia*, Moscow, Nov. 1987.
11. *KNS* 322, 30 March 1989.
12. *Russkaya mysl*, Paris, 20 May 1988.
13. *Ogonyok*, Moscow, No.21, May 1988, pp. 26–8.
14. *Tablet*, London, 19 Nov. 1988.
15. *KNS* 317, 19 Jan. 1989.
16. *Ogonyok*, No.44, Oct. 1989, pp. 9–12.
17. *Ogonyok*, No.48, Nov. 1989, pp. 28–9.
18. *Pravitelstvenny vestnik*, Moscow, 20 Oct. 1989. Translation in *KNS* 338, 16 Nov. 1989.

Chapter Five: The Orthodox Church and the People

1. Quoted in Michael Bourdeaux, *Risen Indeed*, London, 1983, pp. 81–2.
2. Bourdeaux, *Risen Indeed*, p. 49.
3. Jane Ellis, *The Russian Orthodox Church: A Contemporary History*, London, 1986.
4. Alexander Ogorodnikov, 'Religion and *Perestroika* in the Soviet Union', *Christian Community Bulletin*, Moscow, No.6, 1988.
5. 'Same Homeland, Different Future', 17 July 1988. Translation in *Religion in Communist Lands (RCL)*, Keston, Kent, Vol.17, No.2, 1989. Original in Keston College Archives.
6. *Keston News Service (KNS)* 312, 3 Nov. 1988, Keston, Kent.
7. Zoya Krakhmalnikova, 'More on the Bitter Fruits of Sweet Captivity', *Russkaya Mysl*, Paris, 23 June 1989.
8. 'Round Table in Moscow. Orthodox Activists in Discussion with Archpriest Viktor Potapov.' *Orthodox America*, Oct./Nov./Dec. 1988.
9. Press Conference of Russian Orthodox Christians, *Arkhiv Samizdata* 6065, Radio Liberty, Munich.
10. Press Conference of Metropolitans Yuvenali and Filaret, *Arkhiv Samizdata* 6066.
11. *Journal of the Moscow Patriarchate*, Moscow, No.7, July 1987.
12. Reactions to the Patriarchal Message, dated 18 Nov. 1987, *Christian Community Bulletin*, No.6, 1988.

216   GORBACHEV, GLASNOST AND THE GOSPEL

13. Declaration of the *Christian Community Bulletin* Editorial Board, *Russkaya Mysl*, Paris, 18 Jan. 1988.
14. 'Church, State and Believers: The New Situation, Survey conducted by the *Christian Community Bulletin'*, *Russkaya mysl*, 28 April and 5 May 1989.
15. Yevgeni Pazukhin, 'To which Church Does the Street Lead?' *Christian Community Bulletin*, No.8, 1988.
16. *Russkaya mysl*, 24 Nov., 15 Dec., 22 Dec., 1989, 19 Jan. 1990.
17. *Frontier*, Keston, Kent, March–April 1990, p. 18.
18. *Orthodox America*, Oct./Nov./Dec. 1988.
19. 'To which Church Does the Street Lead?', *Christian Community Bulletin*, No.8, 1988.
20. *KNS* 317, 19 Jan. 1989.
21. 'Same Homeland, Different Future', *RCL*, Vol.17, No.2, 1989.

Chapter Six: The Protestants

1. *Information Bulletin*, Moscow, No.3, May 1989.
2. 'Overcoming Administrative Hypnosis', Jan. 1989, *Protestant* publishers. Synopsis later published in *Protestant*, No.9, July 1989.
3. *Bratsky vestnik*, Moscow, No.4, 1989, pp. 60–2.
4. *Prisoner Bulletin*, Elkhart, Indiana, Winter–Spring 1989 (publication by Georgi Vins, international representative of the Reform Baptists).
5. *Article 227*, Friedenstimme, Nottingham, No.19, May–June 1988.
6. *Bratsky listok* (Reform Baptist publication), No.1, 1986, p. 2.
7. *Moscow News*, Moscow, 3 April 1988.

Chapter Seven: The Baltic on Fire

1. Michael Bourdeaux, *Land of Crosses*, Chulmleigh, Devon, 1979, pp. 281–2.
2. See Lorna and Michael Bourdeaux, *Ten Growing Soviet Churches*, London, 1987, p. 155, where a fuller account will be found.
3. *Chronicle of the Lithuanian Catholic Church*, New York, No.70, p. 3.
4. Quoted in Michael Bourdeaux, *Risen Indeed*, London, 1983, p. 101.
5. Declaration in Keston College Archives.
6. *ELTA Information Bulletin*, Aug. 1989.
7. *Keston News Service (KNS)* 255, 24 July 1986, Keston, Kent.
8. *KNS* 270, 5 March 1987.
9. *Independent*, London, 5 Oct. 1987.
10. *Independent*, 24 Oct. 1987.
11. *Sovetskaya Litva* and *Komjaunimo tiesa*, Vilnius, 7 Feb. 1989.

12. For a fuller account of Harri Mötsnik's activities, see L. and M. Bourdeaux, *Ten Growing Soviet Churches*, pp. 44–58.
13. *Ibid*, pp. 47–8.
14. *Molodyozh Estonii*, Tallinn, 5 Oct. 1988.
15. *European Press Service*, 1–5 Sept. 1989.
16. In this section I am indebted to Marite Sapiets, 'Rebirth and Renewal in the Latvian Lutheran Church', in *Religion in Communist Lands (RCL)*, Keston, Kent, Vol. 16, No.3, 1988, pp. 237–49.
17. *Ibid*, pp. 242–3.
18. From a tape recording of the interview.
19. *RCL*, Vol.17, No.1, 1989, p. 82.
20. *Komjaunimo jaunatne*, Riga (in *KNS* 331), 13 July 1989.
21. *KNS* 331, 7 Sept. 1989.

Chapter Eight: Ukrainian Catholics: Tragedy to Triumph

1. See Robert Conquest, *Harvest of Sorrow, Soviet Collectivization and the Terror Famine*, London, 1986.
2. *Prapor*, No.10, 1988, in Bohdan Nahaylo, *Radio Liberty Research*, Munich, 9 Nov. 1988.
3. *Izvestia*, Moscow, 20 May 1988.
4. *News From Ukraine*, Kiev (in English), 18 April 1986.
5. *Journal of the Moscow Patriarchate*, Moscow, No.8, Aug. 1986.
6. *Religion in USSR*, Novosti, Moscow, No.6, 1989, pp. 31–5.
7. *Referendum*, No.6 (*samizdat* journal), published in *Russkaya mysl*, Paris, 4 March 1988.
8. Letter in Keston College Archives.
9. *Ukrainian Press Service*, Rome, 10 July 1989.
10. *Summary of World Broadcasts*, BBC, London, 16 March 1989.
11. *Keston News Service (KNS)* 265, 11 Dec. 1986, Keston, Kent.
12. *KNS* 286, 22 Oct. 1987.
13. *Moscow News*, Moscow, 22 Nov. 1987.
14. *Nauka i religia*, Moscow, No.12, 1987.
15. *Izvestia*, 1 Feb. 1989 (see *KNS* 321).
16. *Trud*, Moscow, 1 June 1989.
17. *Moscow News*, 30 July 1989.
18. *Ogonyok*, No.38, Sept. 1989, pp. 6–8.
19. Unpublished manuscript in Keston College Archives.
20. Transcript from Vatican Radio interview with Metropolitan Yuvenali, 28/29 Nov. 1989.
21. Keston College Press Release, 2 Dec. 1989.
22. *KNS* 340, 14 Dec. 1989.
23. *KNS* 341, 11 Jan. 1990.
24. *Leninska molod*, Lviv, 22 March 1990.

GORBACHEV, GLASNOST AND THE GOSPEL

Chapter Nine: The Quality of Mercy

1. *Russkaya mysl*, Paris, 20 May 1988.
2. 'O miloserdii', *Literaturnaya gazeta*, Moscow, 18 March 1987.
3. *Literaturnaya gazeta*, 4 Oct. 1989.
4. *Keston News Service (KNS)* 252, 12 June 1987, Keston, Kent.
5. *Ibid.*
6. *Ibid.*
7. 'Guarantees of Freedom', *Nauka i religia*, Moscow, No.11, Nov. 1987.
8. *KNS* 324, 27 April 1989.
9. *KNS* 252, 12 June 1987.
10. *KNS* 324, 27 April 1989.
11. 'I Believe in Goodness', *Molodyozh Estonii*, Tallinn, 28 Feb. 1989. Interview with Fr Mark Smirnov.
12. *KNS* 330, 20 July 1989.
13. *Literaturnaya gazeta*, 9 Aug. 1989.
14. *Sovetskaya Rossia*, Moscow, 23 Dec. 1989.
15. *Informatsionny byulleten* (new Baptist newspaper), Moscow, May 1989.
16. *Khristianskoye slovo (Informatsionny byulleten* renamed), Aug. 1989.
17. *Ogonyok*, No.38, Sept. 1988.
18. *Moscow News*, Moscow, 9 April 1989.
19. *Journal of the Moscow Patriarchate (JMP)*, Moscow, No.3, March 1989. (English language version, printed verbatim; printed in Russian version in June 1989.)
20. *Ibid.* pp. 52–4.
21. *Frontier*, Keston, Kent, March/April 1989.
22. *Moscow News*, 8 Jan. 1989.
23. *Sovetskaya Litva*, Vilnius, 30 Dec. 1988.
24. *JMP* (English), No.11, Nov. 1988.
25. *Moskovsky tserkovny vestnik* (new Orthodox monthly publication), Moscow, No.2, May 1989.
26. *Moskovsky tserkovny vestnik*, No.3, May 1989.
27. *Izvestia*, Moscow, 14 July 1989.

Postscript

1. *Independent*, London, 5 Feb. 1990.

Index

Academy of Sciences, 80
Adventist church
  charitable activity, 204–5
  new administrative centre, 205
Afghanistan, 26, 50
  Association of Afghan War Veterans, 101, 104
Akmentins, Dr Roberts, 154–7
Aksyuchits, Victor, 90
Alexander, Archbishop of Dmitrov, 57
Alexi, Metropolitan of Leningrad and Estonia, 149, 183, 198, 200
  comments on need for new law on freedom of conscience, 67–9
  Patriarch, 86, 211
All-Union Council of Evangelical Christians and Baptists (AUCECB), 109–20, 149
  calls for reform, 116–20
  calls for unity, 126–7
  charitable activity, 199, 200–3, 208
  Congress (1990), 117–20
  donations to Armenia, 193
  schism with Reform Baptists, 6, 110, 125–7
  statistics, 128
Andropov, Yuri, 22, 25, 32, 46
Anilionis, Petras (Lithuanian Council for Religious Affairs), 141, 144
  dismissal, 147
anti-semitism, 26, 107, 210
Armenia
  Armenian Charitable Union, 192

conflict with Azerbaijan, 192
earthquake relief, 192, 195
atheism, 18–21, 36–8, 44, 52, 73, 89, 90, 112, 157, 173
  atheist-Christian dialogue, 73, 113
  atheist education, 13, 24, 36, 147
  Nauka i religia, 68–9, 75, 85, 173, 191
autonomous registration of congregations, autonomous churches, 110, 118, 126

Barinov, Valeri, 109, 116, 199
Bessmertny, Andrei, 96, 102, 104
Bible, 19, 75, 83
  cultural heritage, 18
  difficulty in obtaining, 77
  imports, sale/distribution of, 106–7, 114–15, 145, 151
Bieliauskiene, Jadvyga 141
Bloom, Metropolitan Anthony, 183
Boiko, Nikolai, 122
Bolshoi Theatre, millennium concert, 55, 61–3, 94
Bondarenko, Iosif, 112
Brazauskas, Antanas (Lithuanian Communist leader), 140
Brezhnev, Leonid, 8, 10, 14–15, 22, 28, 59, 66, 88–9, 108, 121, 123, 153
British Council of Churches, 74–5, 101, 147
Burlatsky, Fyodor, 33–4, 67, 71, 172
  See also human rights
Bychkov, Alexei, 114, 120